Private sector development

Private sector development
Policies and programs for the Pacific islands

Andrew McGregor
Mark Sturton
Sitiveni Halapua

天 An East-West Center Book
Pacific Islands Development Program
East-West Center

About the Authors

ANDREW McGREGOR was leader of the Private Sector Project, which was conducted by the Pacific Islands Development Program (PIDP) at the East-West Center. Before joining PIDP he was a senior commodity analyst with the United Nations Food and Agriculture Organization (FAO). Dr. McGregor holds a Ph.D. from Cornell University and is currently commercial agriculture advisor to the United States Agency for International Development (USAID) Pacific Regional Office.

MARK STURTON has a special interest in policy modeling—analytical tools for designing economic policy appropriate to the small island economies of the Pacific islands region. He has a Ph.D. from Sussex University and was formerly an East-West Center research associate in charge of the macroeconomic components of PIDP's Private Sector Project. Currently, Dr. Sturton is research director of the National Reserve Bank of Tonga.

SITIVENI HALAPUA is director of the PIDP. Before joining the East-West Center in 1989 as a research associate, he was a senior lecturer in Monetary Economics at the University of the South Pacific. Born in Tonga, Dr. Halapua received his Ph.D. in Economics from the University of Kent, England.

Library of Congress Cataloging-in-Publication Data

McGregor, Andrew.
    Private sector development: policies and programs for the Pacific Islands / by Andrew McGregor, Mark Sturton, Sitiveni Halapua.
        p.   cm.
    Includes bibliographical references and index.
    ISBN 0-86638-155-4 : $10.00
    1. Islands of the Pacific—Economic conditions. 2. Investments—Islands of the Pacific. 3. Islands of the Pacific—Economic policy. I. Sturton, Mark, 1947-   . II. Halapua, Sitiveni. III. Title
    HC681.M42   1993   92-40076
                                                 CIP

The paper used in this publication meets the minimum requirements of American National Standard for Information Sciences—Permanence of Paper for Printed Library Materials

Distributed by
University of Hawaii Press
Order Department
2840 Kolowalu Street
Honolulu, Hawaii 96822

Contents

List of tables

List of figures

Exchange rates

As of December 31, 1990, the exchange rates for one US dollar are as follows:

Cook Islands	NZ$1.701
Fiji	F$1.459
Kiribati	A$1.293
Papua New Guinea	K0.953 (kina)
Solomon Islands	SI$2.614
Tonga	T$1.296
Vanuatu	VT109.22 (Vatu)
Western Samoa	WS$2.333

Foreword

The private sector is crucial to the economic development of the Pacific islands, and it is the primary vehicle by which individuals participate in and contribute to the national development process in their own country. This has been recognized by Pacific island leaders who, for more than a decade, have determined the research issues and guided the research activity of the Pacific Islands Development Program at the East-West Center.

We welcome this publication as a valuable product of the practical research activities being undertaken by PIDP, and we are confident that it will prove of great interest and assistance to policymakers and all those involved with or interested in the development of the Pacific islands region.

We would like to express our appreciation to the Asian Development Bank for providing the financial support for this research project and for the publication of this work.

Honorable Sir Geoffrey Henry, KBE
Prime Minister of the Cook Islands
and
Chairman, Standing Committee
of Pacific Islands Conference of Leaders

Preface

During and immediately after the independence era the public sector was the dominant economic force in the Pacific island economies. However, after the strong economic showing of the 1970s, the export and growth performance of the 1980s has been poor. It has become increasingly evident that the public sector is unable to provide the increase in the standard of living expected and that the onus of development must originate from the private sector. Thus this link between economic development and private sector development and the appropriate role of government was the major focus of the Pacific Islands Development Program's (PIDP) Private Sector Project.

The private sector in the Pacific islands region has often been perceived as commercial trading enterprises to the exclusion of the village and smallholder sector. This dualistic attitude of policymakers is illustrated by the following extract from the 1988 Papua New Guinea budget statement:

> A key strategic decision taken by Government is to stimulate the commercial enterprise sector while at the same time committing public resources to investment in the development of the smallholder sector (Government of Papua New Guinea).

It also has not been uncommon to equate the private sector with the foreign sector. Such misconceptions have tended to distort attitudes and policies toward private sector development. PIDP's Private Sector Project has viewed the private sector in its broadest sense and includes the small semisubsistent farmers wishing to increase their marketable surplus to the same extent as it does the large multinational mining company.

Appropriate government policies for private sector development are also sometimes perceived as a simple matter of privatization and deregulation. Yet the reality is far more complex, especially for decision makers in a small open economy with a narrow production base, a small fragmented domestic market, a low level of human resource development, and underdeveloped physical infrastructure.

The Private Sector Project has researched a variety of interrelated issues, ranging from the macroeconomic environment for private sector investment to support for small and indigenous business. While this applied research was originally explicitly directed at the eight South Pacific Developing Member Countries (SPDMCs) of the Asian Development Bank (ADB),[1] generalizations can be drawn for the region as a whole. The research for this project is based on fieldwork completed in 1990.

The Private Sector Project covers eight countries and a wide range of issues and sectors. Thus, due to the limited resources available to achieve this ambitious task, a heavy reliance has been placed on selected case studies. Accordingly, perhaps the greatest value of the research for decision makers lies in its regional and comparative nature. The countries of the region have much to learn from each other's experiences—both the successes and failures.

---

[1] At the time of the study the SPDMCs were Cook Islands, Fiji, Kiribati, Papua New Guinea, Solomon Islands, Tonga, Vanuatu, and Western Samoa.

Acknowledgments

PIDP gratefully acknowledges the contribution of the Asian Development Bank, which made possible the publication of this book. In addition, PIDP is indebted to Jim McMaster, Dean, Faculty of Management, University of Canberra, Australia, and A. P. Thirlwall, Professor of Applied Economics at the University of Kent at Canterbury, England; both McMaster and Thirlwall made substantial contributions to this book while they were Fellows with PIDP.

Acronyms

ADB	Asian Development Bank
ADFIP	Association of Development Finance Institutions of the Pacific
ASEAN	Association of Southeast Asian Nations
CDI	Center for Development of Industry, EEC
CEMA	Solomon Islands Commodities Export Marketing Authority
CFF	Compensatory Financing Facility, IMF
CMT	cut make and trim
CNMI	Commonwealth of the Northern Mariana Islands
COMSEC	Commonwealth Secretariat
CPDF	Caribbean Project Development Facility
CPI	consumer price index
CSA	commercial statutory authorities
DHT	dry heat treatment
DB	Development Bank
DFI	Development Finance Institution
DWFN	Distant Water Fishing Nation
EDB	post-ethylene dibromide
EEC	European Economic Community
EEZ	Exclusive Economic Zone
ESCAP	Economic and Social Commission for Asia and the Pacific
ESO	Enterprise Support Organization
FAO	Food and Agriculture Organization
FFGEA	Fiji's Fresh Ginger Exporters Association
FIC	Forum Island Country
FIMCO	Friendly Islander Marketing Cooperative, Tonga
FMA	Furniture Manufacturers Association, Malaysia
FNPF	Fiji National Provident Fund
FTIB	Fiji Trade and Investment Board
GDP	gross domestic product

GNP	gross national product
IFC	International Finance Corporation
ILO	International Labor Organization
IMF	International Monetary Fund
IPA	Investment Promotion Authority
JETRO	Japan's External Trade Organization
MAF	Ministry of Agriculture and Forestry, Tonga
MARC	Market Access Regional Competitiveness Project, USAID
MUV	Manufacturing Unit Value
NES	nucleus estate
NGIP	New Guinea Islands Produce, Papua New Guinea
NGO	non-government organization
NIDA	National Investment Development Authority, Papua New Guinea
NLTB	Native Land Trust Board, Fiji
NMA	National Marketing Authority, Fiji
NSC	National Steering Committee
OPIC	Overseas Private Investment Corporation, United States of America
PIDP	Pacific Islands Development Program
PSA	Plantation Support Association, Vanuatu
PSDP	private sector development program
RSBC	Regional Small Business Center
SBC	Small Business Center
SDRs	Special Drawing Rights
SIC	Small Industries Centre
SOE	state-owned enterprise
SPARTECA	South Pacific Regional Trade and Economic Cooperation Agreement
SPDB	South Pacific Development Bank
SPDMC	South Pacific Developing Member Country
SPPF	South Pacific Project Facility, International Finance Corporation
SPRETCO	South Pacific Regional Trade Commission, Australia
SPRO	South Pacific Regional Office, Asian Development Bank
SPTC	South Pacific Trade Commission, Australia
SPTO	South Pacific Trade Office, New Zealand
TCB	Tonga Commodities Board
TCSP	Tourism Council of the South Pacific
TFF	Tax Free Factory
TFO	Trade Facilitation Office, Canada
TPC	Trade Promotion Center

TSA	Tourism Support Association
UNCTAD	United Nations Conference on Trade and Development
UNDP	United Nations Development Program
UNIDO	United Nations Industrial Development Organization
USAID	United States Agency for International Development
USDA	United States Department of Agriculture
USP	University of the South Pacific
VCMB	Vanuatu Commodities Marketing Board
YMCA	Young Men's Christian Association
YWCA	Young Women's Christian Association

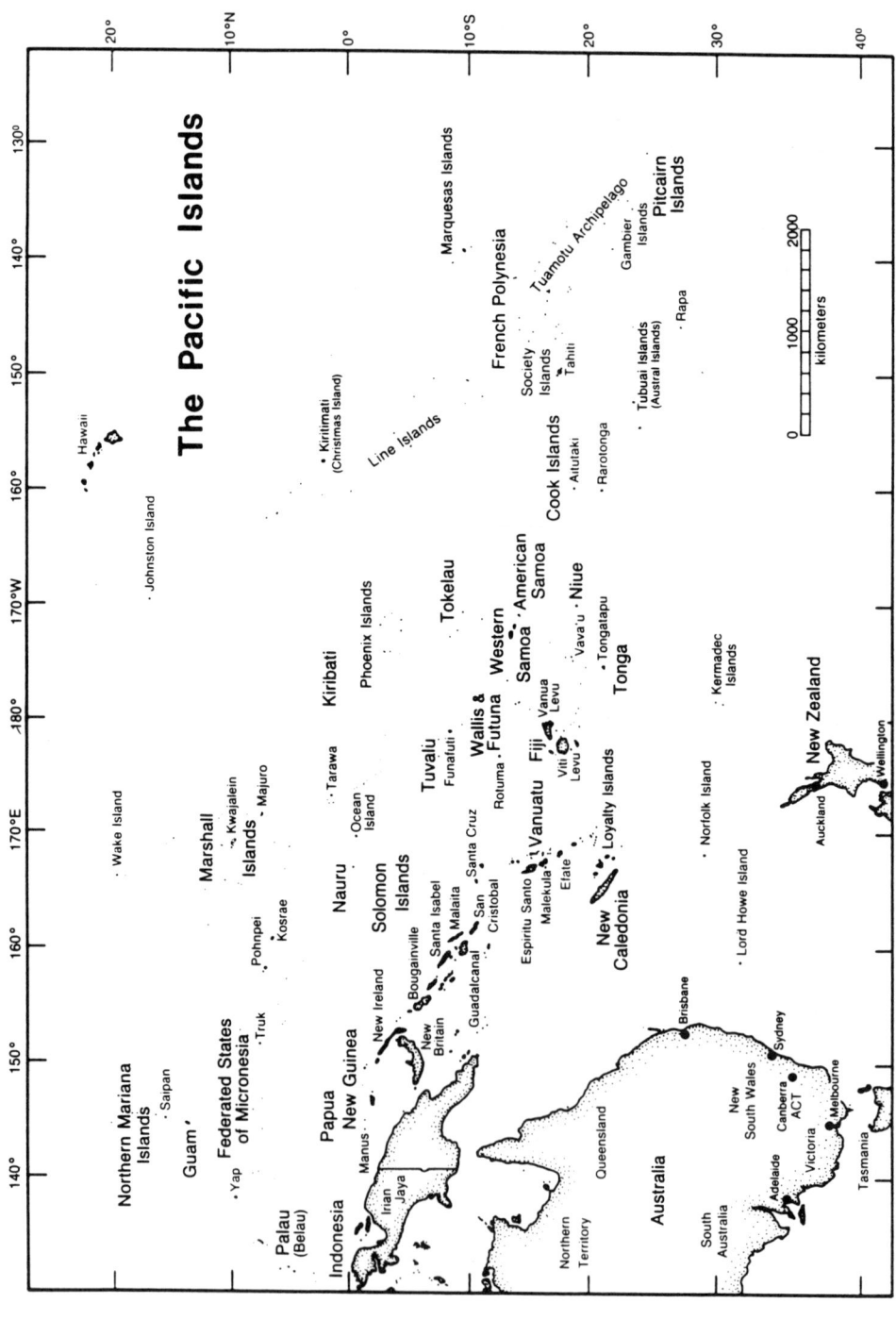

The Pacific Islands

20°
10°N
0°
10°S
20°
30°
40°

130°
140°
150°
160°
170°W
180°
170°E
160°
150°
140°

Hawaii

· Johnston Island

· Wake Island

Northern Mariana
Islands
· Saipan

Guam·

Federated States
of Micronesia
· Yap
·Truk
Palau
(Belau)

·Pohnpei
·Kosrae

Marshall
Islands
·· Kwajalein
· Majuro

Nauru

· Ocean
Island

·Tarawa

Kiribati

Phoenix Islands

Tokelau

· Kiritimati
(Christmas Island)

Line Islands

Marquesas Islands

French Polynesia

Tuamotu Archipelago

Gambier
Islands

Pitcairn
Islands

Society
Islands
·Tahiti

· Rapa

Tubuai Islands
(Austral Islands)

Cook Islands

· Aitutaki
· Rarotonga

2000

1000
kilometers

0

Western
Samoa
American
Samoa
· Niue

· Vava'u

Tuvalu
Funafuti ·

Wallis &
Futuna
Rotuma ·

· Vanua
Levu

Fiji

Viti
Levu

Tonga
· Tongatapu

Kermadec
Islands

Solomon
Islands
Santa Isabel
Bougainville
Guadalcanal
San
Cristobal
· Malaita
Santa Cruz

New Ireland
New
Britain

Espiritu Santo
Malekula ·
Efate ·

Vanuatu

New
Caledonia

Loyalty Islands

· Norfolk Island

New Zealand

Auckland

Wellington

Papua
New Guinea
Manus

Indonesia
Irian
Jaya

· Lord Howe Island

Brisbane

Sydney

New
South Wales

Canberra
ACT

Melbourne

Victoria

Tasmania

Australia

Queensland

Northern
Territory

South
Australia

Adelaide

chapter 1

Economic overview

This chapter describes the major characteristics of economic performance of the Pacific island countries since the independence era of the 1970s, with a special focus on the more recent developments during the 1980s (Thirlwall 1991).

Economic Growth

Although the Pacific island economies maintained a satisfactory rate of growth during the 1970s, performance during the 1980s was dismal. Table 1.1 presents figures for five Pacific island economies.

Over the period 1970-79 economic growth ranged from 4 to 7 percent but fell between 2 and 4 percent in the decade of the 1980s. Given the population growth, gross domestic product (GDP) per capita dropped from an average of 2 percent during the 1970s to approximately zero for the group during the 1980s. During the 1980s Tonga revealed the highest rate of GDP growth per capita with 1.3 percent, and Vanuatu the lowest with a negative 1.1 percent. The adverse impact of high rates of population growth can also be seen in the Melanesian economies. Solomon Islands, which recorded the highest absolute rate of GDP growth, showed a disappointing drop of 0.6 percent in per capita terms. These results reinforce the observation that high rates of population growth can strongly erode the

Table 1.1   Average GDP and GDP growth per capita, 1970-89

	Fiji	Papua New Guinea	Solomon Islands	Tonga	Vanuatu
		GDP growth			
1970-79	4.7	3.8	7.5	3.7	N.A.
1980-89	2.0	1.7	2.9	1.9	1.9
		Per capita growth			
1970-79	2.6	1.7	3.9	2.8	N.A.
1980-89	0.5	-0.4	-0.6	1.3	-1.1

benefits of economic development. Comparisons made in Chapter 2 with other developing countries reveal a declining relative performance of the Pacific islands even when size and economic structure are taken into account.

A degree of caution is needed in interpreting GDP statistics. The compilation of national accounts data is weak in all the Pacific island countries, and the figures presented have been restricted to the more reliable estimates. Consequently, no data have been included for Western Samoa, for which figures exist for only the 1984-86 period. The omission of data for Western Samoa does not alter the overall assessment of the Pacific island economies because the evidence suggests that Western Samoan performance has been one of the poorest. The data problem has been compounded in the Pacific islands region by the incentive to inhibit statistical measurement to retain the least developed status that confers preferential terms on the receipt of aid. Yet the conclusion remains that the economic growth of the Pacific islands during the 1980s has been unacceptably low.

GDP and GDP per capita growth on a year-by-year basis for five countries are shown in Appendix 1. The graphical description reveals not only the underlying trends during the period, but also the substantial year-to-year fluctuations that these economies experience. Cyclical movement in the terms of trade, adverse climatic conditions, and tropical cyclones are the major causes of the fluctuations. Commodity price instability was also found to be a contributing factor (Chapter 2). In Fiji's case the 1980s reveal a typical wave motion, which was generated by a sharp improvement in the terms of trade in the early 1980s, an onset of tropical cyclones in the middle period, and political disturbance at the end of the decade.

Sectoral Structure

Theory and international empirical observation suggest that a strong association exists between increases in GDP per capita and change in economic structure. In other words, growth is positively associated with manufacturing and services having an increasing share of GDP. This theory suggests that little structural change could be anticipated in the Pacific islands given the economic stagnation experienced during the 1980s. Such was the case for Fiji and Papua New Guinea, the two largest economies (Appendix 2). However, the smaller economies represent an anomaly with respect to the relationship between changing structure and economic performance.

In the Fiji case the figure shows a fall in the share of agriculture and industry and the rising importance of services during the 1970s. Economic structure remained virtually unchanged during the 1980s. These events are consistent with economic growth and stagnation during the two periods, respectively. The more recent development of a dynamic manufacturing sector in the Fiji economy at the end of the 1980s has been accompanied by a sharp increase in economic growth. This recent phenomenon is not included in the data set used in the analysis. In case of Papua New Guinea there was an increase in the share of services in the late 1970s while the economy experienced a period of fiscal expansion but a decline thereafter as stagnation set in during the 1980s. During the latter period the share of primary industries increased as new mining ventures commenced. The share of manufacturing, however, remained largely static throughout the 1970s and 1980s.

In the Melanesian cases of Solomon Islands and Vanuatu, data are available for only the 1980s but reveal a decline in the share of primary industries and a rise in services. These developments occurred at a time not only when economic growth was low but also when per capita growth was negative. Interestingly, the data suggest some rise in the share of industry in the case of Vanuatu, which, given the lack of manufacturing development, reflects growth in construction. These results reflect the poor performance of export agriculture, particularly copra earnings, rather than any structural change in these economies.

Information on the Polynesian economies is available only for Tonga, and again the share of the primary sector fell substantially with increases not only in services but also in industry. Tonga has enjoyed some manufacturing growth through its Small Industries Centre (SIC), and the data indicate that the share of manufacturing has increased. However, a significant increase in the share of industries is again attributable to growth in construction. Tonga has experienced a sharp decline in the level and value of copra production, which only in recent years has been offset to some extent by growth in diversified agriculture, particularly vanilla. Given the lack of industrial development in Western Samoa, structural trends are likely to be similar to either Solomon Islands or Vanuatu.

While the preceding analysis indicates that Pacific islands economic growth was poor and that there was little structural change at the aggregate level, it would be inappropriate to suggest that these economies have ossified. In fact, significant changes have occurred during the period at the sectorial and commodity level that indicate the Pacific islands are responsive to changes in economic opportunities. Common to all has been an adjustment to depressed copra and coconut oil prices.

Terms of Trade

A question of emerging importance in the debate on Pacific island economic development is the question of whether there has been a deterioration in the terms of trade between export and import prices. Thirlwall (1991) estimated that the terms of trade had deteriorated during the 1980s for certain Pacific island economies. These findings were strongly refuted in a World Bank (World Bank 1991)[2] review of the Pacific islands stating that "nothing could be further from the truth." The apparent contradictory findings from such eminent sources on this crucial indicator are surprising. Thus an additional set of estimates of the terms of trade were derived.

Two sets of estimates were prepared with the normal indices and five year moving averages, which smooth commodity price fluctuations. Both estimates for each of the six main Pacific island economies are shown in Appendix 4. The same data are presented in Table 1.2 and include the five year moving averages in the terms of trade for the 1970s and 1980s with and without the export of services.

These estimates suggest clearly that Pacific island terms of trade have deteriorated substantially since the beginning of the 1970s but that the rate of decline was generally lower in the 1980s compared with the 1970s. The data indicate the substantial commodity price fluctuations to which Pacific island commodity exports are subject. These findings have an important bearing on the policy prescriptions derived from the Private Sector Project. A detailed discussion of the terms of trade estimation is presented in Sturton (1991).

The decline in the terms of trade (excluding services) should come as no surprise to an observer of commodity price movements. All the major

Table 1.2   Terms of trade for the Pacific islands including annual and five year moving averages, 1970-89

	Fiji	PNG	Solomons	Tonga	Vanuatu	W. Samoa	Coconut/ MUV
	Goods and Services (%)						
1972-80	-3.8	-5.8	0.5	-5.1	-2.9	-4.9	-5.8
1980-87	-1.8	-1.3	-3.6	0.3	-1.7	-6.3	-4.5
	Goods only (%)						
1972-80	-4.1	-5.8	0.5	-6.5	-4.2	-5.0	
1980-87	-2.1	-1.3	-3.6	-3.8	-5.6	-8.1	

2 World Bank. "Toward Higher Growth in Pacific Island Economies: Lessons from the 1980s." Report No. 9059-Asia, January 18, 1991.

commodities that the Pacific islands export, with the exception of gold and sawn timber, have deteriorated relative to the exports of manufactures from the developed countries (comparison is made here with the World Bank's G5 Manufacturing Unit Value (MUV) index). The real price of petroleum has fallen and the general decline in primary commodity prices would also reduce the price of Pacific island imports. However, the price of imports of manufactures has risen relative to primary commodity prices, and these imports typically represent more than 60 percent of total Pacific island import requirements. In summary, it would be counter-intuitive if the terms of trade had improved. The inclusion of services ameliorates this outcome, but the trend is still downward.

An additional factor underscoring the decline in the commodity terms of trade is the importance of coconut products, which have dominated exports of the smaller Pacific island economies. The price of this commodity declined more during the 1970-89 period than all other primary commodity exports from the Pacific islands with the exception of cocoa whose price fell to greater extent during the 1980s. A simple approximation to the terms of trade for these economies is simply the ratio of coconut oil prices to the MUV index, which is given in Table 1.2. The decline in this ratio explains a very substantial component of the deterioration in the terms of trade.

The significance of these results needs emphasizing because of their implications for policy. Clearly, reliance on exports of traditional commodities such as copra has resulted in the erosion of real incomes including the generation of a surplus for development. However, this study does not recommend that the Pacific islands should turn inward as was the conclusion of the debate for the adoption of import substitution policies in Latin America in the 1950s. Development experience has not found this strategy successful, and it is the least recommended for the Pacific islands whose room for industrialization behind protective tariffs is negligible.

While the findings here are at odds with those of the World Bank insofar as the terms of trade are concerned, they are in accord with the main policy recommendation regarding the need to seek out new export opportunities. Indeed, the declining terms of trade emphasize the need for the Pacific islands to seek out new export possibilities. The fruits of export diversification can be shown in the improved terms of trade that result when services are included (Sturton 1991).

Tonga is an example; it was the only country whose terms of trade improved during the 1980s. This result arose not only from the sizable export of services but also from the substantial reduction in coconut exports and development of new high value agricultural exports. Western Samoa provides a counter example of an economy that failed to diversify. It continued to rely on cocoa and coconut products, and the terms of trade declined by a greater amount than all other Pacific island economies. However, while this study emphasizes the need for diversification and reduction in the reliance on "traditional" exports, every effort still needs to be maintained to improve the viability of these commodities through technological innovations and other cost reducing efficiency improvements. In many rural areas, for the foreseeable future, traditional exports provide the only available source of income on a significant scale.

Structure of Exports

The changing structure of exports can be seen in Appendix 3. Tourism receipts, with the exception of Fiji, have been excluded due to data limitations. However, they have become an important component of foreign exchange receipts for many of the economies.

The data for Papua New Guinea describe the changes between minerals and non-mineral exports and changes within the non-mineral sector. The pattern of development during the period indicates further concentration of investment in natural resource exploitation (mining, commodity agriculture, and forestry) and the failure to develop any significant exports of manufactures. By the end of the 1980s the share of "other" exports had fallen to 2 percent of the total.

The data for the Fiji economy indicate a similar dependency on a limited number of exported commodities with sugar and tourism dominating. The 1970s saw the resurgence of sugar production and a static nature in the structure of Fiji's other main exports. The latter part of the 1980s saw some important restructuring of the economy with the share of gold, fish, garments, and "other" items all increasing. These trends have continued with the emergence of a significant manufacturing sector based on garment production for export. Policy reorientation toward an outward looking export strategy coupled with the beneficial impact of the South Pacific Regional Trade and Economic Cooperation Agreement (SPARTECA) trade arrangements have encouraged these developments.

The Tongan economy shows the most marked change in the structure of exports among all the Pacific island countries, although exports as a whole have stagnated with the marked decline in coconut product exports. Coconut products represented nearly 80 percent of exports in the early

1970s, but by the end of the 1980s production had fallen to 20 percent. These trends reflect the unprofitable nature of copra production in terms of returns to labor. Farmers have, however, switched their labor resources to high value niche export crops such as vanilla, watermelons, and squash where Tonga appears to have developed a comparative advantage.

In addition, quite a strong growth has occurred in manufactures, resulting from the establishment of the SIC. While it must be reiterated that export production as a whole has stagnated, the substantial restructuring indicates an economy able to adjust and take advantage of more rewarding activities.

Western Samoa has seen an increase in the share of coconut products, which makes it unique among regional countries. However, this has been the result of the successful development of a coconut cream factory by the private sector. Production of cocoa, a traditional export, has fallen, while the export of taro to migrant Pacific island communities in New Zealand and Australia has become a major activity. However, unlike Tonga, Western Samoa has failed to develop any form of export manufacturing capability despite the fact that it was the first in the region to propose the development of an export free zone.

The Vanuatu economy displays both a concentration of commodity production in a few activities and a static structure during most of the period under review. Coconut production dominates and represents over 50 percent of total exports but, as elsewhere, has declined in significance in recent years. In the latter part of the 1980s attempts to diversify the economy have shown some success with increased production in both cocoa and the beef industry. However, the Vanuatu economy has reduced its dependence on primary commodity production with the establishment of a successful tourism industry whose gross foreign exchange receipts are greater than the total commodity exports. The Financial Center is also an important element of the economic activity whose exports represent approximately one-fourth export receipts.

Solomon Islands is wholly dependent on a limited range of primary commodities for export. However, within this specialization the economy had diversified its structure and reduced its dependence on copra production to less than 10 percent by the end of the 1980s. The main change in structure has been the rapid increase in exports of canned tuna. An efficient palm oil sector and cocoa production have shown growth.

Island production for export is concentrated on a limited number of primary commodities, and this characteristic did not change during the 1970s or 1980s. Only Fiji and Tonga managed to develop any sort of manufacturing sector but this has so far contributed only a minor part of the overall picture. However, the Pacific island producers are responsive to changes in economic incentives, in particular, commodity prices. Pacific island economies thus display sensitivity to price movements but in the period reviewed have failed to diversify into activities that might have led to a more satisfactory growth performance. The emphasis of the Private Sector Project has been on deriving appropriate policies and programs to make this transition via the private sector.

The External Sector

Equilibrium in the balance of payments has been maintained with few exceptions through responsible fiscal and monetary policies. Only in a few instances have imprudent policies led to external imbalance and a decline in foreign reserves. However, the external position in most Pacific island countries is extremely fragile. Current levels of imports are maintained by export of a narrow range of commodities, tourism earnings, foreign aid, and workers' remittances. Many factors affecting the flow of these receipts are outside the direct control of island governments. A variation in commodity export prices, a tropical cyclone, alteration in tastes affecting the demand for tourism, or changes in foreign government aid policy can all adversely affect foreign exchange receipts requiring rapid economic adjustments by the Pacific islands to maintain stability. Given the fragility in the external account, it is in many ways remarkable that adjustment has proceeded as efficiently as it has in most instances.

Some recent trends in the balance of payments of the six countries are presented in Appendix 6. The high dependency on trade is revealed through the ratio of imports to GDP. For the larger economies it ranges from about 40 percent of GDP and rises up to 60 percent in the most dependent cases. The ratio in each country has maintained a relatively constant relationship to GDP. This ratio has risen in times of substantial investment activity such as in Fiji during the beginning of the 1970s when considerable additions were made to the tourism plant and during the early part of the 1980s when several large infrastructure projects were undertaken. A similar trend was indicated in Papua New Guinea at the beginning of the 1980s with investment in the Ok Tedi mine and during a period of fiscal expansion. An upward trend is exhibited in Solomon Islands with a significant expansion in government expenditures at the end of the 1980s. However, the statistics suggest that the relationship between imports and GDP has not changed, which is consistent with a static economic structure; when variation has arisen, it has been due to changes in the composition of demand.

While the demand for imports has matched economic growth (or lack of it), Pacific island exports failed to keep pace with the average growth of exports from non-oil producing developing nations during the 1980s, although performance during the 1970s was satisfactory. These trends are revealed in Table 1.3. The volume of exports (division of export values by unit export prices) also stagnated between the two periods but to a lesser extent. These trends are reflected in the poor growth performance of the Pacific island countries during the 1980s, and the reduction in exports contributed substantially to the decline.

Given the significance of export production in the structure of the Pacific island economies, it is to be anticipated that any variation in export growth would have immediate repercussions on economic performance.

While export growth has declined, the ratio of exports to GDP has remained relatively static for most island economies, as Appendix 6 reveals. Only in the case of the Polynesian economies has this ratio declined. These forces are reflected in the trade deficit, and the ratio of export to imports has not varied significantly except for Tonga and Western Samoa where the ratio has fallen and the trade deficit has worsened substantially.

Transfers including both workers remittances and external aid make very substantial contribution to external receipts in many island economies. External transfers make only a small contribution to the Fiji balance of payments, and in Papua New Guinea the trend has been downward as budgetary support has been withdrawn. In the case of Vanuatu external aid makes a very important contribution to foreign exchange receipts.

Table 1.3 Growth in export values (US$) and volumes during the 1970s and 1980s

	Values (percentage)		Volumes (percentage)	
	1970-80	1980-89	1970-80	1980-89
Fiji	17.4	1.7	3.4	2.5
Papua New Guinea	23.6	2.9	13.8	4.9
Solomon Islands	25.0	-0.1	7.0	5.0
Tonga	10.5	-0.5	3.7	-0.7
Vanuatu	6.5	0.8	-3.0	3.4
Western Samoa	13.6	-3.3	3.9	3.5
Non-oil producing developing nations	21.2	6.8		

However, the trend has also been downward as budgetary support was phased out during the 1980s, although during the 1987-88 period a sizable inflow of Stabex money funded a shortfall in export earnings. For Solomon Islands foreign aid is also very important and rose to high levels during the second half of the 1980s.

In the case of Tonga and Western Samoa transfers include both remittances and foreign aid. While the level of the latter has remained more or less static, the level of remittances has increased very substantially. In both economies the level of transfers has assumed an increasing significance and has balanced the deteriorating trade deficit. However, the reliance on remittances is precarious should barriers to migrant labor arise and as ties to home become weakened through time.

Investment, Savings, and Foreign Transfers

Data on the pattern of investment and savings in the Pacific islands are not obtainable for the complete 1970-89 period. The rate of investment (excluding inventories) achieved in the Pacific islands has been high by developing country standards, reaching in excess of 20 percent of GDP in most years. However, while investment has been high the associated rate of economic growth has been dismal, and an implicit Pacific island incremental capital output ratio is very high by world standards. International comparisons are developed further in Chapter 2.

While evidence on the destination of investment by institution is not presented, the majority has been in the public sector on infrastructure projects, which are often aid financed. Investment in the private sector represents a much smaller proportion of the total and helps to explain the lack of association between investment and growth in the Pacific islands. Public investment in infrastructure has proved to be a necessary but not sufficient condition for growth. This suggests that other binding constraints are in place, notably human resource development, and that more is required to encourage productive private sector investment.

Trends in the Pacific island savings rates, the level of capital inflow, and foreign aid are also indicated in Appendix 5. Domestic savings rates are determined as a residual from national accounts data, and the figures fluctuate substantially due to the unavoidable accumulation of national accounts errors. While investment rates have been high the reverse can be said about the rate of savings. Domestic savings range from negative rates in the case of Tonga and Western Samoa, to a figure of about 8 percent for Solomon Islands and Vanuatu, to 14 percent in Papua New Guinea, and 18 percent in Fiji. The lack of domestic savings is made up through substantial levels of capital inflow (of which development aid forms an essential ingredient) and remittances in the case of the Polynesian countries. Only in the case of Fiji do both foreign investment and aid play a relatively minor part in the economy and remittances are insignificant.

Aid receipts in Papua New Guinea and Solomon Islands represent about 10 percent of GDP, while Vanuatu, Tonga, and Western Samoa receive about 20 percent. In Papua New Guinea and Vanuatu the level of aid has fallen in recent years as recurrent budgetary support has been withdrawn. If this component is ignored, the trend level of aid receipts has either remained static or increased. While there is talk of donor fatigue, there is reason to assume this level of receipts may not continue during the 1990s.

These results suggest that domestic resource mobilization has not been a constraint on investment or growth, although the Private Sector Project makes a strong case for greater efficiency in financial intermediation. The sizable source of financial resources has been channeled into investment that has failed to generate growth, which is therefore inefficient. Clearly, a major challenge for the Pacific islands is how to funnel the large available sources of official aid and remittances into productive activities, namely, private sector investment. While the solutions to this problem are not easy, the process of financial intermediation has failed to establish an adequate conduit. These issues are addressed in Chapter 5.

The high volume of aid receipts in the Pacific island economies has had a variety of consequences not all of which are beneficial. The high volume of aid receipts has distorted the allocation of resources. Scarce human resources are attracted into a "booming" aid sector, and an overinflated public sector has been encouraged to expand (Table 1.4). In the Pacific island economies the aid sector has become associated with "Dutch

Table 1.4 Percent distribution of labor force by activity status

	Fiji (1986)	PNG (1980)	Solomon Islands (1986)	Tonga (1986)	Vanuatu (1986)	Western Samoa (1981)
Employees	42.2	16.1	16.0	47.8	26.0	42.0
Private sector	26.4	N.A.	N.A.	19.5	18.0	N.A.
Public sector	15.8	N.A.	N.A.	28.2	7.9	N.A.
Self-employment	50.3	81.0	84.0	43.2	74.0	58.0
Cash	37.1	39.8	6.1	N.A.	N.A.	3.8
Subsistence	13.2	41.2	77.9	N.A.	N.A.	54.2
Unemployment	7.5	2.8	N.A.	9.0	N.A.	N.A.

Disease" consequences, which lead to currency overvaluation, economic stagnation in other parts of the economy, and a general attitude of dependency. Furthermore, aid can directly undermine private sector development by supporting government participation in production and marketing activities. This has been particularly evident in the agricultural sector (McGregor and Coulter 1991). However, this is not to say that well designed aid programs do not have a crucial role to play in encouraging and facilitating private sector development. An integrated series of proposals to this effect are made in Chapter 9.

The aid situation is compounded in the Cook Islands, Tonga, and Western Samoa with the high level of migrants remittances, which have also reached in excess of 20 percent of GDP. The populations of these three Polynesian countries have in varying degrees access to Australia, New Zealand, and the United States. These economies have responded to the high wages in neighboring countries and to opportunities at home, through exporting their labor. The resulting flow of remittances supports the high level of domestic consumption and the associated level of negative savings. While migration may provide less of an avenue for future generations as immigration requirements tighten, family reunification will still provide a substantial outlet. It might also be expected that second and third generations would be less willing to support relatives in the islands. However, for the foreseeable future the export of labor will have a strong impact on domestic labor markets and consequently domestic production. Only activities yielding a high rate of economic return are undertaken, and others less profitable will be abandoned. The sharp decline of the Tongan copra industry is a prime example. Remittances do, however, potentially offer a substantial source of funds that could be tapped for productive investment. Some recommendations are presented in Chapter 5.

Employment

The pattern of employment in the Pacific island countries is dominated by a large rural sector. Employment in the rural areas has centered around communal subsistence activities, although most households now sell at least some marketable surplus or are otherwise engaged in commercial transaction. Table 1.4 provides basic statistics on participation in economic production in the Pacific islands. The data presented are derived from the latest island population censuses but are not always consistent or presented in a form suitable for cross country comparison.

The data on self-employment provide a rough indicator of the size of the traditional and rural agricultural sector. In some cases it has been divided into a cash and a subsistence component. In all economies, with the exception of Tonga, the rural self-employed sector is larger than 50 percent of employment. In Fiji, the majority of self-employment is for cash farming, reflecting the more monetized nature of the economy, particularly relating to sugarcane production. In Papua New Guinea, subsistence farming is greater than one-half of all self-employment, whereas for Solomon Islands and Western Samoa the data suggest the level of subsistence is even greater. These figures, however, probably reflect differences in census definitions rather than actual differences in activity because the Papua New Guinea economy is one of the most traditional in the region. While the data are obviously imperfect, they do provide an important guide to the structure of the island economies and the importance of the largely subsistence rural sector.

A notable feature of paid employment for the three countries for which data are available (Fiji, Tonga, and Vanuatu) is the high percentage engaged/employed in the public sector. This reflects the leading sector role assumed by governments, which, with the exception of Fiji, is being increasingly driven by aid.

Conclusion

The Pacific island economic performance during the 1980s was generally poor, and rates of economic growth barely managed to keep pace with the expansion in population. The failure of this group of economies to grow reflected poor export performance. In part, the poor export performance was the result of declining terms of trade. Although the rate of deterioration in the terms of trade during the 1980s was less than that of the previous decade, the long-run secular decline in export commodity prices throughout the 1970s and 1980s was a major disincentive to primary commodity production. However, while the declining terms of trade was an important explanatory variable in Pacific island economic performance, it was only one of many contributing factors, which are discussed elsewhere throughout this book.

With economic stagnation came little change in economic structure. Perversely, the level of services rose in some Pacific islands reflecting "booming" aid sectors and large remittance flows. However, although economic structure remained largely unchanged, economic diversification was not insignificant and indicates that these economies are responsive to market forces and appropriate polices. Toward the end of the 1980s Fiji commenced deregulating its economic structure, and a substantial garment industry has been developed. In Tonga substantial shifts in the structure of exports have occurred with a very significant reduction in the reliance on coconut products.

Although overall growth has been poor, investment in the Pacific island countries has been high by developing country standards. The very weak relationship between growth and investment results from the fact that the majority of investment has been in public sector infrastructure projects. This type of investment, although a necessary condition for growth, is not sufficient. If there is insufficient private sector investment, no amount of public sector activity will generate economic development.

Although domestic resource mobilization has been limited in most Pacific island economies, inadequate domestic savings has not inhibited investment or development. Sufficient sources of funds have usually been available from foreign sources. This points to a problem of financial intermediation: how to ensure that the sizable pool of resources flows into productive investment and economically efficient activities. The situation indicates the need to develop appropriate financial institutions, but it is particularly problematic in the Pacific islands, given the lack of private sector entrepreneurship. The sizable volume of remittances in certain Pacific island economies present opportunities to redirect these flows from consumption purposes toward productive investment.

chapter 2

Trade and investment performance in the global context

To evaluate private sector performance, opportunities, and policies, it is necessary to examine the Pacific island countries in the context of the world economy. The Private Sector Project's research concentrated on four interrelated areas: first, on the growth, trade, and investment performance of these economies in the 1970s and 1980s in the context of the functioning of the world economy; second, on the structure and direction of Pacific island trade and policy issues that arise; third, on commodity price fluctuations and how they affect the Pacific island economies; and, fourth, on the prospects for the world economy in the 1990s and the Pacific island economies within the world economy in the coming decade. The findings of this research are presented in Thirlwall (1991) and are summarized in this chapter.

Small countries face obstacles in the growth and development process that are not present in larger countries. First, they tend to be more specialized and less diversified than larger countries, which makes them much more vulnerable to both internal and external shocks.

Second, the population of small countries is usually not sufficient to reap economies of scale. Economies of scale in manufacturing and in infrastructure are difficult to achieve, which makes investment in manufacturing activities and infrastructure more costly and uneconomic; this is more often the case with small rather than large countries.

Third, to the extent that small economies are island economies and geographically remote, transport and communication problems can undermine the competitiveness of these economies. These are some problems that small economies face in the growth and development process, which are not present in larger economies. In addition, most Pacific island countries are particularly prone to natural disasters and operate under land tenure systems that constrain the availability of land and its productivity.

There are, however, some offsetting advantages for the Pacific islands that this project has explored in detail in terms of investment opportunities. These stem from the region's climate, southern hemisphere location, relatively pest free and unpolluted environment, and natural beauty.

The Relative Performance of the Region in the Global Context

An assessment of economic performance of the Pacific island countries was presented in Chapter 1. In this chapter some key economic indicators are considered in the context of the world economy.

The average per capita income of the seven countries for which data are available is approximately US$800. This puts the Pacific island economies somewhere between the 42 low income countries identified by the World Bank with an average annual per capita income of US$290 and the 34 low middle-income countries with an average per capita income of US$1,200.

Compared with other small economies with populations of less than one million, the World Bank's definition of a small economy, only eight actually have a per capita income that is lower than the Pacific islands average. Countries that are richer tend to be tourist destinations in the eastern Caribbean that are in close proximity to the large markets of Europe and North America.

In comparison with other developing countries, how did the Pacific island economies perform during the 1970s and 1980s? These were very turbulent years in the world economy. The Bretton Woods system collapsed in 1971-72. The world went on the floating exchange rates, and inflation generally accelerated. The price of oil rose five times in 1973-74, which plunged the oil consuming countries into recession. The price of oil doubled again in 1979, and in 1980-82 the world economies as a whole experienced a slump greater than that of the Great Depression of the 1930s. The debt crisis emerged during the early years of the 1980s. Its effect lingers on and hampers the growth in development performance in large parts of the developing world, particularly in Africa and Latin America.

Against this background the Pacific island economies both absolutely and relative to many other developing countries did remarkably well in the 1970s. However, in the 1980s their performance was uniformly bad (Table 1.1).

During the 1970s the average annual economic growth ranged from 4 to 7 percent for the four Pacific island countries for which data are available

(Fiji, Papua New Guinea, Solomon Islands, and Tonga) (Table 1.1). This compares with 5.7 percent for all developing countries and 3.2 percent for all small low-income countries over the same period. For the group, growth fell to between 2 and 4 percent in the 1980s, with a similar result achieved for the other Pacific island countries for which data are available. This compares with 3.3 percent for all developing countries and 3.5 percent for low income countries. When population growth is taken into account, GDP per capita dropped from an average of 2 percent during the 1970s to approximately zero for the group during the 1980s. Investment and export performance were examined to explain the overall deterioration in Pacific island growth performance in the 1980s.

A significant relationship between growth and the proportion of gross national product (GNP) devoted to investment was not found in either Fiji or Papua New Guinea. Sufficiently long data runs are not available for the other economies, but a similar result would be expected. However, there is no evidence of a deterioration of investment performance in the 1980s compared with the 1970s. The investment ratio stays up at about 25 percent of GDP, which represents a deterioration of investment performance relative to other developing countries. Thus the growth performance of the Pacific island economies deteriorated relative to their investment performance.

The productivity of investment must be lower in the Pacific island economies relative to other developing countries and must have fallen in the 1980s relative to the 1970s. It is notable that the capital-output ratio estimated from those relationships between the growth rate and the investment ratio turns out to be about six, which is very high by international standards.

The above may reflect the different structure of investment or its lower quality in the Pacific island economies relative to other developing countries or perhaps a greater degree of undercapacity utilization owing to constraints on output. For instance, a high percentage of investment has been in the public sector on infrastructure projects, which have not necessarily translated into increased output, at least without considerable lags. Investment in the private sector on its own would represent a lower rate and would indicate a much poorer investment performance. The data that are available indicate that in Tonga public sector investment was 30 percent of the total investment during the 1980s, while in Western Samoa and Fiji, the comparative figures were 33 percent and 39 percent, respectively. Public investment in infrastructure has proved to be a necessary, but not a sufficient, condition for growth. This suggests that other binding constraints are in place, notably human resource development, and that more is required to encourage productive private sector investment. The policy and institutional requirements to achieve this investment have been a major focus of this investment.

Evidence of a low quality of investment is reflected in terms of the massive slowdown in export growth in the 1980s as compared with the 1970s (Table 1.3). A percentage decline in export growth was also experienced by other developing countries. Yet the output growth decline was not as great as in the Pacific islands. This suggests structural differences and weaknesses in the Pacific island economies reflecting perhaps the greater openness of the Pacific island economies and their greater dependence on imports for the productivity of domestic resources. The ratio of imports to GDP, for example, in most of the islands averages between 50 and 70 percent and in one or two cases is over 70 percent.

The Pacific island economies suffered a serious deterioration in their terms of trade over the last two decades, as shown by the analysis in Chapter 1. The prices of all major commodities that the Pacific islands export, with the exception of gold and sawn timber, have deteriorated relative to the exports of manufactures from industrial countries. Most seriously affected are the smaller island economies that are heavily dependent on coconut products, the price of which has halved in real terms over the 1980s. The point is reiterated in Figure 2.1, which plots the ratio of coconut oil prices to import prices for Tonga.

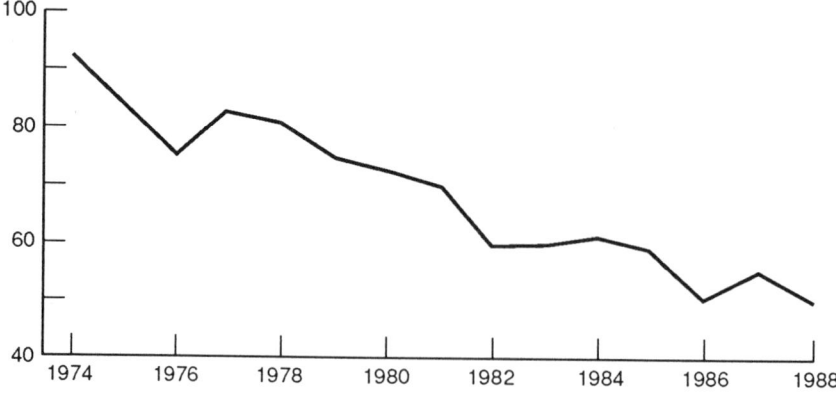

Figure 2.1 Tongan coconut oil prices (five year moving averages) deflated by the import component of the consumer price index, 1974–88

The Direction of Pacific Islands Trade

The relationship between economic performance of the Pacific island economies and world economic growth working through the medium of trade was examined. Four of the six Pacific island countries identified in Tables 2.1 and 2.2 show a significant elasticity of export growth with respect to both the value and volume of world trade. Furthermore, the impact of world trade was large with the elasticity in all but one case exceeding unity. It can be concluded from the statistical analysis that the Pacific islands are sufficiently integrated into the world economy through trade for fluctuations in the world economy to have significant repercussions in terms of their export performance. In other words, export performance is not simply determined by the supply side or by erratic shocks. There are, however, major supply-side constraints to private sector development to which government policy can be addressed, and these have been a major focus of the Private Sector Project.

We now specifically examine the direction of Pacific island trade and issues of trade strategy. Table 2.3 shows the trade flows in 1988 between the

Table 2.1   The elasticity of Pacific island export growth to world trade growth (value)

	Elasticity coefficient	Standard error of estimate	Correlation coefficient
Fiji	1.195	(0.259)	0.587
PNG	1.646	(0.507)	0.412
Solomon Islands	1.579	(0.463)	0.436
Vanuatu	1.095*	(0.727)	0.131
Western Samoa	1.216*	(0.765)	0.144
Tonga	1.798	(0.781)	0.261

* Not statistically significant at the 95 percent confidence level.

Table 2.2   The elasticity of Pacific island export growth to the growth in the volume of world trade

	Elasticity coefficient	Standard error of estimate	Correlation coefficient
Fiji	0.710*	(1.007)	0.032
PNG	5.034	(1.067)	0.597
Solomon Islands	4.337	(1.098)	0.509
Tonga	4.130	(2.050)	0.212
Vanuatu	4.978	(1.150)	0.419
Western Samoa	3.152*	(1.938)	0.149

* Not statistically significant at the 95 percent confidence level.

Table 2.3 Changing pattern of Pacific island trade, 1982-88

Exports		Fiji	Papua New Guinea	Solomon Islands	Western Samoa	Vanuatu	Tonga	Kiribati	Total Pacific Islands	United Kingdom	Australia & New Zealand	United States & Canada	Japan	Rest of Asia	Other
Fiji	a		+0.33	-0.1	-0.6	-0.6	-1.6	-0.9	-3.5	+6.8	+1.0	-5.5	+4.3	-0.2	-
	b		+471%	-33%	-21%	-33%	-46%	-53%	-34%	+30%	+5%	-46%	+215%	-1%	-
Papua New Guinea	a	+0.02		-0.2		-0.01			-0.2	-0.4	-3.7	+0.8	+8.2	+3.5	-4.0*
	b	+200%		-50%		-100%			-50%	-7%	-34%	+42%	+25%	+30%	-15%
Solomon Islands	a	+1.3	0			+0.43			+1.8	-3.9	-1.6	+2.5	-21.0	+25.9	
	b	+100%	0%			∞			+90%	-27%	-32%	+277%	-34%	+530%	
Western Samoa	a	+1.4							+1.4	+7.2	+6.7	-20.4	-7.8	-2.6	+16.2*
	b	+280%							+280%	+7200%	+18%	-73%	-95%	-13%	+274%
Vanuatu	a	-0.01	+0.07	-0.04					+0.1	-0.07	+1.6	-3.4	+4.7	-2.1	-4.0**
	b	-25%	∞	-40%					+50%	-70%	+228%	-13%	+174%	-26%	-13%
Tonga	a	-0.7			+5.0	+0.005			+4.4	-0.1	-29.8	+16.4	+10.4	0	
	b	-17%			+1000%	∞			+95%	-7%	-37%	+174%	∞	0	

a represents change in proportion of exports going to different markets.
b represents the percentage change in the share of the market.

*Germany

**Benelux Countries

Pacific islands themselves and how much each island exports to the rest of the world.

As far as trade with the outside world is concerned, the importance of world markets outside the Pacific island economies varies from one Pacific island country to another.

One important finding is that despite the South Pacific Regional Trade and Economic Cooperation Agreement (SPARTECA) between the Pacific island country economies and Australasia, there is very little evidence that total trade with Australasia has grown more strongly than with other countries. One reason may be that Australasia in the 1970s and the 1980s was one of the slowest growing markets in terms of the rate of growth of import volume. The recent dramatic growth in Fiji garment exports to Australia and New Zealand is an important exception. However, this too is beginning to slow in the face of a prolonged recession in Australia and New Zealand and a reduction in the Australian import quota allocated to Fiji.

On trade between the Pacific islands themselves, two facts stand out. First, intra-Pacific island trade is dominated by Fiji. In 1988 of the US$29.14 million of intra-Pacific island trade, US$22.10 million or 80 percent is accounted for by Fiji. Second, intra-Pacific island trade is absolutely miniscule relative to trade with other parts of the world. In 1988 intra-island trade was only 1.5 percent of the total export value of all Pacific island exports. If this is compared with the earlier 1980s, that level of the value of intra-Pacific island trade has actually fallen.

An Appropriate Trade and Investment Strategy for the Pacific Islands

The Pacific island outputs and exports are dominated by bulk primary commodities such as sugar, coconut products, cocoa, coffee, timber, canned fish, palm oil, and minerals. While the Pacific island countries may have a "natural" comparative advantage in the production of these commodities, they cannot alone provide the basis for sustained development in the future. The expectation is that the terms of trade will continue to move against bulk commodity exports as demand for these commodities grows relatively slowly compared with world income.

In contrast, the demand for other types of goods, particularly most manufactures, horticultural products, and sophisticated services, grows relatively rapidly compared with world income. Thus Pacific island economies, as part of a long-term development strategy, need to diversify their output and export structure toward commodities with more favorable production and demand characteristics, such as various types of manufactures, high-value horticulture and marine products, and service activities such as tourism. The opportunities and requirements for developing high-value exports have been a major focus of the Private Sector Project. At the same time the efficiency of traditional export activities needs to be enhanced as part of the process of broadening and strengthening the economic base of the Pacific island countries.

The vital trade policy question is how to create the appropriate environment for structural change and diversification. Historical evidence supports the view that unrestricted free trade has not always been the route to development. All other countries now developed, with the exception of Britain, achieved structural change and industrialization behind protective barriers of some sort, and even today many successful industrialized countries practice various forms of overt and covert protection. However, historical evidence also suggests that countries that have continued to rely on protection have failed to develop at a satisfactory rate. At some point in the development process, the reduction in protection of import substituting industries, and the adoption of an outward looking strategy, has proved the best vehicle for economic growth and development.

In the case of the Pacific island countries there would appear, with the exceptions of Fiji and Papua New Guinea, to be no room for development through import substitution. The smaller economies have such limited domestic markets that the development of industrialization through import substitution must be slight. Development through necessity will have to be restricted to exports, and the case of Tonga's Small Industries Centre (SIC) provides a good example. In the smaller economies the cost of protection will be high and will place an immediate tax on the consuming population with the benefits accruing to a narrow range of interests.

In the case of Fiji a highly protected industrial sector was encouraged in the 1980s, and the economy failed to register any significant growth. In the latter part of the 1980s a booming garment sector emerged, and the pace of economic growth quickened. At the same time the government began to reverse many of its earlier protectionist policies, although most of the necessary movement to reduce the prevailing high rates of protection needs to be accomplished in the 1990s. There is a consensus of opinion that the protectionist policies of the 1980s directly resulted in the poor growth performance of the Fiji economy. However, it was the development of a domestic industrial base behind tariffs that allowed sufficient entrepreneurial skills to be developed and through which the garment revolution emerged. It is doubtful that sufficient domestic skills would have existed if there had not been a pool of entrepreneurs to draw on. In this sense the Fiji economy is treading a well worn route; that is, development behind protected tariffs followed by a restructuring of government policy reorienting the economy toward an outward direction. This process of restructuring is still ongoing and in Fiji's case needs to be completed before the fruits and rewards of these policies can be achieved.

The Pacific island countries would stand to benefit handsomely from any movement toward freer world trade. Proposals for a wider free trade area with Australasia need to be approached with particular caution. Unequal partners need to be treated unequally if the outcome is to be greater equality. There is a strong case for duty free access into Australia and New Zealand for all Pacific island products, including those presently exempted under SPARTECA, but not for reciprocity. First, there is a limited scope for structural change in any of the Pacific islands without a measure of protection from countries that are already more competitive. Second, the abolition of import duties would deprive governments of an important source of revenue.

It is recommended that the Pacific island economies adopt an outward looking strategy. This infers orientation toward export promotion rather than import substitution. This strategy will entail government support and encouragement but exclude instruments that directly affect the price mechanism and interfere with resource allocation such as tariffs or subsidies. The strategy is, however, not completely "laissez faire" and implicitly involves an element of protection. The Private Sector Project recommends a number of specific programs along with supporting projects that constitute an "outward looking" strategy. These include industry based and supported institutions for export promotion, the establishment of export oriented small industry centers, and various measures and programs directed at enterprise support organizations (ESOs). This strategy, which reflects the outward looking policies adopted by the successful developing countries, particularly those in Southeast Asia, would seem to be the appropriate route for the Pacific islands to follow.

Commodity Price Fluctuations and Their Effect on Pacific Islands Development

The Pacific island economies arc plagued by commodity price fluctuations. The instability of primary product prices plays havoc with individual commodities and is a major source of instability, as well as a contributory factor toward the poor growth performance of the Pacific island countries.

Figures 2.2 and 2.3 show the movement in the prices of major commodities together with the movements in the value of total exports for Fiji and Papua New Guinea. Similar relationships were derived for Solomon Islands, Kiribati, Tonga, and Western Samoa and are presented in Thirlwall (1991). The analysis shows a strong statistical relationship between variations in the value of export earnings and variations in the prices of the major exports. In the case of Fiji, for example, changes in the prices of sugar and coconut oil account for 84 percent of the variation in export earnings. The price variation of each of the individual commodities has strong explanatory power, with all the prices being highly correlated. These results confirm the findings of previous Papua New Guinea studies, which concluded that severe commodity price instability has a disruptive impact on export earnings and hence on economic stability and growth (McGregor and Coulter 1991).

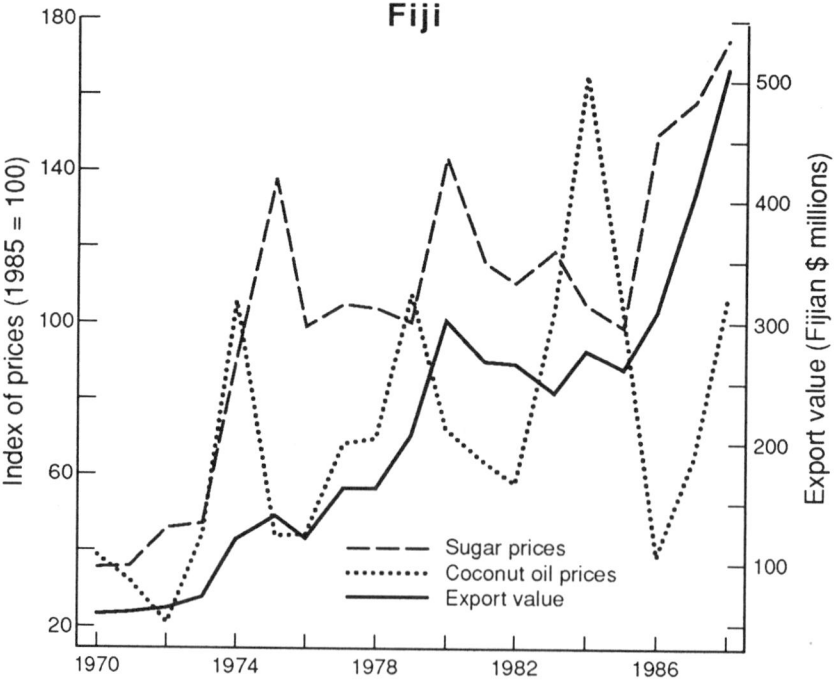

Figure 2.2 Commodity prices and export value

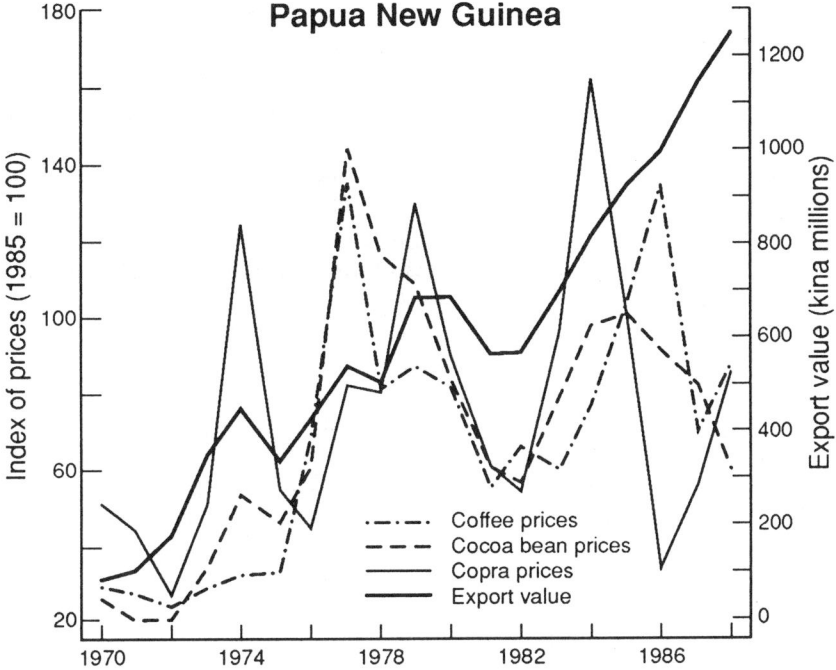

Figure 2.3 Commodity prices and export value

The Private Sector Project's findings, presented in McGregor and Coulter 1991, are that extreme price instability has had a negative impact on investment and maintenance decisions by smallholders, although this impact is less for the plantation sector. This view, however, is not universally supported in the literature.

International compensation for shortfalls in export earnings comes from two main sources: the Compensatory Financing Facility (CFF) of the International Monetary Fund (IMF) and the Stabex scheme operated by the European Economic Community (EEC) under the Lomé Convention.

To date, Fiji, Papua New Guinea, Solomon Islands, and Western Samoa have used the CFF, and all the Pacific island economies (except the Cook Islands) have received support from Stabex. Stabex funds form an important component of Solomon Islands and Vanuatu national budgets. However, compensation from the IMF's Compensatory Financing Facility and the EEC's Stabex scheme has been small in relation to fluctuations in export earnings experienced.

Some individual island countries operate their own internal schemes to insulate producers against price fluctuations. These schemes are analyzed in some detail in McGregor and Coulter 1991, which examines the institutional environment for private sector development. In principle such schemes are to be welcomed from the point of view of maintaining the continuity of production and for overall macroeconomic stability. However, only in the case of Papua New Guinea have these funds had a significant and largely successful impact. These funds have gone a long way to stabilize prices during a turbulent time and have by and large been well managed. The mechanism, legal basis, and management of these funds provide a model for other Pacific island countries wishing to stabilize the commodity returns of growers.

In the absence of international commodity agreements to stabilize prices, international organizations might consider subscribing to a regional stabilization fund or to national stabilization funds within the countries themselves. However, before this could be done great care would need to be taken to ensure that these funds had a sound economic and legal basis and that the necessary management input was in place.

Prospects for the 1990s

As far as the world economy is concerned, the prospects for the 1990s, beyond the present recessionary circumstances, look more favorable compared with those of the first six or seven years of the 1980s. A 3 percent per annum growth is expected in the developed countries and 4 percent for the developing countries as a whole. These figures are based on estimates of forecasting units such as United Nations Conference on Trade and Development (UNCTAD), the World Bank, the IMF, and the world model developed by the National Institute of Economic and Social Research in London. All these forecasting units seem to converge on this figure of roughly 3 percent growth for the developed countries and 4 percent growth for the less developed countries.

The value of world trade is projected to grow 10 percent per annum. This would suggest there will be an external environment that will not be unfavorable for private sector development in the Pacific island countries over the next decade. In fact, if the past statistical relationship between the export growth of the Pacific island economies and world trade's growth held in the 1990s, the average growth of the value exports of the Pacific island economies could be in the vicinity of 10 percent.

However, according to the most recent World Bank forecasts, a substantial improvement in the prices of the region's major commodities cannot be expected in the medium term (Table 2.4). These forecasts follow the World Bank's previous set of more optimistic price projections. Should a cyclical upswing in commodity prices not materialize in the near future there will be no respite for the Pacific island countries in achieving the necessary viability in their traditional exports through increasing efficiency and reducing costs. Sustained development at an accelerated pace cannot be based, if a long-run perspective is used, on primary bulk commodities alone. There has to be structural change, which should not be left entirely to market forces. However, if commodity prices remain low over next few years, it will be more difficult to make a smooth adjustment toward higher value export commodities that have more favorable long-term demand prospects. A major objective of the Private Sector Project was to indicate policies and measures to facilitate this adjustment via private sector development.

Table 2.4 Price forecasts for major commodities exported by Pacific island countries

	1985 (actual)	1989 (actual)	1990	1995	2000	Percentage change, 1989-95
Coffee (c/kg)	321	239	198	280	424	17.2
Cocoa (c/kg)	225	124	127	160	223	29.0
Sugar ($/tonne)	90	282	277	341	457	20.9
Palm oil ($/tonne)	501	350	285	408	425	16.6
Coconut oil ($/tonne)	590	517	336	639	793	23.6
Copra ($/tonne)	386	348	230	387	557	11.2
Logs-Malaysian ($/cm)	136	225	210	260	340	15.5
Copper ($/tonne)	1,417	2,848	2,650	1,874	2,875	-34.2
Gold ($/oz)	318	381	383	500	600	31.2
MUV index (1985 = 100)	100	138.5	147.2	170.4	204.9	23.0

Source: World Bank, International Economics Department, International Trade Division, December 19, 1990.

chapter 3

The macroeconomic environment

This chapter highlights some of the key issues of macroeconomic policy in the Pacific islands that have been identified through the Private Sector Project. The discussion focuses on those elements that directly affect the productive environment, as well as whether the conduct of policy has encouraged or discouraged economic activity and development. Because the private sector is the main vehicle of attaining economic progress, the subject basically concerns whether the macroeconomic environment has fostered a hospitable climate for private enterprise.

The research was divided into four broad areas:

1. Financial stability,

2. A competitive price and cost structure,

3. Trade policy, and

4. Counter-cyclical policy.

Financial stability, the first area, is perhaps the most important ingredient of economic policy for without an orderly economic environment, productive activity will stagnate and fail to reach its potential. Overly expansionary fiscal policies, coupled with excessive domestic credit creation, and foreign borrowing will result in a deterioration in the external account, inflation, and debt service problems. Productive entrepreneurship will be discouraged if foreign exchange and credit are rationed and if prices are rapidly inflating. This section briefly examines the success of the Pacific islands in maintaining financial stability and investigates inflation rates, the balance of payments outcome, and external debt performance.

The second area of interest is whether economic policy has generated a price and cost structure–which has provided an incentive for entrepreneurs to take risk and make profit–that fully uses a nation's resources to the best of its productive potential. The discussion focuses on whether the basic elements of prime cost (wages, exchange rate, and interest rates) have maintained a healthy and competitive economy.

The use of tariff policy is an extremely powerful tool of resource allocation, and much of the debate on the success and failure of economic development in different regions of the world has been attributed to differences in tariff policy. This discussion forms the third area of research.

The fourth important aspect of macroeconomic policy is how successfully the Pacific island countries have responded to changes in the product or business cycle. The Pacific islands are particularly vulnerable to large shocks to their economies. These shocks may arise from the impact of tropical cyclones, the impact of large infrastructure projects, or rapid swings in the external terms of trade. Most of the Pacific islands have very open economies with imports/exports representing 50 percent or more of total production. Productive activity is also largely concentrated in the production of primary commodities for export, which are subject to wide fluctuations in their price. Under these conditions, variations in the terms of trade can impart highly destabilizing influences on fiscal and monetary objectives. As part of the Private Sector Project, research was conducted into these issues of short- and medium-term economic management.

Financial Stability

For the most part the governments of the Pacific islands have followed conservative fiscal and monetary policies, and a sound record of financial stability has been achieved. The small and very open nature of the island economies results in an almost immediate deterioration in the external account if imprudent fiscal and monetary policies are followed. With this awareness, and basically sound management, balance of payments problems and excessive inflation have been avoided. Only in the case of Solomon Islands and Western Samoa and in the last two decades have Pacific island economies pursued overly expansionary fiscal and monetary policies, and only in the case of Western Samoa was an International Monetary Fund (IMF) program required to stabilize and restore external equilibrium. The next sections examine the success of financial management through an examination of recent regional trends in inflation, external debt, and foreign reserve import coverage.

Inflation

Appendix 7 indicates the relative success of different island economies in containing inflation. Given the choice of exchange rate regime, and the openness of the island economies, inflation in the Pacific islands has been strongly influenced by the rate of inflation in their major trading partners. Accordingly, trends in Australia, Japan, and New Zealand are also included for comparison. The situation presented suggests that the Pacific island inflationary experience has been, on balance, adequate considering the openness of the island economies. Certainly, the Pacific island countries have not suffered from hyperinflation, which is common to many African and South American countries. However, rates of inflation have at times been high and the oscillations have been considerable. In the discussion it is worth noting that the inflationary experience in Australia and New Zealand has generally been poor, and given the exchange rate environment, the Pacific islands have had little choice but to inherit this outcome.

Discussion of the individual countries' experience will help in establishing certain key characteristics. Experience in Papua New Guinea is the most favorable of all the Pacific island countries and directly reflects the pursuit of the "hard Kina" policy–the selection of an exchange rate regime to minimize imported inflation. Apart from the two oil price shocks, inflation in Papua New Guinea was held in the 3 to 8 percent range. In terms of inflation Papua New Guinea has out-performed Australia, which is quite an achievement, given Australia is the major source of Papua New Guinea's imports. Fiji's experience is not dissimilar to Papua New Guinea with the exception of the late 1980s when Fiji underwent a large cumulative devaluation of 30 percent to help maintain external stability during a political crisis, which imparted substantial domestic inflation.

Solomon Islands experienced largely reflected imported trends until the mid-1980s when a persistent financial crisis led to a series of devaluations and reciprocal wage adjustments. This resulted in a rising trend in domestic inflation at a time when imported inflationary pressure was downward. Tonga has pegged its currency at par to the Australian dollar throughout the period, and the rapid oscillations reflect not only imported inflation inherited from the oil crises but also the impact of adverse climatic conditions and consequential shortage of foodstuffs in 1985 and 1986.

Apart from the peaks in inflation in 1974 and 1980-81 following the two oil crises, the Vanuatu experience has been moderate with the exception of 1987-88 when inflation revealed a marked rise after a tropical cyclone at the beginning of 1987 and two large devaluations in 1986 totaling 22 percent. In Western Samoa recent trends in inflation have been dominated by the financial crisis the economy experienced in the late 1970s and early

1980s. However, after a successful IMF adjustment and stabilization package, inflation fell to more modest and satisfactory levels.

Inflation in the Pacific island countries has been dominated by the underlying rate of imported inflation. Deviations from this trend have been caused by currency depreciation or adverse climatic conditions. Inflation has been largely cost driven, and monetary expansion has played a relatively minor part of the outcome, with the exception of Western Samoa in the late 1970s and Solomon Islands in the mid- to late 1980s. The minor influence of monetary policy has resulted from the adoption of normally prudent and conservative fiscal and monetary policies.

External debt

Appendix 8 illustrates the Pacific island external debt situation. With the exception of Tonga the external debt of the Pacific islands has risen throughout the period covered from 1976 to 1988. In Fiji, Tonga, and Vanuatu external debt is a small percentage of GDP, and external borrowing has been modest. However, borrowing in Papua New Guinea, Solomon Islands, and Western Samoa has risen to a sizable volume, although the levels are not yet excessive from an international perspective. In the case of Papua New Guinea the government embarked on an expansionary expenditure program at the beginning of the 1980s largely financed from commercial external sources. This led to a rapid build-up of debt from 20 to 40 percent of GDP (data for Papua New Guinea exclude private sector debt and debt service). In the second half of the 1980s (and not fully covered in the diagram) the government reversed its earlier policies and reduced its external commercial borrowings to more appropriate levels.

The expansion in government expenditures in Solomon Islands in the mid- to late 1980s is reflected in the very large increase in external debt from less than 20 percent of GDP to just under 60 percent, placing the country as the most indebted in the group. Western Samoan debt has also reached a high level and reflects the build-up during the late 1970s, a period for which no data were available for this study. However, in the case of Western Samoa the ratio of debt to GDP has remained relatively static during the period for which data are available.

Appendix 9 indicates the debt service position of the Pacific islands, which with the exception of Papua New Guinea and Western Samoa reveals a comfortable picture.

This outcome largely reflects the reliance of the Pacific islands on concessional sources of external finance. The relatively large debt service ratio for Papua New Guinea results from the choice to fund government expenditure from external commercial borrowing. In the case of Solomon Islands the rapid build-up of external debt has yet to have an impact on the debt service ratio. This reflects both the concessional nature of the borrowing and the fact that most of the debt was incurred recently before grace periods had time to elapse. It could be expected that this situation will change quite rapidly in the near future, and the debt service ratio for Solomon Islands will rise to a higher level. For Western Samoa the repayment pattern reflects the historical build-up of debt.

Balance of payments

Appendix 10 indicates changes in import coverage–the ratio of net foreign reserves to monthly imports. Due to the choice of fixed exchange rates and restrictions on capital account, import coverage may be used as a rough guide to the success of monetary policy or the control of domestic credit. Vanuatu is excluded from the analysis because its situation is atypical as a result of the absence of external capital controls and abnormally large reserves of foreign exchange. For many Pacific islands at least three months coverage has been considered a minimum.

With the exception of Western Samoa the Pacific islands reveal a satisfactory performance in maintaining adequate external reserves, although considerable year-to-year fluctuations are indicated. Such variations are typical in economies dependent on a limited range of primary commodities whose production is subject to adverse climatic conditions and whose prices are subject to the vagaries of international commodity cycles.

In the case of Western Samoa the graph clearly reveals the consequences for the external account of rapid fiscal expansion accommodated through monetary creation. The successful stabilization and adjustment program implemented at the beginning of the 1980s was achieved through tight expenditure and credit controls. These policies were maintained during the remainder of the 1980s with the result that by the end of the decade Western Samoa had achieved the highest level of import coverage of all Pacific islands with the exception of Vanuatu.

The example of Western Samoa indicates the rapid deterioration in the external account that can occur in a small Pacific island economy if prudent fiscal and monetary policies are not adopted. Given the very small and open nature of these economies, increases in domestic credit are very quickly translated into deterioration of the external account before excessive inflation is generated. Adjustment becomes necessary at an early stage, and thus a degree of automatic protection is generated against the consequences of poor fiscal management on inflation.

A Competitive Price and Cost Structure

We now turn to the question of whether the Pacific island economies have generated a price and cost environment conducive to encouraging productive investment and economic activity. The majority of products exported from the island economies fall into the category of primary commodities whose prices are determined in international markets and over which island producers have no control. There has been some departure from this norm with the advent of tourism and the development of niche market exports by some countries. However, in general, it is accurate to define the Pacific islands as price takers. In other words, the islands can remain competitive only through attempts to maintain a competitive cost structure. The research examined the three elements of prime cost: wages, the price of foreign exchange, and the cost of capital or the rate of interest.

Wages

Consideration of wages can be divided into two areas: (1) the absolute level of the real wage and (2) the flexibility of wages to meet changing economic circumstances. In the first instance the basic real wage of unskilled labor in the Pacific islands is strongly influenced by the subsistence wage in the rural economy. The level of subsistence production in the traditional economy has meant that households have not been prepared to supply labor below a relatively high real wage by international standards. This has meant that the Pacific island economies have not been able to develop a comparative advantage in many labor-intensive activities that have been exploited by other developing countries. However, as urban populations grow, their traditional rural links weaken this so-called "subsistence affluence." Furthermore, Fiji, the country that has done best in export manufacturing, has a sizable population that has no access to land.

Additional factors of more recent origin, however, have tended to exert an upward influence on the level of the real wage. The first factor concerns the high proportion of economic activity that is represented by government and aid expenditures. Table 3.1 indicates the proportion of GDP represented by government expenditure and foreign aid. Although for Fiji and Papua New Guinea these proportions are relatively low, the levels in the smaller island economies are high. The large volume of demand originating from these sources has resulted in these economies displaying symptoms of what has become to be known as Dutch Disease. Under these

Table 3.1 Public expenditure, foreign aid, and migrants remittances as a percent of GDP during 1987

	Fiji	PNG	Solomon Islands	Vanuatu	Western Samoa	Tonga
Public expenditure/ GDP	29.4	30.9	47.2	56.9	51.4	45.0
Foreign aid/GDP	0.7	6.6	10.7	21.8	15.5	14.1
Private transfers/GDP					36.5	30.7

conditions the aid and public sectors have come to absorb an undue proportion of scarce resources bidding up wages and depressing output elsewhere.

In a similar vein the Polynesian economies of Tonga, Western Samoa, and the Cook Islands have had this problem compounded by the very sizable inflows of migrants remittances. Many household members in these economies have the opportunity to migrate and earn higher wages in Australia, New Zealand, or the United States. However, the reliance on migration as a source of income through migrants transfers has meant that households have been unwilling to supply labor at home at low wage levels.

We now consider the wage flexibility that the island economies display in varying signs of wage rigidity. In Fiji and Papua New Guinea wages were indexed to the cost of living as a result of tripartite agreements between strong unions, employers desirous of industrial harmony, and governments. However, the result was a particularly inflexible system in the 1970s and early '80s. As a consequence under- and unemployment rose to high levels in both economies. In Fiji the reality of economic conditions exerted downward pressure on the real wage by the mid-1980s, and the system came under threat. The economic consequences of the 1987 coups in Fiji brought disruption to the system, and nominal wages have remained unchanged for the last three years. In Papua New Guinea wage rigidity has remained in force through the 1980s, and only now with the advent of the closure of the Bougainville copper mine has any serious amendment to the system become possible.

In both economies it has been frequently argued that although wage indexation was far from ideal, it guaranteed industrial harmony and was therefore justifiable. However, the growing law and order problem, which is evident in both countries, but particularly in Papua New Guinea, must give rise to grave doubts about this belief.

In the other Pacific island economies, wages are determined more through market forces than by any formal wage indexation process. Although frequent adjustments are made, additional research is needed to determine the dynamics of the process. Information on private sector wages is practically non-existent in all these economies.

In summary, the economies of the Pacific islands display varying characteristics of wage rigidity. In Fiji and Papua New Guinea wages have been indexed, but economic realities are forcing changes on the situation, and wages in Fiji are no longer linked to the consumer price index (CPI). In Vanuatu, Solomon Islands, Tonga, and Western Samoa wages are more flexible and are determined to a greater extent by market forces. However, the phenomena of large aid and migrants' transfers have resulted in higher real wage levels. A general conclusion is that various factors in the labor markets of the Pacific island countries have had a negative impact on the private sector's investment demand and profitability.

The rate of exchange

The exchange rate policy was considered from two perspectives: (1) the exchange rate regime adopted by the island governments and (2) the absolute level of the rate of exchange. A discussion of the first concerns the mechanism of determining the rate of exchange in foreign dealings, and the second concerns the profitability of exporting and import replacing activities–collectively known as the traded goods sectors. Given the very open nature of the island economies and their dependence on international trade, an appropriate level of the exchange rate is clearly of fundamental importance.

Most Pacific island countries have adopted an exchange rate regime where the daily rate of exchange is pegged to a basket of currencies. The choice of currencies used in the basket is usually determined by the significance of trading partners in exports and imports. However, a variety of different combinations have been adopted by the island governments. In Papua New Guinea an import weighted basket is used, while in Vanuatu the Vatu was pegged to the Special Drawing Rights (SDRs) until 1988 when a trade weighted basket was adopted. Fiji and Western Samoa follow this procedure, whereas Tonga has pegged its currency, the Pa'anga, to the Australian dollar.

The implication for the island economies of adopting these types of regimes is that the domestic rate of inflation is largely determined by the inflation rate of the respective trading partners. In other words, the rate of inflation in Australia, New Zealand, and Japan plays an extremely important role in influencing the domestic rate of inflation. The advantage of fixing the currency to a basket of currencies is that it averages out the rate of inflation imported from countries with different internal inflation rates. This procedure has proved quite successful in maintaining a relatively low level of domestic inflation, as indicated earlier.

We now consider the real level of the rate of exchange and the ability of island governments to effect a lasting change in the ratio of domestic to foreign prices. Clearly, any attempt to improve profitability in export and import replacing activities through currency depreciation that will be met with compensating rises in domestic costs will render an exchange rate policy ineffective.

Earlier it was noted that both Fiji and Papua New Guinea had a formalized wage indexation process during the 1970s and early '80s. In these circumstances any exchange rate depreciation would have led to a rise in import costs, a rise in the consumer price index, and a compensating rise in wages. Given the very open nature of the island economies, these changes work themselves through the system very quickly. Econometric evidence from the Private Sector Project suggests that a change in import prices fully works its way through the economy within one year. In response to these forces the authorities in both Fiji and Papua New Guinea adopted an approach to an exchange rate policy that in Papua New Guinea came to be known as the hard Kina policy. In other words, the exchange rate policy was geared to minimizing the rate of imported inflation, and no attempt was made to alter either the nominal or the real exchange rate.

Greater flexibility in exchange rate policy has become possible in recent years in these economies as a result of the weakening of the formal wage indexation process. In Fiji after the 1987 coups the government depreciated the Fiji dollar by 35 percent in order to maintain external balance. As a consequence, the profitability of the traded goods sectors was considerably enhanced and provided a considerable boost to the tourism sector. In Papua New Guinea the authorities have recently devalued the Kina by 10 percent for the first time in many years in response to the Bougainville crisis, and a pact with the unions has been achieved to depart from automatic indexation.

In the other Pacific island countries the strength of the wage indexation process has never been as strong, and greater flexibility has been possible. Western Samoa, Vanuatu, and Solomon Islands have more actively used exchange rate adjustment as a tool of macroeconomic policy. However, the open nature of the island economies renders exchange rate deprecia-tion a blunt tool of economic management even in the best of circum-stances.

Wage indexation has rendered exchange rate adjustment an ineffective tool of economic management in the larger island economies during most of the last two decades. However, this situation has been changing with the harsher economic reality being experienced during the latter part of the 1980s. In the smaller economies with less rigid labor markets, exchange rate adjustment is unfortunately at best a blunt tool of economic policy management. These remarks are not intended to say that no scope exists for exchange rate policy in the island economies but rather to point out its limited effectiveness.

The rate of interest

Interest rate policy has not attracted the same concern in the Pacific is-lands as either wage or exchange rate policy. The experience in each is-land has been different, and generalization is not easily undertaken. Compared with the more developed economies, the interest rate policy has not played a critical role in macroeconomic policy. This observation re-sults from the underdeveloped nature of the island capital markets and the lack of integration into international money markets. The lack of moneti-zation of the subsistence sector and the conservative nature of both com-mercial bankers and policymakers have also played their part.

In the 1970s and early 1980s interest rates were largely regulated and in some cases set with a view to maintaining positive real rates and encouraging financial deepening.

In Western Samoa, Fiji, and Papua New Guinea real interest rates on a three month deposit had reached positive levels by the end of the 1980s. After the events of 1987, real interest rates had turned negative in Fiji, al-though at present this situation is reaching positive levels. In Tonga nega-tive rates existed throughout the period and in Vanuatu deposit rates were negative although the large interest rate spread resulted in positive real leveling rates. In Solomon Islands the high rates of inflation resulting from successive devaluations turned relatively high nominal interest rates nega-tive over the rest of the period.

The efficient allocation of resources that flexible interest rates would ar-guably achieve was not widely perceived. Many countries imposed credit rationing to ensure that a certain proportion of commercial bank credit was available to the so-called productive sectors, usually agriculture, manufacturing, and the public sector. These policies were reinforced by conservative managers of overseas banks, whose main interest lay in funding secure loans for working capital and who had no interest in innovation in an uncompetitive market. In short, the commercial banking environment was conservative, uncompetitive, and regulated.

In the latter part of the 1980s with a growing awareness of the benefits of deregulation, which were being expressed by the island countries' metropolitan neighbors, many Pacific island countries began the slow process toward deregulation. Papua New Guinea deregulated in 1986 but experienced difficulties at the time as both credit and interest rates exploded after a boom in commodity prices. Regulation was reintroduced but has lately been relaxed, and Papua New Guinea now appears to have maintained a successful transition to a more flexible system. Fiji deregulated interest rate controls after the 1987 coups, but with the subsequent lack of demand for credit the success of this policy is difficult to determine.

Western Samoa deregulated in the earlier part of the 1980s based on an awareness that the much higher rates of interest available to the closely related migrant communities in New Zealand and Australia had led to an outflow of resources. While capital controls existed, they were rendered largely ineffective because of the ease with which migrants were able to transfer funds. The same forces exist in Tonga, and the authorities have now responded by allowing some upward mobility in rates. Since independence Vanuatu has maintained a deregulated environment consistent with its offshore financial center.

The island economies are thus evolving and undergoing change in their policies toward financial markets and interest rates as they search for more flexible systems. As in the case of the deregulation of labor markets, these trends should result in economies that can more readily adjust and respond to changing economic circumstances.

Trade Policy

A very critical element of economic policy is a country's application of tariffs and quotas on international trade. Present evidence suggests that those countries that have refrained from using widespread protection to encourage industrialization and development have performed better than those economies that have adopted inward looking import substitution policies behind protective barriers. In general, protection is not as wide-spread in the Pacific islands as compared with many other developing countries such as the economies of Latin America. The small size of the Pacific island economies prohibits the use of protection beyond certain limits. However, protection has been used both deliberately and unwittingly.

The main user of protection in the Pacific has been Fiji, which adopted protective import substitution policies in the 1970s and '80s. By the mid-1980s these policies came under scrutiny after a period of economic stagnation, and policies were drawn up to move toward a more open oriented economy. The use of licenses has been withdrawn for many industries and replaced by tariffs, usually at very high levels. The policy is to slowly reduce these rates to more appropriate levels.

In other Pacific island countries, protection has not usually been an explicit objective of policy. Rather, it has been for the result of expansionary fiscal policy. Island governments rely heavily on trade taxes to raise revenue. Expansionary fiscal policies of island governments, often facing deteriorating external terms of trade, require budgetary caution if inflation and balance of payments problems are to be avoided. This will frequently involve additional revenue measures involving tariffs. The rise in general tariffs not explicitly protecting any given industry has had the effect of protecting domestic production and penalizing exports. Governments have attempted to counterbalance these trends with rebates on imports. However, the high rate of trade taxes in most island economies raises costs of intermediate inputs (mostly non-traded goods) and the price of labor, which largely consumes imported items. These forces generally go unnoticed but have a negative impact on economies that are already distorted through large aid and remittance transfers.

Counter-cyclical Policy

Pacific island countries experience substantial fluctuations in their economies due to large cyclical swings in their terms of trade and to adverse climatic conditions affecting agricultural production. Rapid swings in the price of major export commodities have been the main focus of concern. In the upswing a substantial increase in export receipts is usually associated with rising government revenue and leads to expansionary expenditure programs. The infusion of export receipts into the banking system increases the size of the monetary base and leads to strong credit growth and rising demand. The additional demand and expansion in fiscal policy is inflationary and may result in upward pressure on wages. In the downswing the reduction in export receipts leads to a series of contractionary forces. Government revenue falls and the deficit rises, placing an additional burden on the banking system. The associated reduction in export receipts contracts the monetary base, and interest rates rise as extended credit cannot quickly be recalled. The situation is aggravated by additional demands from the government. Furthermore, wages that can move upward freely are usually sticky downward.

Two types of major policy strategies have been developed to counteract the undesirable impact of sudden swings in export commodity prices. The main concern of fiscal policy is the design of a program that focuses on the medium term and does not respond to short-run influences. This requires a medium-term economic forecast to be projected, which can form the basis of fiscal planning. In the upswing fiscal policy is not allowed to respond, and a balance of payments surplus results, provided monetary policy is coordinated. In the downswing a fiscal and balance of payments deficit results but will be corrected during the next phase of the cycle. These strategies can work well, provided the economic forecasts are sound. The trick is to forecast the difference between a short-run hiccup and a long-run secular shift in the terms of trade. In recent years Pacific island economies have experienced declining terms of trade, and it would not be an appropriate strategy to simply ride out the troughs because the trend has been downward. In practice it is by no means easy to obtain an accurate forecast.

On the monetary front stabilization schemes can have an important part to play in sterilizing the impact of commodity price fluctuations. Stabilization funds are usually considered in the context of the primary producers as a means to reduce income fluctuations and to provide a secure environment for investment. However, stabilization schemes also have an important macroeconomic function. In theory the central bank maintains the fund. In the upswing a royalty is collected by the bank and accumulated with the assets of the stabilization fund, which are not invested in the domestic financial system. The foreign reserves of the bank rise proportionately, and the monetary impact is sterilized with no associated extension of credit in the banking system. In the downswing the reverse situation occurs and a royalty is paid. Foreign reserves fall, and domestic liquidity is prevented from contracting. From a central bankers' perspective this policy is automatic and requires no intervention in the market. In island economies with undeveloped money markets, the usual instruments of monetary policy are not available, and the automaticity of the stabilization schemes is attractive.

In practice the only island country to employ counter-cyclical policies has been Papua New Guinea. Fiscal policy is planned with a medium-term horizon, but unforeseen circumstances like the closure of the Bougainville mine make this difficult. Commodity price stabilization schemes are also employed, but in practice their impact has been quite limited. The schemes usually sterilize a very limited part of the overall fluctuation, which may be only 10 to 20 percent. The associated macroeconomic impact is thus quite small. In summary, while Papua New Guinea has set up a battery of counter-cyclical measures their usefulness has not been as effective as theory would suggest.

Conclusion

This discussion on the macroeconomic environment has suggested that the island economies have been largely successful in maintaining financial stability and providing a secure environment for private sector development.

On the more complex issues of ensuring that market prices reflect their economic costs, the results have been mixed. In Fiji and Papua New Guinea the wage system has been inflexible and resulted in loss of jobs, associated law and order problems, and until recently an inability to use the exchange rate as an instrument of economic adjustment. In the smaller economies the labor markets have been less rigid, but other factors have helped maintain wages at high levels, although exchange rate adjustment has been more frequent.

Macroeconomically, interest rates have been less important than either wage or exchange rate policy. However, a general movement has occurred toward deregulation in the island economies in the latter half of the 1980s.

Protective policies have been employed both deliberately and inadvertently in the island economies and have biased the resource allocation process. Fiji embarked on a substantial phase of protective import substitution policies in the 1980s. The economy stagnated, but policy is now becoming more open oriented, and growth has accelerated. In the other island economies protection has been unintentional and less substantial but has also biased development. These governments have yet to realize the benefits from a shift to a more open, deregulated, and growth-oriented economic policy.

Counter-cyclical policies have been employed in Papua New Guinea and a variety of strategies developed. While economic theory indicates the benefits to be gained from these stabilization policies, the rewards have not lived up to their expectations. The other island governments have not utilized counter-cyclical policies to nearly the same extent.

In conclusion, macroeconomic policies have been evolving, and the island economies are now more adaptable and in a stronger position to meet the challenges of the coming decade than they were at the beginning of the 1980s or at the time of independence.

chapter 4

The microeconomic policy environment

The previous chapter showed that in general the Pacific island countries have followed conservative fiscal and monetary policies and have a sound record of financial stability. Furthermore, Chapter 1 revealed that there has been a high level of public investment in physical infrastructure, although more is required to meet necessary requirements in areas such as roads, telecommunications, and ports. The analysis of private sector trade and investment opportunities, summarized in Chapter 7, indicates that the region has a comparative advantage in certain lines of export oriented activities, such as marine products, high value niche market agriculture, and in certain lines of manufacturing such as quality garments and furniture. Inherent comparative advantage, sound macroeconomic policy, and basic physical infrastructure are essential conditions for private sector development and growth. However, in most of the Pacific islands these have not proved to be a sufficient condition. Clearly, there are other constraints at play, and more is required to encourage productive private sector investment. This chapter tries to identify some of these other factors. The focus is on the broad areas of the microeconomic environment, development finance and financial intermediation, and the institutional environment for private sector development.

It is encouraging to note that the Pacific island countries themselves recognize that investors have doubts about some conditions prevailing in the islands and that incentives and other measures are required to offset them. According to Thomson (1989), there is a high degree of self-analysis and awareness of problems. All island countries accept that land tenure difficulties would be a justifiable concern for prospective investors in their countries. The lack of domestic capital is also identified as a strong disadvantage. Other shared constraints are lack of skilled manpower, lack of managerial and marketing skills, inadequate infrastructure (particularly telecommunications and domestic roading and shipping), excessive distance from markets, small domestic markets, and lack of continuity of raw

material supply. Some Pacific island countries criticize their own administrative and political structures for inefficiency, politicized civil services,
and over-involvement of government in the productive sector (Thomson
1989).

The discussion in this chapter places particular emphasis on incentives.
The Private Sector Project reviewed the key policy issues in relation to the
effectiveness of incentives, the appropriateness of regulatory mechanisms,
and the influence of government policies and programs on the risk climate
for private sector development. A summary of findings and major recommendations are presented here.

Incentives

The key policy issues examined

The incentive policy issues examined included:

- How effective have the incentive policies of Pacific island countries been in stimulating private sector development?

- What types of incentive measures have been the most effective in
  achieving their objectives?

- How effective have incentives been in promoting foreign investment in the Pacific islands?

- Are incentives an efficient means of stimulating investment and
  new enterprise development by the local indigenous business
  community?

- Should incentives focus more on human resource development
  and less on subsidizing investment in the physical plant and capital equipment?

- What are the likely benefits and costs of harmonizing the incentive measures offered by the Pacific island countries by translat-
  ing them into a common code?

- What other policy measures are more effective than fiscal and financial incentives for stimulating private sector development?

- What sectors of the economy have been targeted for incentives
  and why?

- Why and by what means should incentive measures be monitored
  and evaluated for their cost effectiveness?

- Have the incentive measures effectively been promoted to foreign
  investors and the local business community?

- How effective are the systems for processing and administering incentive measures?
- What role could export processing zones play in the Pacific island countries?
- What additional measures could be implemented to more effectively promote export development?

Project findings

The effectiveness of incentives are undermined by cumbersome administrative procedures. Although some variations exist among the Pacific island countries, the effectiveness of incentive measures in attracting new investment has been substantially reduced by the cumbersome administrative processes associated with application and approval systems. In general, the application processes involve considerable uncertainty, frustration, and unreasonable delays for the firms. A swift response to project proposals is especially important for small enterprises considering establishing operations in the smaller Pacific islands. An entrepreneurial investor of the type likely to invest in, say, Tonga or Western Samoa is distinctly different from the large multinational investor who can mobilize substantial funds and is usually interested in investing in natural resources and a large tourism plant. The magnitude of the profits from these investments is sufficiently large, and the time–scale sufficiently long, to sustain prolonged project negotiations. In contrast, the entrepreneurs by nature require quick decision on their investment proposals, and, in the context of a small island economy, such investors are likely to be the major source of foreign investment and technology transfer and thus have considerable significance.

The precise criteria for eligibility for different incentives should be publicly available. In addition, the amount of discretion regarding the disposition of an individual application could be reduced, thus avoiding unwarranted political interference in granting incentives. Thus considerable scope exists for improving the administration of incentives in most Pacific island countries.

Incentives offered in the islands are similar to those offered by competing countries. With some exceptions the general level and types of incentives offered in the region are similar to those offered in Southeast Asia. However, it is not recommended that the Pacific islands try to compete by offering even more generous incentives, without a reasonable expectation that this will affect investment decisions at the margin.

The value of traditional incentives in attracting incentives is probably exaggerated. The slow growth rates of the manufacturing sectors in most Pacific island countries clearly demonstrate that the proponents of incentives may have exaggerated their value in promoting growth. The Private Sector Project's research indicated that the level of industrialization was well below that of developing countries as a whole and more akin to the level of the least developed countries.

Other important factors are in attracting foreign investment. Surveys of investment decision making found that long-term profitability and a basic comparative advantage are far more important than the availability of such factors as five-year tax holidays and other short-term concessions. Also of critical importance is the appropriateness of the macroeconomic policy framework and the long-term microeconomic policy measures that regulate the competitive environment. The Pacific island countries shape-up well in terms of financial stability but not so well in terms of cost competitiveness. Other important factors include the living environment for expatriates, which includes personal safety and the quality of health and educational services, as well as the policy on work permits. Events in Papua New Guinea highlight the sensitivity of foreign investment to law and order issues and the impact of political instability on the level and type of foreign investment. The availability of a productive, reliable labor force is highly valued, as is preferential access to overseas markets offered by trade agreements, which were found to be key factors in the rapid development of the Fiji garment industry.

Incentives are inadequate in the crucial area of human resource development. Few indigenous businesses in the Pacific islands invest sufficient resources in conducting their own in-house training programs, although almost all would benefit from increased work skills and labor productivity through training and other forms of staff development.

Export processing zones and small industry centers have a role in attracting manufacturing investment. The Tongan experience has shown that small industry centers can make an important contribution to manufacturing investment in the Pacific islands. Apart from physical infrastructure, they provide access to land where its availability on a long-term basis is difficult to obtain. Furthermore, they provide the prospective investor with tangible evidence of the government's sustained commitment to manufacturing development and reduce the perceived risk associated with the investment.

Small industry centers can make a greater contribution to local and indigenous participation in export manufacturing than has been the case with the Tongan SIC.

Incentive monitoring is lacking. The island governments do not monitor the effectiveness of incentives and make little or no attempt to measure their cost and benefits. As a result it would appear that some incentives are more generous than necessary to attract foreign investment.

The marketing of the incentive package was shown to be as important as the package itself. This has been illustrated by the Fiji experience. In highlighting the availability of the tax free system, the Fiji Trade and Investment Board (FTIB) brought opportunities in Fiji to the attention of investors. This increased level of awareness of Fiji has been one of the key successes of the tax free system. A bold approach that is aggressively marketed is what succeeds in attracting the attention of overseas investors.

Major recommendations

The major recommendations are presented in McMaster (1990b) and summarized below:

Investment promotion

Most Pacific island countries could substantially improve their systems for investment promotion and approvals by:

- Allocating responsibility for investment promotion to a single central agency and adopting a "one-stop approach,"

- Aggressively marketing the incentive packages that are available to investors,

- Undertaking a program in that agency of staff development and training,

- Improving systems for the evaluation and processing of applications for incentives,

- Providing information to improve the risk assessment of investors.

Fiscal incentives

Several new grant schemes are recommended to encourage export market development, technology development and acquisition, new product development, the improvement of manufacturing and agroprocessing systems, feasibility studies, and in-house staff development and training.

Some current incentives, such as Fiji's 13-year tax holiday for export firms, seem overly generous, with more being given away than is necessary to attract foreign investment. Such excessive incentives need to be phased out over time. Some Pacific island countries, particularly the microstates, with cost disadvantages, might need to offer relatively more attractive incentives to "level the playing field" in attracting foreign investment. However, even in such cases careful consideration needs to be given to whether marginally more attractive fiscal incentives will make the critical difference in attracting foreign investment.

Financial incentives

Incentive schemes should be established or strengthened so that commercial banks will increase lending to the productive sectors through the use of reserve bank powers and credit guarantee schemes.

Approved foreign investors in priority areas should be given access to debt financing from the Pacific islands development banks. This is to offset the major constraint imposed by the high rates of interest in Australia and New Zealand. The development banks have a role to play in ameliorating the perceived risks for bona fide foreign investors by taking equity in selected projects that are in the national interest.

Incentives for local versus foreign investment

Higher priority should be given to the development of more effective incentives and other enterprise support measures to encourage the growth of local investment and entrepreneurship, particularly in the microstates. Appropriately designed small industry centers have been identified as having a major role to play in this respect. Proposals are made for the establishment of business incubators, nursery factories, and village factory schemes.

Much more needs to be done in promoting and explaining existing incentives to the local business community.

Human resource development incentives

Human resource development is identified as an area warranting a significantly higher allocation of resources, especially in private sector staff training and staff development schemes. A major overall shift in emphasis is recommended from traditional fiscal and financial incentives to incentives directed at the neglected area of human resource development. For example, the Singapore government has developed an effective scheme for encouraging firms to develop their own on-the-job training programs by directly subsidizing the cost of training by paying firms cash grants for approved training activities. Such a scheme could be introduced in the Pacific island countries.

Export incentives and support systems

Country studies have identified the need to strengthen export development support systems and to introduce new incentive measures to promote export development. Specific recommendations include:

- The development of a South Pacific Regional Trade Commission Network, with new offices in Brussels, Hong Kong, Los Angeles, Tokyo, and Vancouver, in addition to the offices in Auckland and Sydney;

- The development of a Regional Trade Data Bank and information service;

- Institutional strengthening of national trade and investment agencies;

- The introduction of Export Market Development Schemes and New Product Development Assistance Schemes;

- The establishment of export credit schemes in the Pacific island countries that do not have such schemes and the strengthening of such schemes in countries that do.

A common code and a harmonizing of island incentives

Many similarities exist in the investment incentive measures of all Pacific island countries, which has prompted debate on the feasibility of all islands adopting a common code of industrial incentives. Thus the Private Sector Project considered the feasibility of harmonization. While there are sound theoretical arguments for a common code and the harmonization of incentives, the research concluded that there was little practical prospect for the harmonization of incentives in the foreseeable future. However, the Forum Secretariat could play a valuable role in assisting member countries to simplify and improve their investment legislation and to modernize their approach to investment promotion.

Monitoring

Effective systems should be established for monitoring the cost effectiveness of incentive measures and the economic value of the allocation of incentives to different sectors of the economy by collecting data and conducting research on the costs and benefits of incentives and concessions.

The Regulatory Framework

Almost all governments in the region have announced policies or expressed strong commitment to deregulation, privatization, and commercialization of public enterprises, as well as measures to increase competition. However, there are considerable lags between the annunciation of appropriate policies to improve the business environment and the implementation of these policies. In a number of instances policy conflicts need to be resolved.

The Fiji experience

Fiji, of all the Pacific island countries, has perhaps the most comprehensive program of deregulation and is the farthest down the road in terms of implementation. In 1989 the government announced its new economic strategy, one where the thrust of development was to be achieved through export led growth. The mini-budget announced the gradual deregulation of the economy and the elimination of Fiji's import-substitution protective policies that had dominated development in the early 1980s. These measures were to be coupled with tax reform to promote economic efficiency, deregulation of the labor market, and restraint on government expenditure to avoid crowding out private sector development.

Accordingly, the Fiji experience became a major focus of the Private Sector Project, and the findings of this research are reported in McMaster (1990b). Highlights that are of relevance to the region are discussed briefly below.

The import-substitution era. Fiji, during the decade following independence, vigorously followed an industrial policy based on import-substitution industries, combined with a general emphasis on self-reliance. In addition to providing generous financial and fiscal incentives to entrepreneurs to enter manufacturing, Fiji provided protection from imports through a complex system of licensing, quantitative controls, and tariffs.

These policies led to an increase in manufacturing in a wide variety of areas. However, as the first phase of easy import-substitution came to an end, further movement along the import-substitution path simply meant that there were severe scale penalties: there was much duplication with consequent low levels of capacity utilization. In addition, high levels of protection, seemingly for unlimited periods, and the lack of government monitoring of firms given assistance, tied to lack of competition, led to industrial stagnation. However, from 1982 garment exports began to expand at an increasing rate with the modifications to the South Pacific Regional Trade and Economic Cooperation Agreement (SPARTECA), which gave a special quota to the Australian market.

Price control licensing and tariff reduction. A key element in Fiji's deregulation program has been a policy for progressively lifting price controls on products along with the reduction of tariffs. In the mini-budget of 1989 new rates of nominal tariffs in the order of 50 percent were installed and as part of the 1990 budget were reduced to 40 percent together with further removal of licenses. It is the intention in the next two budgets to reduce tariff rates by an additional 10 percent in each year. In the same mini-budget the government indicated its intention to look at the wide range of commodities presently under price control.

Fiji's price control system was designed to ensure that local producers do not take undue advantage of the protection they receive against imports. The expectation was that the reduction of tariffs and the phasing out of licensing would increase competition from imports and negate the need for price control. Given Fiji's rate of inflation rate in recent years, this policy has achieved a fair degree of success and should give confidence to other Pacific island countries in adopting similar reforms.

Yet while much attention has been given to deregulation, Fiji still maintains an extensive system of price controls (mainly markup control), which is no longer appropriate to a more deregulated economy. In most instances these controls (with the exception of house rentals) are ineffective and impose unnecessary bureaucratic barriers to efficient business operation. Furthermore, licensing is now being used as an instrument to encourage indigenous Fijian business participation–perhaps the government's highest priority. Thus policy conflicts, or at least the instruments used to implement these policies, need to be resolved.

Deregulation of labor markets. The government's announced policies toward deregulating the labor market are welcome. Wages since the early 1970s have been largely determined through a central fixing system, which has not proved efficient. Wages were set according to cost of living changes and led to a particularly rigid economic environment. Before the events of 1987 the system changed to incorporating terms of trade changes, but a guideline was still administered economy-wide. After the events of 1987 wages through economic necessity were strictly controlled by central government edict. However, in line with its other deregulatory policies the new focus of policy will be to abolish centralization and let market forces determine wage levels. New legislation is proposed freeing the labor market and requiring a secret ballot before strike action can be called. The experience of Fiji in deregulating its labor market will be highly relevant to Papua New Guinea, which of all the Pacific island countries has the most regulated formal sector labor market. High wages and low productivity of labor have made Papua New Guinea uncompetitive in areas such as export manufacturing. As a result of labor market distortion Papua New Guinea faces high urban unemployment and serious associated law and order problems, which in turn undermine investor confidence. Comparative wage rates in selected countries are presented in Table 4.1.

Corporatization and privatization. A key element in Fiji's deregulation program is the implementation of a long-term program to reduce the size of the public sector by privatizing a number of public sector income earning agencies. However, apart from the corporatization of the Post and Telecommunications Department and the Pine Commission, implementation has been slow and more difficult than was perhaps envisaged. Other Pacific island countries such as Kiribati and Western Samoa, which are committed to programs of privatization, were found to be encountering

Table 4.1 Comparative wage rates in the manufacturing sector, selected countries

Country	Year	Hourly wage in US$	Ratio of Fiji to country rate (%)
Australia	1986	6.96	14.8
Bangladesh	1984	0.16	643.8
China	1987	0.20	515.0
Fiji	1988	1.03	100.0
Federal Republic of Germany	1987	9.74	10.6
Hong Kong	1987	1.91	53.9
India	1984	0.42	245.2
Japan	1987	13.53	7.6
South Korea	1987	2.50	41.2
Mauritius	1987	0.43	239.5
New Zealand	1986	5.30	19.4
Papua New Guinea	1988	1.45	71.0
Philippines	1988	0.45	228.9
Singapore	1987	2.29	45.0
Sri Lanka	1987	0.21	490.5
Thailand	1986	0.63	163.5
Tonga	1986	0.59	174.6
United States	1987	9.91	10.4

Source: Calculated from data in International Labour Office, 1988. Data have been converted using the average of 40 hours per week, 160 hours per month, and 1,920 hours per year. Local currencies have been converted to US$ using the average exchange rate for the relevant year as given in World Bank's World Tables for 1989-90.

similar problems of implementation. The issue is not just handing over shares in the enterprises of these countries from the public sector to the private sector. The breaking of monopolies is a delicate matter because of the small economies of the Pacific islands, but the issue has to be tackled if free competition and consumer interests are to be given precedence. At times running contrary to privatization in some islands is the pressing need for greater indigenous community involvement in business and the fear that privatization will not be to their benefit. The suggestion has been made in Fiji, for example, that commercialization and corporatization of the public sector is a better goal than straight-out privatization if indigenous Fijians are to gain a bigger share of business activity. Issues of privatization, particularly in the context of investment opportunities are dealt with in detail in McMaster (1990c) and summarized in Chapter 8.

Taxation reform. Fiji's deregulation program includes comprehensive taxation reform directed at broadening the tax base and minimizing market distortions to improve the business environment. Effective July 1, 1992, a value-added tax was introduced, effectively replacing all current indirect taxes, i.e., customs duty, excise tax, hotel turnover tax, etc. This should allow government to reduce the high marginal rates on personal income tax with the aim to improve incentives to earn extra income. Such reforms substantially reduce the scope for tax avoidance and thus can be considered as highly equitable. The Fiji government has expressed its intention for this tax reform to be accompanied by restraint on the growth of government expenditure. The research indicated considerable scope for other Pacific island countries, regardless of their size, to adopt similar tax reforms. It is strongly recommended that other Pacific islands obtain technical assistance to establish comparable tax reform systems.

Some policy and implementation conflict. While Fiji has made commendable overall progress in implementing these reforms conflict and inconsistency exist between government policy announcements on deregulation and their implementation. Furthermore, superimposed on the process of deregulation has been the incremental addition of new regulatory measures. The tempo of change in the government's bureaucracy needs to be quickened so as not to stifle investment, both foreign and local. There is also a need to resolve apparent differences of emphasis and even philosophy between the various institutions involved, such as the Ministry of Trade and Industry, the Ministry of Finance, the Reserve Bank, the Development Bank, and the Fiji Trade and Investment Board. Conflicting interpretation of policy by institutions serves to confuse investors. Investors need clearly laid out rules and procedures with a minimum of discretion, particularly in areas such as domestic borrowing by foreign corporations and in foreign exchange transactions.

Regulation and export agriculture development

The policy and other requirements to encourage private investment in agricultural development, particularly with respect to new export commodities, constituted a major focus of the Private Sector Project. Hence a detailed study of the institutional and regulatory environment as it pertains to private investment in the agricultural sector was undertaken. The findings of this research are presented in McGregor and Coulter (1991), with the major conclusions discussed briefly below.

The overall conclusion of this research was that the Pacific island governments generally have not created a regulatory environment conducive to private investment in new commodity development. The problem for export agriculture in the Pacific islands is not overregulation but rather the lack of appropriate regulation. Government–as the Hawaii papaya and Fiji ginger studies have shown–can play a crucial role in creating an environment that will encourage sustained private investment. Its vital responsibilities include (1) certifying that the quarantine and quality standards of the importing countries have been met and (2) providing the institutional and legal environment to facilitate industry self-regulation. Government also can facilitate the flow of technical assistance to the commercial sector.

It was also found that government and statutory agency involvement in agricultural production and marketing has been lackluster and is likely to be an obstruction to long-run commodity development. Government agencies in the Pacific islands have proved to be particularly inept in handling the development of fresh commodities, as illustrated by the detailed study of Fiji's papaya industry. The overall conclusion was that the Pacific island governments, where practical, should privatize government commodity agencies. However, in the process the government's crucial regulatory functions should not be ignored as Western Samoa's experience has shown with the abolition of the Cocoa and Coconut Board.

The Private Sector Project advocates the establishment of a system of industry self-regulation with respect to developing a viable horticultural export sector in the Pacific island countries. The Papua New Guinea Coffee Industry has successfully moved in this direction. The important role of government in establishing the necessary legal and institutional arrangements to enable industry self-regulation to function effectively was stressed. The movement toward appropriate systems of industry self-regulation has many advantages. It usually would create a more favorable environment for private sector growth by reducing both the negative aspects of excessive government regulation and control and the slowness of governments to respond to dynamic market situations. Industry self-regulation is likely to react more rapidly to industry needs and provide greater flexibility in adjusting to changing export market requirements.

Conclusions relating to the regulatory environment

The Private Sector Project's research (McGregor and Coulter 1991, McMaster 1990b, McMaster 1990c) has shown that the regulatory environment for private sector development could be improved through:

- Deregulation of labor markets, particularly in Fiji and Papua New Guinea,

- Comprehensive tax reform,

- Phasing out of ineffective subsidies, particularly those relating to inputs,

- Reduction or elimination of price control,

- The elimination of import licensing and a reduction in the level of protection via tariffs,

- Privatization of most commodity boards,

- Withdrawal of government enterprises from the production of private goods and services,

- Greater use of contracting out by government,

- Promotion of self-regulation by industry associations,

- Elimination of barriers to entry and competition.

The priorities, requirements, and the degree of implementing progress vary from country to country. Overall there is considerable scope for improving the regulatory environment for private sector development. Yet the overall finding of the various studies is that regulatory frameworks in the Pacific island countries generally have not been a major factor in inhibiting private sector development. The degree of regulation varies widely from country to country; however, on the whole the economies have not suffered from excessive or restrictive business and employment regulations.

The Risk Climate

A complete analysis of the risk climate in the Pacific island countries and its influence on private sector development is extremely complex and is beyond the scope and resources of this book. There are many dimensions of risk analysis and large variations in the nature and types of risk that affect private sector investment, growth, and development. The risk climate also is perceived differently by foreign and local investors and various interest groups. However, arising out of the research some useful observations can be made concerning the perception of the risks associated with investing in the Pacific island countries.

Some observations concerning perceived risk of investing in the islands

Insufficient information for adequate risk assessment. Figuring high in the potential investor's mind in approaching investment in the Pacific island countries are the perceived risks involved. To many overseas investors unfamiliar with the terrain and track record of the Pacific islands, these risks are difficult to quantify and assess. With inadequate information, potential investors will err in favor of risk aversion and not invest or embark on a conceived project. Some proposals are made for improving information flows to investors and thereby their risk assessment analysis in this important stage in their approach to investment. The expectation is that better information will lead to an increased flow and quality of investment into the region.

A generally favorable environment for foreign investment. Many elements that make up the risk environment are outside the direct control of government; however, government can play a large role in creating a favorable environment for private sector development. All the Pacific island countries have made a concerted effort in this respect. They have developed positive policies toward private sector development and have given high priority to programs designed to accelerate private sector growth–albeit often with implementation and institutional problems. Foreign investment is welcomed in most sectors of the economy, and the incentives for new investment are generous and in some cases unnecessarily overly generous. Foreign exchange is convertible, and repatriation of capital and profits generally is free from restrictions. Business regulations generally are not too restrictive.

The political climate in the islands. The South Pacific had been regarded as having a tranquil political climate characterized by moderation, democracy, and orderly procedures. But this image has taken a bit of a battering recently with the 1989 Bougainville State of Emergency and ongoing crisis, the 1988 Vanuatu Constitutional Crisis, the 1987 military coups in Fiji, and even anti-government political agitation in the Kingdom of Tonga. While some would say that the way in which these crises were played out demonstrates the enduring sense of moderation and consensus-orientation in Pacific island politics. However, from the overseas investors' point of view such political developments impose risks that they would not have to encounter in investments in more stable political environments.

The closure of the Bougainville copper mine is a disaster of an unprecedented scale for Papua New Guinea. Togolo describes the Bougainville Crisis "as the most threatening event to national unity since independence, as well as being expensive in terms of lost government revenue and export earnings" (1989:23). Not to mention the disaster that it has been for the overseas investors who have financed the project (despite the high rate of return over the life of the project), investors are now more cautious and are less likely to proceed with projects that are marginal in terms of the economic rate of return on investment. In addition, more resources are devoted to risk avoidance strategies such as a more thorough analysis of traditional land ownership issues, options for landowner equity participation and employment, relationships with provincial and central government, environmental impact analysis issues, and social/cultural impact issues.

The 1987 political crisis in Fiji came at a time when Fiji tourism arrival trends showed sure signs of lucrative gains for the Fiji hotel industry. Tourism figures plummeted, and while they have since recovered to pre-coup levels, investors in the industry suffered severe losses directly from this political upheaval. The Fiji case is a good example of how difficult the political risk assessment is for overseas investors because the conventional well-informed assessment of Fiji prior to the coups did not foresee an unstable political environment developing in Fiji. Numerous reports of international agencies, including the Asian Development Bank (ADB), alluded to Fiji's political stability as a major attraction for investors. Similarly the social disintegration that was being forecast after the coups has not as yet materialized.

Some analysts argue that political instability and authoritarian governments are not necessarily a deterrent to investment. For example, in Fiji's case the F$290 million Denarau Island Resort attracted its Japanese investors just after the 1987 coups. This has been followed by a high level of foreign investment in the Fiji Tax Free Factory Scheme, particularly garments. The Fiji experience, as elsewhere in the world, indicates that as long as firm economic guidelines are in place and money making opportunities are not compromised, then overseas investors will not be unduly affected by the political environment. However, this argument appears not to hold for domestic investment, at least in the case of Fiji where domestic investment remains at a very low level following the 1987 coups.

Overseas investors in some Pacific island countries complain of insufficient central government resolve in handling provincial problems and blockages caused by localized political squabbles. The Porgera gold mine in Papua New Guinea is a case in point.

Risk and land issues.   Landowners' increasing demands for higher and continuing compensation for development projects is a risk over which investors are showing considerable concern. Central government is often seen to be powerless or unwilling to take unpopular measures in settling landowner demands so that investment projects of national importance can proceed. Compensation is not a concept that investors have a problem with. Where they do have problems are in the volatility of compensation rates and the uncertainty, arising from communal land-owning systems, of who is conducting the compensation negotiations and how binding the compensation settlements are. Togolo points to the difficulty of investors in being understood in a Melanesian context and the need for payments to be varied to suit unique circumstances. He concludes that a "more realistic category of compensation needs to be framed to reflect the relative sacrifice born by different peoples in association with a mining project."

It is undeniable that many Pacific island countries have land tenure systems that are a strong disincentive to investors, but some of the negative overseas perceptions of investment conditions in the Pacific islands related to land are exaggerated and straight-out misinformed. This has not helped the perception of the investment climate. A good example is the persistent comment that land ownership by other than indigenous Fijians is not allowed in Fiji. In fact 10 percent of the total land area is classed as freehold land, which includes some of the best agricultural land and which can be purchased by foreigners. Most of the remainder is administered by the Native Land Trust Board (NLTB) or the government and can be leased to tenants regardless of their racial or national status. However, in the agricultural sector, particularly for the sugar industry, uncertainty does exist with respect to the status of native leases that are due to expire around the end of the century.

In Vanuatu the ownership of all land is reserved for indigenous ni-Vanuatu. This constitutional requirement is often perceived as an overwhelming constraint on foreign investment in the agricultural sector. However, this has not necessarily been the case as foreign investors in the cattle industry on the island of Espiritu Santo have shown. Here investors have been able to secure long-term leases on very favorable terms. Ironically, foreigners have found it much easier to obtain long-term access to land than ni-Vanuatu wishing to migrate from land deficit areas. Such a situation is not uncommon in a number of other Pacific island countries. All the countries in the region could benefit from establishing institutions similar to Fiji's NLTB.

Small industry centers and reducing risks associated with land in manufacturing development. The Tongan experience has shown that a small industry center can contribute significantly to investor confidence by providing access to land where its availability on a long-term basis is difficult to obtain. Furthermore, they provide the prospective investor with tangible evidence of the government's sustained commitment to manufacturing development and thereby reduce the perceived risk of investing.

Risk and the economic environment. The creation of a favorable economic climate for private sector development is more directly influenced by government policies than is either the political or social/cultural climate. Chapter 3 reported that macroeconomic policies have generated a stable financial system in almost all the island nations. Fiscal and monetary policies generally have been conducted so that inflationary pressures have been avoided and the balance of payments outcomes have been favorable. On the basis of these factors most Pacific island countries would rate well in comparison with other developing country regions, but the narrowness of their economic bases and the associated vulnerability to external economic influences beyond their control give cause for concern. The area of greatest economic weakness has been in developing policies to ensure that the cost of labor reflects the market conditions of the island economies. In Papua New Guinea the practice of wage indexation coupled with a high urban wage structure has resulted in labor costs being too high to attract investment in export oriented manufacturing industries. Fiji has embarked on a program of labor market deregulation, the progress of which will be viewed with considerable interest throughout the region.

Security of investments. The Pacific island countries have a laudable track record on the question of appropriation of private property, with properly negotiated and compensated transfers being the norm. Most island countries have legal frameworks that provide for the security of private property. Law and order risk issues are a real worry for investors in Papua New Guinea and to a lesser extent in Fiji. The prospect of seemingly arbitrary deportation of foreign nationals can seriously undermine investor confidence as some recent events in Vanuatu have shown. Some of this confidence, however, has been restored by successful appeals to the Vanuatu legal system.

Other risks. Climatic risks have also been a major concern to investors in many Pacific island countries where the increasing incidence of tropical cyclones in the 1970s and 1980s, which caused considerable crop and property damage, inflated insurance rates for properties such as waterfront hotels and caused investors to shy away from otherwise profitable opportunities. The isolated island nature of the Pacific island countries imposes risks of supply of raw materials and transportation of products. Vulnerability to airline service cancellations affect many industries in the region.

Other risks to be considered by overseas investors include the possible incidence of corruption in political and bureaucratic echelons, the unfamiliarity of legal frameworks and business regulations, and the possibility of punitive taxes. On the last risk the islands' incentive schemes and past record should provide overseas investors with the assurance they need that tax risks are manageable. The structure and administration of the legal systems in the Pacific island countries is one with which an investor familiar with the legal systems of Australia, New Zealand, and the United Kingdom would feel comfortable. The risk of encountering corruption in the establishment or pursuance of an investment in the region is on the whole far less than that in most Asia-Pacific countries. It is true that there have been increasing allegations of corruption in the governments of some Pacific island countries, but most analysts would agree that the rot of corruption has not set in and the element that does exist can, with vigilance, be rooted out.

Dearth of sound information for adequate investor risk analysis. The above are some of the perceptions that overseas investors encounter and assess in their consideration of a Pacific island country as an investment location. There tends to be a dearth of sound information on the constraints and risks facing potential investors in the region with, for obvious reasons, a concentration on information regarding the positive advantages. Poor information leads to poor investment and over time a lower level of investment in the region. Proposals for improving information systems for existing and potential investors are made in Thomson (1989) and are summarized in Chapter 9.

Some suggestions for improving the management of the risk implicit in Pacific islands investment

Issues of risk need to be tackled head on. There is a requirement for a comprehensive and honest appraisal of the risks implicit in investing in the Pacific island countries. Due to its independence Pacific Islands Development Program (PIDP) would be well placed to coordinate this exercise–however, adequate funding would be essential. This appraisal should take in the perceptions of investors who have regional track records of both success and/or failure and the experience of some prominent investors who decided not to go ahead with regional investments because of overexposure to risks. With a clearer agreement on what the investment risks in these countries are, it is recommended that a regional and national effort, through workshops, seminars, and the like, be devoted to a consideration of which of these risks can be eradicated, ameliorated, reduced, or just better understood. A further step to be taken, when these risks have been better presented and understood, is for regional investment promotion agencies to include risk explanation and management as part of their presentation portfolios. A direct approach to risk will relieve the potential investor of the need to second-guess the risks involved in investing in the Pacific island countries.

A role of aid donors and international agencies. Overseas Private Investment Corporation (OPIC) can insure U.S. investments overseas against the risks of political violence, expropriation, inconvertibility of local currency, and/or loss of business income for the above reasons. There would be merit in the governments of Australia and New Zealand providing an OPIC-type political risk insurance scheme to further encourage their private sectors to invest in the South Pacific islands.

The role of development finance institutions. Viable private sector business ventures in the region should be supported at their inception with adequate equity capital as distinct from loan funds. The regional and national development institutions need to step up their ability and inclination to participate in equity funding of new ventures. The development banks will need to plan a lead role in this respect. As is the case with the International Finance Corporation (IFC) these institutions should aim at sale of equity to the private sector when a venture has been successfully established. However, the involvement of development banks in venture capital development is not ideal and should be seen as an interim measure.

Consideration should be given to the development of a Pacific island venture industry with free and active participation from overseas venture capitalist interests. The Private Sector Project makes detailed proposals for establishing a regional venture capital industry, which are summarized in Chapter 9.

chapter 5

The financing of private sector development

This chapter discusses the role of development finance and institutions in promoting the growth of the private sector in the Pacific island countries. Development finance is concerned with the provision of real resources, through savings and investment, in order to raise the per capita GDP. There are basically three methods of financing planned expenditure on new investment goods: (1) self-finance involving financing investment out of accumulated own savings; (2) direct finance involving a separation between the savings units and the investment units, with the latter borrowing directly from the former; and (3) indirect finance requiring a financial intermediary that accepts saving deposits and provides loans to deficit spenders.

The main financing sources of both private and public investment in the Pacific islands are self-accumulated domestic savings, official financial development assistance, personal remittances, and external commercial borrowing. Of these, official financial development assistance is by far the most important as it has managed to finance and maintain high levels of domestic investment in excess of domestic savings. In addition to official development assistance, private transfers through remittance flows have played a major role in financing the high rates of domestic investment in the Cook Islands, Tonga, and Western Samoa.

Despite very high rates of domestic investment, the domestic savings remain at low rates for the Pacific island countries. Fiji is the exception where domestic savings has financed more than 90 percent of domestic investments during the last decade.

The low domestic savings rates in the region in relation to high domestic investment rates can be attributed not only to the high spending propensities of consumers but also to the high inflation and monetary policy controls on nominal interest rates that promote financial repression in the

Pacific islands. As a result, public investment continues to be financed largely from official foreign transfers.

It is therefore argued here that a proper interest policy is necessary to encourage domestic financial savings, enhance the allocative function of financial institutions, promote the growth of instruments of savings, and facilitate financial stability in the Pacific island countries.

There is, however, an important distinction between the financial measures for the promotion of investment in physical assets and those for financial savings mobilization. These two different aspects in connection with the role of financial institutions in the region often involve conflicting policy considerations: the aspect of investment that creates its own savings and the aspect of saving that provides a precondition for investment.

In this connection, the Private Sector Project considered the role of financial institutions in the Pacific island countries and focused on four broad issues and their policy implications:

- Financial Intermediation

- Financing of Investment

- Financial Savings

- Financial Resource Allocation

Financial Intermediation

The process of economic development in the Pacific island countries has been associated with a growing gap between investment and domestic saving. High investment rates are accompanied by an inadequacy of supply and demand for savings instruments. Because the supply of and demand for equity instruments have remained underdeveloped in the Pacific islands, the private nonfinancial sectors have met most of their financing requirements by borrowing from the domestic commercial banking system.

The major components of the portfolio of savings instruments in the island countries consist of:

- The informal market loans;

- The inflation hedges, especially in idle land;

- The foreign-currency assets, especially in Pacific island countries with offshore banking systems;

- The commercial bank time and saving deposits.

Due to low levels of savings, external finance—especially bank advances, bonds, and equity shares required for private sector development—can be raised on domestic financial markets to a limited extent because of the low level of savings.

The role of financial institutions in private sector development relates to the process of financial intermediation. Financial intermediation arises as purchasing power in the form of credit and is channeled, by a financial institution, from the economy's savers to its investors. In other words, the financial institutions provide a link—hence "financial intermediary"— between the surplus units (savers) and the deficit units (investors). In this connection, the role of financial institutions is essential for the speed, direction, and stability of private sector development.

The process of financial intermediation contributes to the development of the private sector in four ways:

1. It helps to augment domestic savings in the form of financial assets from any given level and distribution of domestic income; it also serves to increase the total amount of the investable resources available to the private sector.

2. It helps to increase the productivity of investment by enhancing the efficient allocation of investable funds.

3. It helps to reduce the cost of providing the investors with financial resources.

4. It provides a set of policy instruments for the stabilization and promotion of economic growth.

The process of financial intermediation, in the Pacific island countries, has been concentrated in the commercial banks. The major source of short-term loans for the economy as a whole is the commercial banking system, which offers demand and savings deposits and lends to the private and government sectors.

Recently, however, new types of specialized financial institutions have been established such as the national provident funds, development banks, insurance and life insurance companies, the investment finance corporations, and the home finance corporation; gradually they have assumed an increasing role in both the mobilization of contractual savings and the allocation of investable resources. These institutions have become the principal sources of domestic long-term borrowing.

Through the obligatory bond holdings of commercial banks and non-bank financial institutions, a substantial proportion of the total investable resources has been diverted from the private to the public sector.

The pension funds collect contractual savings from wage and salary earners in return for pension rights and invest in primary securities as well as in private sector projects. Development banks engage primarily in the onlending of both domestic and foreign funds and have become the main vehicles for channeling foreign grants and concessionary loans to the private sectors of Pacific island economies.

The insurance companies offer a variety of insurance policies and consequently serve as collectors of small savings, which are then invested in public securities and private mortgages. The investment finance corporations obtain their finance by issuing shares and bonds (debentures) and use the proceeds for investment in lending to and equity participation in private companies. A home finance corporation tends to rely for its initial finance on the government and foreign borrowing and lends to those who wish to build or buy their own homes with mortgages.

Financing of Investment

The experience of the Pacific island countries has been that the increasing effect of the financial institutions' activities on the direction of economic development reflects the change in the way that investment is financed. It should be emphasized that the role of financial institutions in economic development relates to the relationship between saving and investment. In general, there are three ways of financing investment in the island economies: self-finance, direct finance, and indirect finance. The increasing effect of the financial institutions' activities on the direction and speed of economic development reflects the change in the way that investment is financed with more emphasis on indirect finance.

These three different methods of financing investment, though closely interrelated, can best be discussed separately in relation to the role of financial institutions within the cultural and economic context of saving and investment in the Pacific island countries.

Self-finance

Self-finance involves financing investments out of accumulated own savings. The three main sources of self-financed accumulation are households, business firms, and government. The saving of a Pacific island household is shaped and conditioned by several factors of which the important determinants include the level and distribution of income, the cultural attitude toward accumulation of wealth, and the availability of safe, liquid, convenient, and rewarding ways of accumulating financial savings.

In the Pacific island countries the level of income as indicated by per capita income is relatively low; most of the income is either consumed or channeled into cultural and religious obligatory activities. Usually, a community with a low per capita income tends to be associated with low savings. Even though the statistics on household savings are difficult to obtain in most island countries, the data on gross domestic savings show that they have been low and, in some cases, even negative. With the help of private remittances and official grants, some countries have been able to maintain a high level of consumption in excess of their incomes.

Internal finance and income distribution

Self-financed investment is also influenced by the horizontal and vertical distribution of income. The former refers to the distribution of income between different types of income, for instance, profits and wages. The vertical distribution of income refers to the distribution of income between sectors or industries. In the case of Fiji, for example, the estimated propensity to save out of export income was found to be substantially greater than that of non-export income. The low propensity to save out of income from non-export activity reflects the presence of subsistence production in the non-export activity. However, it is not an exaggeration to state that export production is the most capitalistic form of economic activity in a Pacific island economy. As for the effect of different types of income on saving, in Fiji, for example, private saving depends to a very considerable extent on non-labor income (e.g., business income).

The dependency of private savings on non-labor income is to prevail in most Pacific island countries. The predominance of non-labor income, as a major determinant of private savings, reflects not only the absence of capital markets but also the limited access of small firms and self-employed producers to external or institutional sources of funds.

This finding has important policy implications for the appropriate distribution of the relative burden of direct taxation between labor and non-labor income. Thus, as the share of private non-labor disposable income expands, self-financed investment becomes an important source of private sector growth in a Pacific island economy.

Self-accumulation and cultural values

The development of an indigenous entrepreneurial class has scarcely occurred in most of these countries. As a result, self-financed investment in many private productive undertakings is largely the prerogative of expatriate entrepreneurs, a few indigenous businesspersons, and foreign-owned firms.

Nevertheless, saving out of private income is usually a major source of self-financed investment. The stereotyped image of an indigenous entrepreneur with "a Western value and belief system" is a Pacific islander who has a desire for thrift and who ploughs private income into an expansion of private gain. This entrepreneurial quality is not entirely consistent with the cultural values of many Pacific societies. According to the cultures of some of these societies, the sharing of available labor, land, and income is not a choice but rather a social duty.

Indeed, the traditional right to share material wealth tends to undermine the incentives to save and invest. At the same time, sharing in terms of fulfillment of social obligations is usually perceived as a "cultural investment" to ensure against old age as well as to acquire potential material possessions in case of future need. This may help to explain why semi-commercial producers in Pacific island countries often channel a significant proportion of their meager income into social and religious activities. Consequently, the ability and willingness to accumulate resources for private investment purposes tend to be weak.

Related to the cultural context of the basic problem of low savings are two conflicting ideologies that prevail in many Pacific island countries today:

Individualism	Communalism
• Self-interest is the guiding principle	• Kinship interest is emphasized
• Private property must be respected and protected	• Communal and tribal property must be respected and preserved

- Decisions as to what and how much to save as well as how to save are linked through market forces and price mechanisms

- Such decisions are shaped by kinship relationships and social obligations

- Accumulation or saving is necessary for the survival of the market system

- Sharing rather than accumulation is central to the communal system

- Sharing is a choice

- Sharing is a social duty, i.e., a social obligation but not a choice

Consequently, the difficulty of increasing financial savings in many Pacific island countries is determined to some extent by the degree of influence of each of the two conflicting philosophies described above.

With expanding trade and communications, the population has been increasingly exposed to the high material standards of living elsewhere, particularly in metropolitan countries. This situation tends to fuel the revolution of rising material expectations and hence to raise the minimum cultural standard of living throughout the Pacific island countries. As a result, even when real income and foreign remittances from abroad rise, little is likely to be accumulated for investment purposes.

However, it should be mentioned that the continuing inflows of personal remittances received from kinsmen working abroad reflect the importance of communal ideology in the Pacific island societies.

When these situations are taken into account, a potential source of saving could be provided by the government. In principle, the government could generate saving that might not otherwise exist and mobilize saving that would otherwise remain idle. In this case, the government's propensity to save can partly compensate for the inability and unwillingness to save out of private domestic income. Thus the government has to ensure that the proportion of domestic income is adequate (such as a surplus of tax revenue over current expenditure) and that the resulting unconsumed resources are channeled into public and private investment projects through financial institutions.

Therefore the government's willingness and ability to save must be substantially improved in order to ensure that its propensity to save is greater than that of the private sector. Thus in many Pacific island countries, there is not only a greater need for improving the tax system and raising government savings but also a greater reliance on financial institutions for the channeling of available domestic saving for investment projects. For example, a proportion of the domestic and foreign savings collected by the government could be deposited with the financial institutions that channel these funds to private investors. In this way, the financial institutions, especially the commercial banks, could extend credit to private entrepreneurs without inflationary effects, as well as moderate short-term adversary balance-of-payments effects. This procedure would permit the banks to play a more effective role in the provision of long-term finance.

With the financial system still in an early stage of development in most Pacific island countries, access to safe, liquid, and rewarding ways of accumulating savings is extremely difficult for the majority of households in large subsistence sectors.

Direct finance

Direct finance exists in most Pacific island countries in two forms: equity shares and bonds. In this case, there is a separation between the saving units and the investing units, with the latter borrowing directly from the former. Compared with self-finance in which the saver and the investor are the same economic unit, direct finance permits a divorce between the ownership of saving and the control of its use. This also means that the ownership of a public or private investment project can be more widely spread, and more reliance can be placed on some form of external finance. The government and public and private firms are able to obtain part of the funds required to invest in production of goods and services by issuing marketable interest-bearing debt instruments, such as bonds and bills, and marketable dividend-earning shares.

However, the use of these financial instruments proves to be rather limited in the context of the Pacific island countries. With the financial system still in an early stage of development, entrepreneurs who want to borrow risk capital have encountered difficulties, especially the fact that a well-functioning securities market does not really exist in any of these countries. Due to the absence of a securities market there is a lack of liquidity in the financial investments in the form of shares and bonds made by domestic banks and other financial institutions. However, investment in this type of financial assets is not possible for the vast majority of domestic producers with only small incomes to save.

Government securities and non-inflationary finance

Consequently, the government continues to be the principal issuer of securities (bonds and treasury bills). Insofar as investment in government securities is concerned, the government issues are purchased mainly by domestic financial institutions such as commercial banks, insurance companies, and pension funds.

The experience in Fiji reflects some of the main characteristics of the distribution of government securities common to many Pacific island countries. Since the establishment of the central banking system in 1973, the government has made a deliberate effort to borrow as little as possible from the central bank to finance its development projects on the grounds of its alleged inflationary consequences. As a result, the domestic financing of the government deficit has consisted largely of non-bank financial resources, mainly borrowing from the Fiji National Provident Fund (FNPF) and the insurance companies. It should be mentioned that the FNPF, which was established in 1966 to provide a superannuation fund for all wage earners, is a collector of compulsory saving in the sense that employee-employer contributions, based on wages and salaries, are mandatory. Consequently, the growth of wage income has helped expand the "institutionalized forced" savings and lending by the FNPF. In other words, the FNPF guarantees the existence of compulsory savings out of wages and salaries, which are then used to purchase government securities.

Of the FNPF's total assets between 1974 and 1984, for instance, the development loans to the government accounted for 39.5 percent; the loans to the private sector constituted 23.5 percent; the loans to the Housing Authority accounted for 17.5 percent; while the loans to other statutory bodies and local authorities accounted for 19.5 percent. In other words, for the period 1974-84, 76.5 percent of the assets of the FNPF were development loans to the public sector (government and statutory bodies) and only 23.5 percent were loans to the private sector. In addition to the FNPF, the insurance companies are both collectors of small savings in Fiji and holders of part of the government's domestic debt.

Altogether, about 65 percent of the domestic financial resources available for financing government deficits between 1975 and 1984 originated in prior private savings (i.e., FNPF funds, insurance companies, non-financial firms, etc.), leaving about 35 percent to be provided by the domestic banking system. The second largest holders of the Fiji government domestic debt were the commercial banks with about 23 percent. Fiji's central bank was responsible for about 12 percent of the domestic financing of deficits during this period.

These statistics suggest that government deficits have not been primarily financed through inflationary means by the banking system. Nevertheless, borrowing from banks could be inflationary if the central bank does not want interest rates to rise, thereby providing funds to the commercial banks to maintain liquidity.

However, some firms in the economy have used part of their undistributed profits to buy government bonds when the alternative of either investing in plant and machinery or buying shares in other companies have been less attractive. Nevertheless, the private ownership of government securities is attractive to a very small, high-income, and hence high-saving section of the population.

Equity participation

Except for the methods of financing the capital expenditure of the few multinational firms operating in the region, the investments of domestic firms or companies have been rarely financed by the issues of shares and bonds (or debentures) to the general public. Some recent instances in Papua New Guinea are an exception. This method of finance is usually not feasible in the Pacific island countries mainly because of the lack of a stock exchange or a money market for this purpose. This has meant that the domestic firms that want to borrow risk capital or debt capital (bonds) face difficulties and rely for finance on retained profits and bank loans.

This difficulty has been partly moderated by the equity participation of the specialized financial institutions such as the development banks, the investment finance corporations, pension funds, insurance companies, and unit trusts while relying for finance on own accumulated savings. These institutions gather together small amounts of individual saving into large sums and take up investments in equity shares or purchase bonds (or debentures) of domestic firms with such needs.

Usually, a development bank is not permitted to commit to a single enterprise in the form of equity participation more than 10-20 percent of its unimpaired paid share capital and reserve fund. In addition, a development bank's equity is normally not permitted to exceed 25 percent of the paid-up capital of the assisted enterprise.

However, the development bank's equity participation is granted only when it is considered to serve as a catalytic agent for the establishment as well as for the expansion of an enterprise. Thus the development bank provides equity finance not in the hope of obtaining a greater share of potential future profits but rather in the hope of supporting the infant stage of risky but viable enterprises. The development bank usually intends to dispose of such equity investments to domestic entrepreneurs when appropriate.

The Investment Corporation of Solomon Islands, which was established in 1988, is one of the examples of a government-owned specialized financial institution that is not functioning well. It was established primarily to hold government equity investment in commercial enterprises. Subject to ministerial approval, the corporation may form subsidiary corporations under the Companies Act; form partnerships and enter into joint ventures; purchase and dispose of equity or other commercial interests in companies, partnerships, enterprises, or joint ventures; make or grant loans to enterprises in which it holds a commercial interest; borrow monies and issue securities, including guarantees and debentures; establish and manage unit trusts; and make such unit trusts available to the public. The corporation may issue shares, as well as issue stock, bonds, bills, or other promissory notes. The main source of funding for equity purchase has been borrowing from the banks as well as from the government.

The other major non-monetary financial institutions, which devote at least a small part of their funds to investments in equity shares, include provident funds and insurance companies. Nevertheless, these two types of financial intermediaries play a very important role in the mobilization of domestic savings in the island economies.

Overall, very few financial intermediaries engage in long-term financing and participate in the equity capital of domestic enterprises in the Pacific island countries. As a result, the domestic firms and producers have little choice but to make the best from own-saving and debt finance. Of even more importance, most of the agricultural producers in the Pacific island countries have a highly variable income because of external price fluctuations, natural disasters, etc., with which to pay the fixed annual interest payments.

Indirect finance

In the private sector, indirect finance requires a financial intermediary that accepts saving deposits and provides loans to deficit spenders. Thus the act of saving is separated from the act of investment, which is at the heart of the problem of adjustment between saving and investment decisions. The act of saving is therefore freed from the problem of lack of investment opportunity in a Pacific island country. In addition, indirect finance as an integral part of financial intermediation breaks down the limitations of self-finance. Without financial intermediation, producers can finance only their investment requirements from their own accumulated savings or from direct borrowing in the form of equity shares.

It is important to stress that the entrepreneurs' ability to borrow often depends on own finance. However, the lumpy investments ordinarily associated with the adoption of improved technologies and hence improved productivity are normally well beyond the capacity of self-finance. In addition, the limitation of self-finance is one of the major problems that impede the speed and direction of private sector development in the Pacific island countries.

The increasing role of indirect finance in financing the private sector's investment has been associated with financial development. In some cases, the gross national savings are increasingly deposited in financial institutions that use these funds to increase their loans to private and government sectors. In the private sectors, domestic entrepreneurs usually invest more than they save, and for them the financial institutions are an important source of additional finance. Not only commercial banks but also development banks and pension funds have become an important source of funds for the private sector.

Bank's time deposits and ability to make new loans

Because the commercial bank remains the principal source of indirect finance in most island countries, a major question is how to increase the proportion of domestic savings that should be placed with commercial banks. The increase in the ratio of financial assets, mainly in the form of bank deposits to gross domestic income, is due to two effects: (1) an increase in the ratio of domestic savings to gross domestic income and (2) a substitution of financial assets for real assets. In both cases, the results represent a potential claim on a bank's cash reserves and overseas funds, which has some bearing on a bank's ability to extend new loans to the private sector.

The potential claims by depositors on the assets of the commercial banks can be exercised after a fixed period if they are savings and time deposits. Thus the greater the ratio of savings and time deposits to total deposits, the more potential claims the commercial banks can make on their cash and foreign exchange reserves by granting new loans to private entrepreneurs with acceptable credit worthiness and collateral. Accordingly, the commercial banks can make available to private entrepreneurs the command over real resources that the time and savings depositors are forgoing for a specified period, normally between one and 24 months.

Financial Savings

It has already been pointed out that the crux of the problem of private sector development in years to come is how to increase the quantity and quality of the resources available for capital formation, or how to control consumption and increase saving and investment. It is therefore important to consider the possibility that an expansion of the financial system will stimulate domestic savings in the Pacific island countries.

This section is not concerned with the determinants of saving behavior as such in the Pacific island countries. Rather, it deals with the ways in which financial intermediaries help the mobilization of domestic savings in these countries. The basic function of financial institutions is to offer claims to savers (capital suppliers) that are more attractive than the claims that they themselves obtain from investors (capital users). In this way, an extension of the banking system provides a stimulus to domestic saving that might not otherwise exist as the total abstention from consumption is increased.

However, the financial institutions offer an extremely limited range of saving instruments with certain expected returns and a high liquidity of which savings and time deposits are the most important. Nevertheless, the availability of such financial assets could induce some economic units to save more. With the limited range of financial institutions, the allocation of a given volume of savings over available financial assets is influenced by (1) the expected returns, e.g., the interest rates paid on savings and time deposits; (2) the level of risk in the portfolio, e.g., the solvency of the intermediary; and (3) the costs related to moving into and out from that portfolio, e.g., the liquidity of the financial assets. The lenders (or savers) will choose the type of financial asset that best suits their preference for yield, risk aversion, and liquidity.

Two main types of saving instruments constitute by far the greatest share of financial assets outstanding in the Pacific island countries, namely:

- Non-income-earning assets, basically currency and demand deposits.

- Income-earning assets, of which the main form is time and savings deposits with commercial banks.

These are now briefly discussed:

Non-income earning financial assets: currency and demand deposits

In the private sector, part of the private sector's financial savings takes the form of currency and demand deposits. However, there is a tinge of irrationality in holding non-income-generating currency and demand deposits when other income-earning assets are available in the country. Nevertheless, it is important to remember that the production in semi-subsistence sectors of island economies is small in scale and normally uses simple traditional technologies. In addition, self-accumulated saving is the principal method of financing the modest investment requirements of these semi-subsistence producers. Consequently, part of the process of self-financed investment in these countries involves the accumulation of savings first in the form of currency and demand deposits and later in form of planting materials, physical capital, etc.

However, as has happened in many Pacific island countries over the last few years, the rise in the nominal interest rates coupled with the fall in the rate of inflation has led to the rise in the opportunity cost in terms of the interest income forgone in holding currency and demand deposit balances. As a result, some of the financial assets that have high expected returns were substituted for small and risky self-financed investment projects with a low return. This effect has tended to reduce the demand for non-income-earning financial assets. Such is the portfolio effect of financial intermediation in terms of the substitution of high income-earning financial assets for low and/or non-income-earning assets.

Income-earning financial assets: time and savings deposits

The shift away from self-financed investment projects with low returns and from non-income-earning financial assets has been reflected by the growth in the demand for time and savings balances. In the Pacific island countries the time and savings deposits with commercial banks constitute the main form of income-earning financial assets available.

The change in the ratio of financial savings in the form of time and savings to gross domestic product, which occurred in many Pacific island countries especially during the latter part of the 1980s, was mainly a result of (1) the substitution of high income-earning financial assets for low income-earning financial assets and physical assets and (2) the increased domestic savings associated with economic growth.

Portfolio substitution effect

In the absence of a capital market in most Pacific island economies, the portfolio substitution effect is associated with a breaking down of the traditional link between saving and investment. In sectors where the prospects for investment are not so attractive, some economic units have substituted financial assets in the form of savings and time deposits for physical assets. The important implication of this effect for private sector development is that more long-term funds will be available at the financial institutions to finance viable investment projects. Consequently, the portfolio substitution effect of financial intermediation helps to stimulate real investment.

The substitution of demand deposits for income-earning financial assets such as savings and time deposits is largely a function of the bank deposit rate. In particular, a rise in the bank deposit rate is expected to induce a fall in the ratio of demand deposits to savings and time deposits. The increase in the rate of return on savings and time deposits has been associated with a decrease in the demand for demand deposits in most Pacific island countries. This situation has some bearing on the commercial banks' lending policy. In general, the higher their savings and time deposits in relation to their demand deposits, the more claims the banks can make on their cash and foreign assets by extending loans to government and private producers.

Growth of financial savings

An important question, in the absence of a securities market operation, is whether the increase in the ratio of broad money (currency plus demand, time, and savings deposits) to gross domestic product in many Pacific island countries represents an increase in the overall savings ratio. This ratio can be used as a measure of the flow of loanable funds in the economy for two reasons. First, it gives an indication of the size of financial resources available for self-finance. Second, it provides an indication of the ability of the banking system to extend new credit to finance private investment.

Net current transfers have played an important role in the process of domestic savings in some island countries. With the help of remittances received from relatives and friends abroad, the people of Western Samoa, Tonga, and Kiribati, for example, have been able to maintain a high level of consumption in excess of their incomes. Consequently, the gross domestic savings (gross domestic income less consumption expenditures) of these countries have been negative.

Moreover, the gross national savings (the gross domestic income plus net current transfers from abroad less total consumption expenditure) have been positive. In addition, the ratio of gross national savings to gross do-

mestic income has tended to increase in recent years. In the case of
Western Samoa, this increase was mainly caused by the increase in government savings as a fraction of gross domestic product, which rose from
25 percent in 1983 to 37 percent in 1987. It also should be mentioned that
the increase in government savings was greatly influenced by an austerity
program introduced as a crucial part of the conditionality of the
International Monetary Fund (IMF) assistance to cover the country's balance of payments problems in the early 1980s.

Because remittances are mainly in the form of foreign financial assets,
they must to a large extent pass through the domestic banking system for
liquidity conversion. Therefore, there is potential for raising the level of
financial savings out of private remittances from abroad. However, financial savings have been relatively low in Western Samoa and Tonga. In
Western Samoa, for example, the level was about 8 percent of the gross
domestic product in 1987 compared with the overall savings ratio of 37
percent in the same year. This situation stems from holding gross national
savings mainly in the form of physical assets such as private dwellings,
private vehicles, church buildings, etc. Nevertheless, the share of financial
savings in gross national savings has increased from -10.2 percent in 1983
to 21 percent in 1987.

The important implication of this finding is that the increase in the ratio of
financial savings to gross domestic product has been a reflection of the increase in the overall savings ratio over the period. This finding is important because it implies that the portfolio substitution effect, already discussed, was associated with an increasing saving effect. At the macro
level, therefore, the process of financial intermediation in Western Samoa
not only involved the reallocation of wealth but also entailed the change in
the level of savings. This may be attributed to several factors of which the
most important was the increase in the level of the real deposit rate between 1983 and 1987. Both the bank deposit and the lending rates, which
were highly positive in real terms during that period, tended to encourage
financial savings and at the same time discourage the private sector's demand for credit.

The 1991 World Bank report on the Pacific island economies states that
deposit rates remain highly negative in most Pacific island countries.
However, the figures for the 1985-90 periods, which are given in Table 5.1
for a selected number of Pacific island countries, show that some countries
have negative deposit interest rates and some have positive ones.

Table 5.1   Three-month deposit interest rates for selected Pacific island countries

Year	Solomon Islands Interest rates			CPI	Real interest
1985	8.31	-	8.51	8.7	-0.29
1986	10.09	-	10.24	23.6	-13.5
1987	10.11	-	10.20	6.3	3.4
1988	8.75	-	10.56	17.1	-7.4
1989	9	-	12	10.8	-0.3
1990	9	-	12	10.2	0.3

Year	Fiji Interest rates	CPI	Real interest (one-year deposit)
1985	8	4.4	3.6
1986	8	1.8	6.2
1987	8	5.7	2.3
1988	8	11.9	-3.9
1989	7.5	6.1	1.4
1990	n/a	n/a	n/a

Year	Western Samoa Interest rates	CPI	Real interest (3-month deposit)
1985	12	9.1	2.9
1986	12.5	5.8	6.7
1987	10.25	4.6	5.7
1988	10.25	8.7	1.6
1989	7	6.2	0.8
1990	n/a	n/a	n/a

Year	Tonga Interest rates	CPI	Real interest (3-month deposit)
1985	6	1.4	4.6
1986	6	29.1	-23.1
1987	6	7.5	-1.5
1988	6	11.3	-5.3
1989	6	4	2
1990	7.5	9.8	-2.3

Year	Papua New Guinea Interest rates			CPI	Real interest (3-month deposit)
1985	8.25	-	11	4.3	5.3
1986	7	-	8.75	5.3	2.6
1987	8	-	9.25	3	5.6
1988	8	-	9.5	3.9	4.9
1989	8	-	10.25	4.5	4.6
1990	8	-	11	6.3*	3.2

* First nine months.   (con.)

Table 5.1   Three-month deposit interest rates for selected Pacific island countries (con.)

Year	Vanuatu Interest rates		CPI	Real interest (2-6 month deposit)
1985	6.37 -	8.5	2.7	4.7
1986	4.5 -	8.79	5.7	-0.9
1987	3 -	5.75	15.9	-11.5
1988	4 -	10	8.7	-1.7
1989	6 -	8	7.7	-0.7
1990	6 -	8	5.6	1.4

Financial Resource Allocation

One principal effect of the shift of resources to the financial institutions is the increased efficiency in the allocation of investable resources. A considerable proportion of their funds came from household units that otherwise would have used these resources for less productive investment if not consumption purposes. In addition, small savers in the rural areas and elsewhere do not always have direct access to sound investment opportunities in other sectors of the economy.

Moreover, the intermediaries, which can afford to employ a variety of experts, should create a small pool of expertise that could provide management advice and technical guidance to domestic producers who seek financial assistance from them. In this connection, the financial institutions can help to direct savings from diverse sources to productive investment projects in the country.

By extending credit for investments in projects with high rates of return, the financial institutions improve the efficient allocation of financial resources. However, if additional savings are transferred to financial intermediaries, which in turn lend only to well established firms that are able to pay higher interest rates and use credit to finance luxury consumption goods and thus divert to consumption purposes those resources that would otherwise be available for investment purposes, the overall allocation of bank credit will not be improved. In general, commercial banks show a particular reluctance to lend to rural producers in the Pacific island countries. As discussed earlier, most of these rural producers have highly variable incomes with which to service their debt.

As long as commercial banks remain the principal source of external finance for the credit requirements of the Pacific island economies, the government has to direct bank lending toward private sector development by applying appropriate methods of credit controls. In most Pacific island countries, selective credit allocation policies consist of:

- Quantitative control of credit.

- Selective control of credit.

- Selective control of the interest rate.

These are discussed briefly below:

Quantitative control of credit

Normally, the central bank has the power to influence the lending policies of the commercial banks. Specifically, the central bank uses the legal reserve ratios to influence the cash reserves of the commercial banks. Commercial banks have to meet their loan commitments while maintaining cash reserves including their balances at the central bank, which they regard as adequate to meet the demand for their depositors. If their actual cash reserves are less than they desire, they will lend less to their customers. If banks have more cash reserves than they desire, they will lend more to their customers if the potential borrowers have the desired credit worthiness and collateral.

However, with an insufficient effective demand for loans in many Pacific island countries, the commercial banks tend to keep high levels of cash reserves. It is important to emphasize that it is not the level of the legal reserve ratio that counts but rather the margin of "free" cash reserves remaining with the banks. In the case of Fiji, the statistics of the margin between the actual and the statutory required cash and securities balances held by the central bank between 1974 and 1983 show that the banks were not in any danger that their balances at the central bank would fall below the legal minimum, and thus they were under no pressure to reduce loans or to refrain from increasing them. In the Pacific island countries, the statutory control governing the magnitude of the reserve ratio can be viewed as a form of "moral suasion" approach in accordance with the banks' desire to restrain or to expand lending.

Other instruments of direct credit controls used by the central banks in some Pacific island countries are the ratio of advances to total deposits and free capital and reserves, and the ratio of total lending to the level of foreign reserves. The increase of bank advances produces a greater demand for foreign currency, which may have to be bought from the central bank, thus reducing not only the commercial banks' reserves but also their foreign exchange reserves.

Another method of direct credit control in operation similar to that in Western Samoa is the legal permissible growth in commercial bank credit, which is linked to the growth in time and savings deposits. Furthermore, the allowable increase in commercial bank credit is disaggregated as between (1) the private sector and (2) the public sector. Thus, given the official target average increase of 13 percent set in 1989, the growth rate of lending to the public sector is not permitted to exceed 5 percent, leaving the remainder to the private sector.

Selective control of credit

In addition to the system of quantitative control in operation, specific restraints are placed on the use of bank credit for certain purposes. Specific rules were formulated for the operation of a selective control of bank advances that restrict the availability of bank credit to certain kinds of potential borrowers. The broad classes of bank advances receiving selective credit preference in most Pacific island countries are (1) advances to agriculture, (2) advances to export and import substitution industries, and (3) advances to tourism industries. The bank decides the acceptable type of collateral for the loan in each case.

At the same time the banks are usually requested not to increase, without central bank approval, advances for luxury imports or in some cases advances to importers if the loans are to be used to buy foreign exchange and to provide advances for non-residents.

Furthermore, some selective credit criteria include "financial layering" or the on-lending of funds from commercial banks to development banks. The commercial banks' holdings of development bank bonds are usually eligible for agricultural loan ratio calculations. In some cases, however, the development banks' bonds, which were earmarked as a "proxy" for agricultural loans, could not be included in the computation of the government securities reserve requirements. This situation has encouraged some commercial banks to take up more development bank bond issues and thereby has afforded more scope for direct lending to agricultural producers via development bank loans.

Selective control of interest rates

Bank credit is sometimes channeled at subsidized or low interest rates to priority sectors. In Tonga, for instance, the development bank charges relatively higher rates of interest on enterprises that are either fully or majority foreign owned. Projects for developing agriculture or for creating foreign exchange pay lower rates of interest per annum than projects pertaining to low priority sectors.

Implicit in this strategy is the underlying assumption that the demand for bank credit is interest elastic in the country. If this assumption is not valid, the interest differentials would have no effect on the allocation of bank credit between the low and high priority sectors of the economy.

On the one hand, especially in the short run, the selective control of the interest rate deprives the bank of opportunities to earn higher profits by lending to willing and creditworthy borrowers at higher interest rates. On the other hand, it is usually argued that the adoption of a low interest rate policy from a long-run standpoint is in the interest of economic development. The resultant increase in domestic investment and thus income will lead to a greater volume of financial savings, which in turn increases the role of financial institutions in financing capital formation.

Conclusions

The major conclusions relating to financial intermediation and the development of the private sector are as follows:

1. One of the biggest problems for private sector development in the Pacific island countries in years to come is how to increase the supply of savings for domestic private entrepreneurs who rely on external finance and can effectively invest it.

2. The Pacific island countries need to encourage the development of financial institutions in order to build up their supply of investable resources and then allocate them to productive use.

3. There exists a degree of complimentarity between self-finance and indirect finance in the island countries.

4. The problem associated with the lack of a domestic securities market has been partly moderated by the specialized financial institutions such as the development banks and provident funds.

5. The growing dependency on debt finance rather than on equity finance has not been in the best interest of most Pacific island agricultural producers who always have a highly variable income because of external price fluctuations, natural disasters, etc., with which to meet the fixed interest obligations.

6. A significant amount of the domestic financial savings have been diverted by the commercial banks, provident funds, and insurance companies away from the private sector and invested in government securities (bonds and treasury bills).

7. The problem associated with dependency on self-finance has two main aspects in the context of the Pacific island countries. First, the lumpy investment often required to expand the production scales are normally well beyond the capacity of self-finance. Second, the reliance on self-finance has also been associated with the dependency on self-management rather than on the professional assistance of banks to make important investment decisions.

8. Because the commercial banks remain the principal sources of indirect finance in the island countries, a major question is how to increase the proportion of domestic savings that is placed with the banking system. This has an important bearing on the banking system's ability to extend new loans or to buy new equity shares in the private sector.

9. To some extent a shift has occurred from self-finance to indirect finance in the Pacific island countries as a result of increases in the domestic real interest rates. This situation produced two effects, namely, a decline in the ratios of demand for money balances to the gross domestic product and a rise in the ratios of time and savings deposits to the gross domestic product.

10. Recent increases in real domestic interest rates have meant that additional medium-term funds have been available to finance planned investment.

11. Administrative selective credit controls are aimed at influencing the pattern of investment expenditure and the allocation of real resources in a way that satisfies the government's development policy.

12. The shift of resources to financial institutions has implied an increased efficiency in the allocation of investment resources.

13. In general, it is the inadequacy of financial savings, as well as the lack of tradition in seeking investment opportunities, that limits the pace of financial development in the Pacific island countries.

14. Regarding policy implications, the financial institutions should actively help to stimulate the effective demand of local producers

for credit finance. The act of saving itself does little to produce a range of viable investment projects in the private sector.

15. To encourage private investment, the specialized financial institutions that engage in long-term financing and equity participation should organize themselves so that they can provide a wide range of technical and management advisory services and also help identify viable investment opportunities and effective organization of production and marketing. It is suggested that the government examine the possibility of using public funds for the costs involved in developing these particular activities.

16. As long as the commercial banks remain the principal vehicle for saving mobilization in the Pacific island countries, they will channel part of their funds to specialized financial institutions that engage in direct long-term lending to the private sector.

17. The specialized financial intermediaries should be more active in mobilizing savings. To assist in this process, it is suggested that the government consider the possibility of allowing the development banks to provide deposit facilities for their clients.

18. A flexible interest rate policy is necessary to influence the change in the composition of bank deposits in favor of savings and time deposits, which in turn enhance the banks' ability to make new longer-term loans available to the private sector.

chapter 6

The institutional environment

All Pacific island countries have policy objectives of investment promotion, entrepreneurial development, and the enhancement of national marketing and product development skills. The challenge is to translate these policies into effective programs to encourage investment and to promote exports. Governments have a key role in providing an institutional environment conducive to the needs of entrepreneurial investors. This role goes beyond providing investors with an attractive package of fiscal incentives.

The Private Sector Project reviewed the overall performance of the institutional structures and arrangements that have been established to promote, direct, and regulate private sector activity. The country and sector experience in the region has been varied. Some institutions have been very successful, while the performance of others has fallen below the expectations of policymakers and planners. In a few instances sound economic policies have been thwarted by inappropriate and ineffective institutions, which has had a negative impact on private sector and entrepreneurial development. Important lessons in institution building and requirements can be learned from these experiences. Several regional projects to facilitate private development have been identified.

As part of the Private Sector Project, a number of in-depth case studies were undertaken dealing with institutions affecting private sector development in five broad areas. These are:

- Trade and investment support institutions,

- Enterprise support organizations,

- Institutions to facilitate private investment in agriculture,

- Institutions and infrastructure to promote investment in export manufacturing,

89

- Development finance institutions with particular emphasis on the region's development banks.

The detailed findings of this research are presented in McGregor and Coulter (1991), Cole (1990), Thomson (1989), and Briscoe et al. (1990), which draw on various sub-studies. This chapter provides a distillation of the various findings and recommendations concerned with institutions affecting private sector development.

Trade and Investment

The South Pacific has also had a strong tradition of expatriate entrepreneurial traders who purchased domestic product and exported it through their own marketing channels. The transference of this role to local traders has been difficult for a variety of reasons including communal pressures and loyalties and lack of overseas marketing connections and skills. The Pacific island countries still have economic roots in communal production and the sharing of the fruits of labor; in this milieu it has been difficult for indigenous middlemen to operate successfully.

During the colonial era exports from the Pacific island countries were largely in the hands of expatriates whose marketing skills and connections receded from the island countries with the passing of that era. Their marketing channels had been, and in some cases still are, through the colonial-based corporations that developed mining operations, coconut plantations, and other agricultural estates. These corporations had head offices in metropolitan centers that handled the marketing function of the islands' production. One of the principal faults of this system was the lack of transference of marketing and product development skills to the nationals of the Pacific island countries. Yet until recently, the nascent private sector in these countries carried out overseas marketing without the benefit of government support mechanisms. Furthermore, governments, and agencies, played no active role in investment promotion.

Trade and investment promotion bodies

The last few years have seen rapid developments in terms of marketing support and investment promotion. On the surface, the private sector would seem to have a plethora of marketing and other assistance available to it from the wide range of aid agency support schemes and governments promising marketing support where possible. In reality, however, the picture for a potential exporter is in most cases confused and shallow. The very range of support institutions, the lack of focal points of assistance, and the persistent lack of follow-through of this assistance militate against effective use of the marketing support available.

Thomson (1989) contains a comprehensive review of regional and international agencies involved with trade and investment promotion. These included:

- The Forum Secretariat

- Regional Trade Commissions, i.e., the Australian South Pacific Trade Commission (SPTC) and the recently established New Zealand government's South Pacific Trade Office (SPTO)

- The EEC's Center for Development of Industry (CDI)

- Canada's Trade Facilitation Office (TFO)

- Japan's External Trade Organization (JETRO)

- The Commonwealth Secretariat (COMSEC) Export Market Development Division

- The Economic and Social Commission for Asian and the Pacific (ESCAP) Trade Promotion Center (TPC)

The Pacific island governments rely mainly on these overseas agencies when called on to support their private sectors in the development of marketing skills and channels. Fiji and Papua New Guinea have made the best use of the available services. Much more can be done in terms of extending the scope and network of the services provided and, more important, achieving better use of existing services. A major challenge is to achieve an improved dissemination of information regarding the services available from the various agencies.

National trade and investment promotion and regulatory bodies were also reviewed:

- The Overseas Missions of the Pacific island countries (Thomson 1989)

- Fiji Trade and Investment Board (FTIB) (Chandra 1990; Thomson 1989)

- Papua New Guinea National Investment Development Authority (NIDA) (Millett 1990b)

- Tongan Department of Commerce and Labour (McGregor 1989)

The FTIB and NIDA were found to represent the two extremes of the impact of the institutional environment created by government on private investment. Both institutions offer important lessons for the other Pacific island countries.

Fiji's FTIB has been the key in promoting Fiji as an attractive and profitable destination for foreign investment and increasing the exposure of Fiji manufacturers to foreign markets and suppliers. This has been done with the backdrop of difficult circumstances. Most of this cost of promotion has been borne by aid agencies. Other Pacific island countries can similarly use aid funds to market themselves and their products, particularly in Australia, New Zealand, Europe, and the United States. The FTIB is an institution that other Pacific island countries would be wise to emulate.

In contrast, NIDA, established to promote and to control foreign investment in Papua New Guinea, has been a major constraint on investment activities. Deficiencies in the NIDA administration, as seen by business, are processing delays, confidentiality, consistency, reliability, effectiveness, and practicality. NIDA has now been abolished and it will be replaced by an Investment Promotion Authority (IPA). This creates direct costs to the potential investor and uncertainty, both of which inhibit investment.

Recommendations for strengthening and developing trade and investment institutions

The major recommendations can be summarized as follows:

The establishment of a South Pacific Regional Trade Commission (SPRETCO). The majority of Pacific island countries will never be able to afford their own overseas trade commissions, and without them it will be very difficult to maintain sustained marketing support for island exporters. The success of the SPTC in Sydney and the opening of the SPTO in Auckland have paved the way for a Regional Trade Commission service, and the emergence of the Trade Division of the Forum Secretariat as the focus of regional trade promotion activities provides a logical base for SPRETCO.

The concept of SPRETCO is a rationalization of existing services, rather than the creation of yet another regional institution. SPRETCO will entail the establishment of a central service to which the private sector of the South Pacific can turn for sustained marketing and trade promotion assistance.

The expansion of the SPRETCO network into the markets of importance to Pacific island exporters should be based on two policies: first, use of the wide range of existing aid agencies described above and, second, the establishment of trade commissions in selected markets of importance, e.g., Tokyo, Los Angeles, Vancouver, and Brussels. It is hoped that the Los Angeles component of the trade commission network will develop under the Market Access and Regional Competitiveness (MARC) project of the United States Agency for International Development (USAID) that has recently been approved. In the establishment of these trade commissions, the successful model of the SPTC should be followed, i.e.:

- Funding the establishment and running costs of the trade commission is the responsibility of the host government as a South Pacific regional aid project;

- Trade commissions should be staffed by a mixture of expertise from the host country and the island countries, with emphasis on the private sector;

- A minimum of bureaucratic red tape and a maximum of accessibility for island exporters should be the hallmark of these offices.

The successful precedence of the SPTC and SPTO as effective aid measures should give confidence to other aid donors in supporting this proposal. These offices would also be in harmony with the trend toward support of regional programs rather than bilateral ones, as well as assist aid donors such as Japan that wish to raise the South Pacific percentage of their global aid programs but have trouble in identifying suitable projects to do so. It should also be pointed out that Japan has already established the Association of Southeast Asian Nations (ASEAN) Promotion Center on Trade, Investment and Tourism so the extension of this precedent to the opening of a SPRETCO office in Tokyo should not be difficult. As a further extension of SPRETCO's coverage, the past offer of the Australian government for Forum Island Country (FIC) to have access to the worldwide services of the Australian Trade Commission offices could be utilized.

Apart from the obvious attractions of economies of scale and outside funding achieved by SPRETCO, and the fact that without it most of the Pacific island countries will never have overseas trade commission services outside of the narrow confines of the South Pacific Regional Trade and Economic Cooperation Agreement (SPARTECA) countries, SPRETCO's scope for regional coordination in trade and investment development is very attractive. Such coordination has been much discussed over the last two decades, but the track record for implementation has been uninspiring.

An expanded role for the Trade Division of the Forum Secretariat in the promotion and policy of FIC trade and investment. There is a need for a central point of reference in the variety of trade promotional programs and agencies available to the exporters of the South Pacific, and the Trade Division is best qualified to be that point.

It is recommended that the Pacific island countries turn their attention to further strengthening of the Trade Division through the establishment of SPRETCO and the appointment of the Trade Division as SPRETCO's headquarters. In the latter role the Trade Division is not expected to lay on the heavy hand of regional bureaucracy; it is instead, through a defined set of motivational objectives, expected to facilitate contact between island exporters and the SPRETCO offices. This is to ensure that follow-on activities are available to FIC exporters; it also facilitates the coordinating and pace-setting role that the scope of this regional exercise demands. It is essential that the private sector deal directly with SPRETCO and not be required to channel requests through the Ministry of Foreign Affairs of their respective countries. It is also important that the staff of SPRETCO have strong private sector backgrounds.

The establishment of a computerized regional trade data bank and information service for the enhancement of marketing facilities for island exporters. A regional trade information data bank is seen as essential to serve as the prime focus of private enterprise and public sector enquiries to provide details of Pacific island export capability and island company information. It is an essential part of any trade development and promotion agency that it has an up-to-date and comprehensive trade information service to provide the resource intelligence required for an effective marketing program. An effective regional trade information data bank would need a central coordination agency. Again the Trade Division of the Forum Secretariat is recommended as the most appropriate office particularly if this service is developed closely in tandem with the proposed SPRETCO. The private sector of the Pacific island countries would have access to the trade data bank through terminals in their national trade promotion offices and Chambers of Commerce. Of most importance, existing trade promotion offices such as SPTC, SPTO, Forum Secretariat, FIC Embassies and Consulates, CDI, and ESCAP's TPC would be linked to the regional trade data bank.

A reorientation of the priorities of the overseas missions. The low percentage of the time that the Pacific island countries' overseas diplomats devote to trade promotion roles and activities is surprising, given the small size of these missions and the limited resources available. It is recommended that there be a reorientation of these foreign missions toward trade and investment promotion roles and activities. This should be reflected in the allocation of staff time and in the selection and training of staff to staff overseas missions.

Greater emphasis of Pacific island countries on their national trade promotion institutions. Domestically there is much that can be done with existing resources to support and facilitate marketing assistance to exporters. To tap into these systems requires coordination and promotion at home with export marketing development agencies clearly identifiable and readily available to service private sector needs. Fiji's FTIB has proved very successful in encouraging trade and investment and provides a model for other regional countries. There is scope for intra-regional technical assistance. Furthermore, aid donors have expressed a willingness to support such a program of institutional building. Where further marketing expertise is seen as desirable a wide range of training options are freely available; these include attachments to the SPTC and SPTO and the potential for governments to second such personnel to private enterprise.

Small Business Enterprise Support Organizations (ESOs)

In the development of regional economies there lies a great challenge in finding ways to effectively facilitate a high level of indigenous participation in the small business sector. Small business offers the countries of the region the greatest potential for economic growth, employment generation, and expansion of the tax base.

Much has been written about the problems encountered in the South Pacific by people wishing to establish and sustain their own business. The problems and constraints are reviewed in detail in Briscoe et al. (1990). A great deal of effort across the region is now being devoted to small business by development governments, aid donors, and non-government organization (NGO). As a result a bewildering range of organizations are involved in promoting new business or offering services to small firms and potential entrepreneurs. But how effective are the services being provided and how well are the limited resources of the region being used? The Private Sector Project examines the activities of ESOs in the region. The problems faced by the ESOs are reviewed on the basis of which a number of specific strategies for improving support services to entrepreneurs and small businesses are made. These are reported briefly below:

Many programs offered are one-dimensional. They typically are not a part of carefully planned coordinated strategies. An organization might offer a course or two, loans at favorable interest rates to a target group, or first-contact counseling services but rarely in an integrated package of services tailored to the specific problems of local entrepreneurs. Integrated and phased development programs are required whereby the investment of resources is dependent on the successful completion of appropriate training and where continuing support is available after business start-up. However, it is not difficult to understand why so many agencies continue to rely on one-dimensional programs rather than on more effective integrated packages. Comprehensive packages of services are costly to administer, and the agencies themselves are chronically short of financial, human, and technical resources. Thus an agency often faces the choice of offering the occasional short course or doing nothing. Individual agencies offering one- or even two-dimensional programs are unlikely to have much impact on the development of indigenous entrepreneurs.

Proliferation and duplication. For a Pacific island country there can be a bewildering array of agencies promoting business development. In Fiji, for example, these include government agencies, particularly the Fiji Development Bank and the National Training Council, the Employers Federation, Chambers of Commerce, the International Labor Organization (ILO), and the programs of bilateral aid donors. In addition, there are a host of other groups involved with small business development, including several churches, the YMCA and YWCA, service clubs, the Fiji National Youth Council, the Hags Schedule Foundation, the Fiji Council of Social Services and many of its member NGOs, the Foundation for the Peoples of the South Pacific, U.N. agencies such as Food and Agriculture Organization (FAO), United Nations Industrial Development Organization (UNIDO), and United Nations Development Program (UNDP), and educational institutions such as the Fiji Institute of Technology, the Suva Campus of the University of the South Pacific (USP), and the Fiji extension center of USP. Such a profusion of sources of help is likely to create confusion not only in the minds of would-be entrepreneurs but also in the operations of the agencies themselves. While in a few cases there is direct competition between organizations, usually they are only dimly aware of each other's existence and frequently do not have a clear idea of the kinds of services other agencies are offering. Inevitably, duplication and overlap occur, mistakes are repeated, lessons are forgotten or are not passed on, and opportunities are overlooked. Business training is one area where greater coordination of effort can be particularly valuable.

Inadequate monitoring. Underresourced agencies find it almost impossible to adequately monitor the results of their work. They also find it difficult to give the degree of individual attention necessary to get viable self-supporting projects off the ground. Typically, funding agencies are unable to spend enough time assessing the viability of a proposal and remedying deficiencies. It is crucial that projects are visited after they have been funded. The mere act of visiting a project can be enough to revive a venture that had been allowed to lapse. Projects die for the most spurious of reasons: for the want of a spare part, a machine breaks down and a project is lost.

Staffing problems. The human resources needed to staff ESOs are in short supply in the region. It is not surprising, therefore, that ESOs must frequently make do with business advisers who often are inappropriately trained, inexperienced in running businesses, or unfamiliar with the communities in which they are working.

Civil servants and bankers, however well educated and experienced in their respective professions, are usually not the best people to help small businesses. Typically, they have no experience in running a small firm on a shoestring, and their training is usually highly specialized and does not encompass the range of skills needed to make a new business viable. Bringing in foreigners with the necessary skills also is not the answer. They find it hard to communicate to local entrepreneurs or to identify with the problems encountered. Nor do they know the community well enough to help entrepreneurs find the needed resources or to anticipate problems and opportunities peculiar to the locality.

Appropriateness and accessibility of services. A common criticism of business support services around the world is the tendency to offer services because they are easy to offer rather than urgently needed. Hence the proliferation of courses in bookkeeping, which are easy to organize and implement but which usually confuse participants by teaching them more than they need to know about the subject.

Methods of instruction tend to be too reminiscent of school. Presentations are academic and teacher-centered. Materials used often are inappropriate to the region and too generalized. Programs that apply business and management concepts to the special problems of specific industrial sectors are few.

Access to services is also very unevenly distributed. Most people of the region live in rural areas, but most enterprise support services are available in capital cities. Even where business advisory services are available, they often are based in premises that are intimidating to the potential entrepreneur. Banks and government buildings are not likely to be the most inviting settings for someone who has a tentative idea and is afraid of being laughed at. Informal store-front facilities with easy access from the street are more likely to tempt the novice businessperson. Hours of operation also should be given careful consideration. Many of the most promising potential entrepreneurs are already working for someone else and cannot easily get away during banking hours for long discussions about business ideas.

Crucial to raise the level of managerial skills. For each of the countries surveyed in the Private Sector Project, inadequate managerial skill was pointed out as a leading constraint to more effective performance on the part of entrepreneurs. Government needs to introduce appropriate measures to strengthen entrepreneurial skills as a matter of policy. Effective business training programs can be carried out through both formal and informal channels. The early exposure of school children to business courses can be beneficial in acquiring basic business skills and instilling entrepreneurial attitudes. Such training can be augmented by informal training schemes aimed at serving a wider section of the population.

Need for NGO commercial associations and community organizations to play a larger role in business training. A good example would be initiatives taken by the Fiji Employer's Consultative Federation and the Vanuatu Finance Centre Association. Both of these groups have prepared a proposal to provide training and technical assistance to small indigenous business.

Strengthened credit facilities for small businesses. Major weaknesses lie in certain aspects of trading bank lending. Not only should these institutions attempt to be more flexible in lending practices, but they also should seek to be more innovative in serving the needs of small enterprises. The kinds of activities that often need to be strengthened include project appraisal, advisory assistance, and market surveys. Innovative ways for improving banking services to remote communities, including outer islands, also deserve attention.

Scope for developing special schemes for indigenous business development. Such schemes could be operated as part of development bank activities, as is the case of the "Stret Pasin Stoa" scheme in Papua New Guinea, which is now being adopted by the Fiji Development Bank. Other avenues and sectorial areas also should be considered.

Recommendations for ESOs

The key recommendations arising from the Private Sector Project are as follows:

The establishment of national Small Business Centers (SBCs). To simplify the lives of potential entrepreneurs the establishment of one-stop SBCs at the national level is recommended, as well as at the subnational levels. These centers will keep track of enterprise support services already available in a community, identify gaps in existing services, and develop strategies to fill those gaps. A key purpose of the SBCs will be to simplify the lives of potential entrepreneurs by providing easy access to a comprehensive library of resources and services. Some of these services will be offered by the center itself, and some by other agencies to which the entrepreneur can be referred by the SBC. Another central aim of the SBCs will be to ensure that the enterprise development services in a nation are coordinated and tailored to the specific problems and needs of local entrepreneurs.

Private/public/NGO partnership. To ensure that the SBCs make effective use of local resources, each center also should seek to involve local businesses, educational institutions, relevant NGOs, labor unions, and service clubs, as well as appropriate governmental and intergovernmental agencies. This chapter considers the benefits that might accrue from such cooperation and how such a partnership might be structured and financed.

A regional nucleus organization; the use of the USP's extension infrastructure. The setting up of a regional nucleus organization to facilitate effective cooperation and coordination of enterprise support services and resources across the region is recommended. A key element in the implementation of these proposals is the use of the extension network of USP. It is recommended that the continuing education arm of USP take an initial leadership role in launching the regional nucleus organization and promoting the development of national and subnational SBCs. USP has an extension network with ten national centers. At its main campus in Suva, it offers a degree program in Business Studies as well as certificate, diploma, and degree programs in Management and Accounting. Clearly, there would be cost advantages in utilizing existing USP resources where possible. Appropriate sectors of the University also could take a leadership role in promoting the development of SBCs and a regional nucleus organization. This has been identified as a project amenable to funding by the ADB.

Integrated development programs. The programs of the SBC network should be designed to provide comprehensive, integrated packages of services targeted to appropriate groups, communities, and industrial sectors. The network should avoid the piecemeal, fragmentary offerings typical of most existing ESOs. Briscoe et al. (1990) outlines a range of strategies for offering integrated services, including successful models from overseas and from the region. Specific recommendations are presented for integrated development programs in the following areas:

- The establishment of small businesses in the tourism industry,

- The development of small businesses by young people.

Institutions to Facilitate Private Investment in Agriculture

The development of the various countries in the Pacific island countries has, in varying degrees, been dependent on primary industry particularly agriculture. This situation is likely to continue in the future, despite developments, in the tourism, manufacturing, and service sectors. Experience has shown that institutional structures and arrangements have been a key determinant of the level and success of private sector participation in this sector. Furthermore, it is an area where government policy and actions can have a major influence, both positive and negative, on private sector activity and investment. The Private Sector Project dealt with the key areas of management and extension, development banks, research, and marketing, with the research being based on a number of in-depth case studies. The detailed findings and recommendations from these studies are presented in McGregor and Coulter (1991) and discussed briefly in this chapter.

Management and extension

The vast majority of the region's population, particularly in Melanesia, is involved in semi-subsistence agriculture. The availability and distribution of land mean that new commodity development is likely to be smallholder based. Furthermore, a smallholder production system, if well managed, can afford major advantages in the production of new high value crops. However haphazard, the smallholder production and marketing systems, which are typical of Pacific island agriculture, are not conducive to new commodity development.

In terms of entrepreneurial and management experience Pacific island smallholders are ill equipped to make the transition to modern commercial export-oriented agriculture. While the traditional extension arrangements have been adequate for stable semi-subsistence production systems, they have proved to be unsatisfactory in the promotion of crop intensification and diversification policies.

In the smallholder sector the dearth of skilled and ongoing managerial expertise is not offset to any significant degree by the government-operated extension services. Instead of being at the vanguard of agricultural development, extension has tended to be a marginal activity. Ministries of Agriculture throughout the region have operated diffuse extension services with weak links to research, usually conducted by the same government departments. Invariably, these services get deeply involved in the administration of agricultural programs, the collection of statistics, loan recovery, and other non-agricultural activities. While these arrangements have been adequate for stable semi-subsistence production systems, they have proved unsatisfactory in the promotion of crop intensification and diversification policies or in handling a crisis such as the outbreak of coffee leaf rust in Papua New Guinea.

Governments have been reluctant to make the necessary political and substantial financial commitment to upgrading and restructuring their agricultural extension services. The severe budgetary constraints faced by most governments have been a major factor. Thus projects generally have relied heavily on the reallocation of existing resources, with little change in the basic structure. In situations where substantial additional resources have been committed to upgrading extension services, implementation has tended to be slow. For instance, part of the World Bank loan to Papua New Guinea for the Agricultural Support Services Project had to be canceled due to difficulties in recruiting the necessary professional and support staff. In the smaller countries the problems facing the government extension service are less intractable, and cost-effective means of increasing their efficiency are likely to present themselves.

The dearth of management skills also extends to the plantation sector. At independence Papua New Guinea's plantation sector was without adequate management, which was the result of a deliberate disinvestment policy of foreign plantation companies and owners. In Vanuatu the plantations were expropriated from their French owners leaving them devoid of any management. Fiji's copra estates have been declining since the Second World War and are operated with minimal management and technology inputs.

The traditional Pacific island plantations gave no attention to training at any level. They operated on minimal technical input, with labor not expected to know anything other than how to wield a bushknife and harvest crops. Furthermore, there were no training institutions geared toward providing the necessary skills for modern plantation management. The advent of new high yielding varieties has meant that comparatively sophisticated management needs to be supported by a stable labor force with the necessary skills.

In Papua New Guinea some use of management agencies is needed to help bridge the management gap. These agencies played an important role in the transfer of ownership of plantation land from foreign to Papua New Guinea nationals. In Vanuatu a low-key version of the same concept has been directed at providing ni-Vanuatu with the technical and management skills they need to run the plantations abandoned by the French settlers. The project makes proposals for strengthening and expanding the role of management companies.

Proposals for commercial management services

The Private Sector Project investigated the prospects and requirements for expanding the role of private extension and management as a means of redressing the management gap in both the plantation and smallholder sectors.

The following six recommendations arising from this research are presented in McGregor and Coulter (1991) and summarized briefly below:

1. The use of a nucleus commercial management unit is proposed to enable smallholders to successfully participate in new high-value crop development. This recommendation represents a modified version of the standard nucleus estate (NES) model that has successfully been applied to the Papua New Guinea oil palm industry. The NES model would be directly applicable to horticultural commodities requiring substantial central processing such as macadamia nuts. However, in most cases of horticultural development the nucleus unit would not necessarily be involved in any production, and its emphasis would be on providing management. The experience of Hawaii's highly successful papaya industry and Fiji's tobacco industry indicated that this approach could be adopted to the development of a commercial smallholder-based horticultural export industry in the Pacific islands.

    The Private Sector Project research examined in detail the technical and supervisory practices, managerial discipline, and cultural sensitivity necessary to improve the farmers' skills and maintain efficiency and quality standards for the demanding agricultural products market. The need for innovative interaction between the "director" and the "doer" is stressed. Important components of this interrelationship include (1) provision for the planning, research, and managerial inputs required for the cultivation, harvesting, and marketing of the commodity; (2) the manner in which field extension services are applied; and (3) the levels of technical diffusion and material and financial support needed for viable sustained production.

2. Selected industry associations can provide a focus for developing private sector extension capability. A strong commercially oriented industry association would be well placed to provide extension and other services to its members and other suppliers. It is encouraging to note that Fiji's Fresh Ginger Exporters Association (FFGEA) is now developing its own extension service. In Tonga, for instance, there is an array of producer-based organizations that have been formed to act as producer lobby groups to organize growing and to act as service organizations to the industry. These include the Friendly Islander Marketing Cooperative (FIMCO). Some of them could offer opportunities to develop their own industry-oriented extension services. On a much larger scale, in Papua New Guinea the coffee and cocoa industries have established vertically integrated companies that have research and extension responsibilities. A particular advantage of using industry associations or companies is that they are an acceptable focus for aid donors and technical assistance. For example, USAID is already assisting FIMCO, which is Tonga's largest vanilla exporter. Following on from this success, USAID is now finalizing the design of its regional Commercial Agricultural Development Project, which will have as one of its main components the support of commercial industry associations. Support to these groups will be in two broad areas: (1) marketing and product development and (2) production and extension.

Aid and technical assistance can be crucial during the start-up phase of such organizations. However, the operations of commercial grower organizations should aim to achieve self-sufficiency as quickly as is reasonably possible, which could be achieved by a levy on members. In this respect the government can play an important role by providing the legal environment that ensures compulsory membership.

There may be scope for some of these industry groups to take commercial advantage of traditional production and organization methods. For example, in the case of Tonga—how might the traditional Tongan *toutu'u* land-use system and *toungaue* labor organization system be incorporated into programs to expand Tonga's non-traditional exports.

3.   Commercial smallholder extension services can be developed to support traditional export commodities. Smallholder production of traditional export commodities such as cocoa and coffee could not sustain the intensive management and extension support required for high value crops such as papaya. Yet these industries could benefit from an industry focused and operated extension service. The experience of the Fiji sugar industry and, more recently, that of the Papua New Guinea coffee industry support this view.

Scope exists for some of Papua New Guinea's better plantation management companies to provide extension services to smallholders. However, this needs to be introduced on a gradual basis, with the most essential element being an effective market oriented monitoring system so that the private agency cannot take advantage of a monopoly situation and shelter behind the same sorts of inefficiencies as the government system had. Such a scheme would need to be project oriented and be formally linked to credit delivery through the development bank, although the commercial banks may also wish to be involved.

4.   Use of management agencies can be expanded for the plantation sector. The concept of management agencies is directed toward small- to medium-sized plantations–holdings usually in the range of 20 to 200 ha. The objective is to bring high level management skills to relatively small-scale developments at an affordable price. Essentially, this goal is accomplished by spreading overheads over a number of projects. These agencies have important training functions at all levels from management to labor so that the project will be viable and eventually self-sufficient. They can also have input purchase and produce selling roles that create economies of scale and bargaining power for their clients. They must also ensure that measurable yardsticks are met.

There is now some question whether the management agent system is economically viable in the longer term with sustained depressed commodity prices. The solution clearly is not for the owners to replace the management agent with their own ill qualified, albeit lower cost, manager. However, the current crisis highlights the training role of management companies, which should leave the project with the option of being able to competently manage itself. A managing agency will not always be the appropriate management vehicle in the Pacific islands plantation sector. With an emerging cadre of plantation managers, owners in the future will have the option of employing their own experienced managers rather than relying on the services of a management agency. Land pressure may also mean that the project owners, with loan repayment, will demand that the plantations are split up and distributed to shareholders as viable producing blocks. Thus the better management agencies probably will eventually evolve into farm management consulting companies, which are common in Australian and New Zealand agriculture.

The better management companies have made a major contribution to Papua New Guinea's export agriculture and rural economy. New Guinea Islands Produce (NGIP), the focus of a Private Sector Project case study, played a lead in the rehabilitation of the cocoa industry during the 1980s. Most of this process has involved the transfer of land from foreign ownership to Papua New Guinea groups. The company has been instrumental in the diffusion of high yielding planting material and the adoption of modern husbandry and management techniques. A significant demonstration effect has occurred among smallholders.

In the final analysis the success of these companies will be measured by their ability to pay back their clients' loans. This has been made increasingly more difficult in recent years by the prolonged depression in commodity prices. The response of the NGIP to depressed prices has been to reduce unit costs and to improve quality to capture market premiums. Major emphasis has been placed on cost control, which has involved seeking less expensive sources of materials combined with better utilization and mobilization of labor. A company such as the NGIP is well placed to assist its clients in surviving the current price crisis and in so doing to protect the lending of the banks.

Successful Papua New Guinea companies could play an important role in initiating the diffusion of management services in the region. Expanding traditional commodity exports remains a priority in most development plans, and throughout the region there is an increasing desire among landowners to acquire and develop (or rehabilitate) plantations. Yet the appropriate management skills, and modern plantation technology, is lacking to successfully achieve this goal on any scale. In situations where infrastructure is not developed, a company may be required to provide services beyond just plantation management. In Fiji, for instance, the development of the cocoa industry is constrained by the absence of high yielding planting material, poor processing, and inefficient export marketing by a government authority. Following the NGIP model it would be appropriate for the management company to operate a centralized fermentary and manage its own seed garden to facilitate the introduction of high yielding planting material. It could also be involved in export marketing at least in a joint venture with a Papua New Guinea marketing company.

5. The government and aid donors have a role in promoting private management and extension services. The nexus between management and the critical mass of production to support that management can be broken only if the government defrays some of the overhead costs by using aid or loan funds. Start-up costs will be high particularly if a new country or a new industry is involved. The costs and benefits of establishing a particular management system must be carefully evaluated with the view to minimizing costs, particularly with prevailing commodity prices. The Papua New Guinea experience, however, indicates the value of using a quality management agency, and the firm offering the cheapest service may certainly not be the best. Thus in developing a management system for a new country and or new industry, the start-up and overhead costs could be justifiably subsidized until sufficient economies of scale can be achieved. The subsidy should be explicit and for a finite period. The ongoing costs of any agency should be borne by the project and not by any outside body.

A commercial management and extension industry may be best developed as a project. A commercial management sub-component of a regional development project could be one approach.

For governments and aid donors wishing to promote the use of private management and extension services, strong arguments exist for building on successful companies and organizations. The Private Sector Project identified several successful institutions. However, successful institutions tend to be scarce, and care must be taken not to overload them beyond their capability. A particular problem lies with producer-based organizations. These institutions have become particularly attractive to competing aid donors as they scramble to implement their new policy mandates of supporting the private sector. The perspective should not be lost that these are commercial organizations that must eventually become financially self-sufficient.

6.   The region's development banks must play an active catalyst in the development of private management and service companies. For the plantation sector the tripartite agreement between the landowners, the development bank, and the management agency is the essential interdependent linkage that makes the system work. All parties benefit from the agreement. The risk exposure of the development bank is reduced by diminishing the danger of a competent manager being dismissed for frivolous reasons such as vetoing expenditure unrelated to the project's approved development program. If the agency is reputable and technically able to conduct the proposed program, the loan should be repaid. Of course, risks still exist from the vagaries of world markets, but these too are minimized by sound and qualified management. The banks should be able to simultaneously increase their level of lending to the agricultural sector and reduce their level of arrears and bad debts, and thus should be prepared to make long-term investments in commodity agriculture, where hitherto they would not.

A formal link with the banking system will also be important in the successful development of commercial smallholder extension services. A fledgling smallholder service company or commercial industry association is likely to need assistance with establishment capital. It will also require working capital on an ongoing basis to finance the operations of its farmers. The level and efficiency of credit delivery are likely to be enhanced with the lending agency able to deal with one entity rather than numerous small farmers. The high risks associated with providing short-term production credit to small farmers is greatly reduced if the nucleus service unit is the sole marketer or processor.

Agricultural research

Agricultural research and development programs are generally deficient in the Pacific island countries. The overwhelming priority of the three major tertiary institutions in the region is undergraduate teaching. The limited research that is undertaken tends to be basic, rather than applied, in nature. Furthermore, there is virtually no link between these universities and industry as has been the tradition with U.S. land grant colleges and New Zealand agricultural universities.

In accordance with British colonial tradition, applied agricultural research in the region has tended to be vested with government Ministries of Agriculture. In recent years these institutions have been starved of funds and expertise. This has occurred despite the overwhelming international evidence of the high returns that can be achieved from applied agricultural research. The operating budgets of the research divisions of Ministries of Agriculture have been prime targets for cuts as governments have faced increasing budgetary pressures. They have difficulty in servicing the extension requirements of existing crop technology, let alone any research dealing with new crops and processing technology. The research that is conducted lacks focus and has tended to be out of touch with industry requirements. There has been a marked decline in the quality of government research output at a time when industries' technological demands have been increasing.

In the face of the failure of the governmental research, Papua New Guinea's major commodity industries have taken the lead in developing their own research capability. The Cocoa Board was the first to establish its own research organization in 1981, following the incorporation of the Cocoa Industry Company. In 1986 the Coconut Industry was included with the formation of the Papua New Guinea Cocoa and Coconut Research Institute. Papua New Guinea has now established an international reputation in cocoa breeding. Studies have revealed an exceptionally high rate of return from this research.

The success of cocoa research, as it is with coffee, is attributed to the ongoing core funding derived from a compulsory industry levy imposed by the boards. This is kept quite separate from the industry stabilization funds. The core funding is supplemented by government allocation, project oriented aid grants, and revenue generated by the institute. The institutional structure of these industries has enabled substantial industry focused research programs to be mounted. However, both research institutes are under-capitalized and are facing difficulties in funding current research programs with the depressed commodity price outlook.

Major recommendations:

- Industries should become increasingly responsible for directing and funding their own research.
- Government needs to play a facilitating role in providing a legal and institutional framework to allow industry levies to be im-

posed and to provide a conduit for aid funding and technical
assistance.

* The Pacific island countries need to develop new export commodities such as horticulture and spices. The successful development of such industries will require a substantial research effort.
  However, a new export commodity, which has yet to develop a
  significant income generating base, will find it more difficult to
  finance its own research. Inevitably, there will be some reliance
  on government assistance, particularly because production is
  likely to be smallholder based. However, there must be industry
  input into identifying problems and setting priorities.

Export marketing

*Government and statutory authority involvement in agricultural export
marketing.* The Pacific islands region has a long history of direct government and statutory authority involvement in commodity exporting. An assessment of the impact of this involvement was thus a major focus of the
Private Sector Project. In-depth studies were undertaken of government
and statutory agencies directly involved with export marketing. These in-
stitutions included Fiji's National Marketing Authority (NMA), the Tonga
Commodities Board (TCB)[3], Western Samoa's Produce Marketing
Division and Cocoa Board, the Papua New Guinea Copra Marketing
Board, the Solomon Islands Commodities Export Marketing Authority
(CEMA), and the Vanuatu Commodities Marketing Board (VCMB).
Studies were also conducted of regulatory institutions, specifically, the
Papua New Guinea Cocoa and Coffee Boards. The detailed findings of this
research are reported in McGregor and Coulter (1991).

Eight common themes emerge from the research regarding the rationale
for government involvement in export marketing. These include:

1. In the Pacific islands it is often perceived that farmers are exploited by middlemen, and thus direct government involvement is
   necessary to protect the interest of farmers. Such was the rationale for the TCB, the NMA, and the takeover of cocoa marketing
   by the VCMB.

2. In some cases government involvement in export marketing has
   been justified by lack of private sector interest or capability in

---

[3] In 1991 the TCB commercialized, and Tonga Investment Ltd. was created in its
stead.

taking on these functions. In the past low levels of entrepreneurial development in the Pacific islands gave some validity to this argument. Even today it can sometimes be difficult to attract the private sector to market specialized commodities. There have been occasions when the performance of private traders has been so poor that it necessitated direct government involvement, which was one of the major reasons for creating the Tonga Copra Board in 1941.

3. Price stabilization is a major feature of the Papua New Guinea commodity boards. In addition, Tonga's TCB, Solomon Islands' CEMA, Vanuatu's VCMB, and Fiji's NMA do have, or have operated, price stabilization schemes of various types.

4. Research and promotion can be more effectively undertaken on behalf of an industry where there are powers of compulsion to levy all members. This has been an important aspect of the operation of the Papua New Guinea Coffee and Cocoa Boards.

5. Direct government involvement in export marketing has sometimes been justified on the basis of a pacesetting role, either in terms of opening up new markets or establishing quality standards. This was the justification for giving Fiji's NMA the exclusive right to export papaya to the Japanese market. The Vanuatu's VCMB has the exclusive right to develop the kava exports, a market with vast potential, on the basis that it "is more attune with the cultural sensitivities of the crop than private exporters."

6. Commodity boards have been used as a mechanism to regulate industries in areas such as the enforcement of quality standards and industry entry. This has been the function of Papua New Guinea's Cocoa and Coffee Boards and an objective of Solomon Islands' CEMA.

7. There are certain commodities, due to the nature of the product and the structure of the market, that are better handled by a large marketing organization to take advantage of economies of scale. Copra is a good example.

8. Accessing foreign aid has been a factor in encouraging direct government involvement in marketing activities. Aid donors have been anxious to provide certain forms of marketing infrastructure and agroprocessing facilities. The traditional policy of donors and recipient governments is that such aid should not be provided directly to the private sector. Thus government departments or agencies have operated these facilities.

9. However, in recent years international opinion, and the opinion of many governments and international development agencies, has therefore turned strongly against commodity marketing boards. As a consequence, countries have abolished marketing boards or sold them to private enterprise. A number of reasons account for this shift:

- Marketing boards in many countries have become very inefficient, incompetent, and in some cases corrupt.

- There has been a growth in private sector marketing firms.

- The belief that private enterprise will exploit farmers has often proved wrong.

In the Pacific islands the experience has been mixed. The direct government and statutory agency involvement in export marketing has been lackluster and probably has been a negative influence on long-term commodity development. Government agencies tend to be particularly inept at handling fresh commodity development. Marketing boards have exhibited poor performance in terms of profitability, efficiency, and encouragement of entrepreneurial development. In some cases copra marketing is an exception.

In contrast, Papua New Guinea's regulatory commodity boards have been successful in achieving and promoting orderly marketing in a cost-effective manner, and they have facilitated increased private sector investment activity. This experience contrasts with that of many other developing countries. The key underlying factors that have contributed to Papua New Guinea's success are listed as follows:

- Effective, and transparent, legislation that promotes orderly marketing and inhibits political interference;

- The separation of stabilization funds from marketing agencies;

- A well defined system of financial accountability;

- General grower and exporter support for the boards and their operations;

- The promotion of efficient private sector involvement in marketing;

- Competent and capable key staff in each of the boards;

- Limited but effective government representation on the boards.

These factors are all seen as necessary for success and should be borne in mind by other Pacific island countries that may wish to replicate the Papua New Guinea experience.

Major recommendations

The major recommendations arising from the various marketing institution case studies are presented in McGregor and Coulter (1991) and summarized as follows:

Papua New Guinea. While Papua New Guinea's regulatory boards have performed well, several reforms are required if they are to continue to achieve what is expected of them. These are as follows:

- Industry interests other than growers should be represented.

- Progression should occur from industry nominated representatives to industry elected representation.

- The boards should be subject to technical as well as financial accountability.

- The boards should develop corporate plans that incorporate national and commercial objectives.

- An international marketing strategy should be developed to capitalize on the quality improvements that are being made.

Fiji. The NMA should cease operations as it has no regulatory functions and its continued direct marketing operation has on balance a negative impact on commodity development. It is recommended that self-regulating industry councils (boards) be established under an umbrella enabling Commodities Board Act. Subordinate to this enabling Act, regulations would be made for individual commodities (e.g., ginger) or groups of commodities (e.g., horticultural exports) as required. Tropical fruit is identified as a priority. The individual commodity councils would be empowered to:

- Issue licenses,

- Set and enforce grading and quality standards,

- Set grower prices when appropriate,

- Impose and administer levies to finance industry-wide research and industry-wide development,

- Formulate industry policy within the confines of national development plans.

It is further recommended that the post-harvest treatment facilities at Nadi international airport be privatized. The most appropriate organization to take on this function would be the Fiji Fresh Produce Exporters Association. Priority also needs to be given to the strengthening of government produce inspection functions.

Tonga. The success of the Friendly Islands Marketing Cooperative (FIMCO) in vanilla and fish marketing indicates that the export and physical marketing functions of the former TCB can be handled more than satisfactorily by the private sector. Regulatory functions should be passed on to the Ministry of Agriculture and Forestry (MAF). However, the quarantine section of the MAF needs to be substantially upgraded to take on quality assurance responsibilities.

Western Samoa. The Western Samoa Copra and Cocoa Boards have recently been dissolved as part of the ADB Agricultural Loan Agreement. They are to be replaced by a commodity pricing and market information unit, which is to be situated in the Department of Commerce and Industry. A more appropriate strategy would have been the privatization of the exporting and physical marketing functions of the boards and the modification of the role of the boards to a regulatory one. It is recommended that Western Samoa establish a similar commodity institutional structure that is proposed for Fiji.

Solomon Islands. The Commodities Export Marketing Authority (CEMA) has already adopted a regulatory-type approach for cocoa and spices by encouraging private marketing. However, this has been done without implementing effective controls. The introduction of a Papua New Guinea type cocoa quality management system is seen as a prerequisite for improving grower returns. The CEMA should retain its monopoly status with respect to copra exporting.

Vanuatu. The Vanuatu Commodities Marketing Board (VCMB) should retain its monopoly status with respect to copra; however, improvements in operational efficiency are necessary in areas such as storage and stevedoring. Monopoly control of cocoa export marketing should be relinquished, and a Papua New Guinea type cocoa quality management system should be adopted. The active participation of the private sector in the development of new export commodities such as kava should be encouraged.

Institutional Support Arrangements for the
Development of Export Manufacturing

Faced with declining terms of trade for their commodity exports, the Pacific island countries are looking increasingly to export manufacturing as a means of expanding their economic base and providing employment opportunities for their growing populations.

For a long time the development literature indicated that small countries could not aspire to significant industrialization. However, technological improvement, reduction of scale penalties, and the spectacular industrial success of relatively small developing countries, such as Hong Kong, Singapore, and Taiwan, have led many small countries to reassess their position and to strive for industrialization. Perhaps even more significant for the small island countries of the South Pacific has been the spectacular export manufacturing success of Mauritius, a small island economy heavily dependent on a sugar monoculture.

The South Pacific Regional Trade and Economic Cooperation Agreement (SPARTECA) between the Forum island countries and Australia and New Zealand signed in 1982, and the restructuring of labor intensive manufacturing in those countries, has provided the impetus for the development of manufacturing. The impact has been most spectacular with respect to Fiji garment exports.

Several infrastructure/institutional development programs and projects have been initiated to encourage investment in export-oriented manufacturing in the Pacific island countries. The Private Sector Project focused on the experience of Fiji and Tonga. The findings of this research are summarized below:

Major conclusions regarding the institutional environment for entrepreneurial investment in export manufacturing

- Smallness and isolation are not insurmountable constraints in the successful development of export manufacturing in the Pacific island countries. The development of the Tongan knitwear industry (a specialized niche market development) is particularly encouraging for the smaller countries of the region.

- The two major limiting factors are the lack of suitable entrepreneurs who are willing to invest their capital and skills in the Pacific islands and the absence of institutional structures and administrative systems that can expeditiously accommodate such investors.

- Entrepreneurs require quick decisions on their investment proposals. Institutional arrangements and administrative procedures can be designed that yield timely decisions yet at the same time safeguard against unscrupulous operators. A "one stop shop" for foreign investors is a necessary condition to achieve this goal.

- Small industry centers/industrial estates can make an important contribution to manufacturing development in the Pacific island countries. Apart from physical infrastructure, they provide access to land where its availability on a long-term basis is difficult to obtain. Furthermore, they provide the prospective investor with tangible evidence of the government's sustained commitment to manufacturing development.

- The Fiji experience has indicated that export manufacturing can successfully commence in advance of establishing a physical tax free zone. It also shows the value of a strong domestic manufacturing sector for export manufacturing development.

- The active promotion of Fiji's tax free system by the Fiji Trade and Investment Board was a major factor in its success.

Proposals for expanding the role and effectiveness of small industry centers

The development of well planned and located industrial estates with the proper mix of infrastructure and technical support services is a complicated exercise requiring the professional services of experts in areas such as civil engineering, urban planning, environmental planning, and financial analysis. Most Pacific island government ministries do not have the necessary professional expertise to undertake industrial estate development without the services of foreign technical assistance. In most cases, international agencies could play a valuable role in providing such technical assistance as well as loan or grant funds to support the development of industrial estates.

A shortcoming of the Tongan Small Industries Centre (SIC) is that it has not encouraged indigenous participation in export manufacturing development. Recently, some innovative approaches have been developed to assist the development of small manufacturing firms. These approaches include incubator centers, nursery factory schemes, and village factory schemes. The basic aim of incubator centers is to assist small businesses during their first few years of operation when their chance of failure is highest. Services such as secretarial support, administrative assistance, facilities support, and business expertise are provided in a controlled environment. Small businesses fail for many reasons, including under-capitalization, lack of a market for their products, high cost of raw materials, inappropriate technology, economic recession, low level of labor skill and productivity, and poor management. A new venture in a Pacific island country is likely to face more than one of these factors. The business incubator seeks to effectively link technology, capital, talent, and business know-how to accelerate the growth of new enterprises. It is recommended that such a concept should be made an integral component of any Pacific island small industry center project.

The village factory model has been pioneered in Malaysia. Here the Furniture Manufacturers Association organized a group of furniture manufacturers to relocate their factories along side each other at an industrial estate, which is called a "furniture village." The co-location of small factories producing the same type of products has generated considerable economic advantages in the supply of support services. The members of this furniture village share the costs of a furniture design service and special professional assistance to improve quality control, assistance with the acquisition and use of new technology, and assistance with international marketing. The design unit has helped village members to re-design their products to suit the particular needs of their overseas market segments. The central unit provides services to village members for production, management assistance, marketing, packaging, transport, and quality control. The Malaysian Iron and Steel Industry Association is also adopting a similar village-type concept for foundries. This concept appears to be an effective way to assist small firms to improve their technology, productivity, and export potential and would be applicable to a Pacific island country like Fiji, which has a well developed industrial structure.

Development Finance Institutions (DFIs)

The South Pacific Development Banks

All the Pacific island countries have established development banks, through assistance from the ADB, as government instrumentalities to take the lead role in encouraging domestic private sector development. All South Pacific Development Banks (SPDBs) have been assigned the following functions:

- Promote economic growth and development in line with national policies,
- Provide finance for primary production and for the establishment of commercial and industrial undertakings,
- Provide assistance to new and ongoing business ventures.

To allow them to carry out their tasks, the SPDBs have access to grant funds and soft-term loans. Generally, low interest rates are charged, minimal security is taken over the activities for which they lend, and profits are not expected.

By and large the SPDBs have not met the expectations of policymakers or the ADB. Not surprisingly, the SPDBs are subject to considerable pressures from political leaders who see them as active supporters of government policies and objectives (particularly in rural constituencies); they have substantial numbers of accounts in arrears and devote more time attempting to collect debts than initiating new and imaginative projects that could create employment and exploit national resources.

The Private Sector Project analyzed the reasons for the shortcomings and made recommendations for their redress. Details of these findings and recommendations are presented in McMaster (1990b) and reported briefly here. A regional project initiative involving institutional building has been identified. The analysis and recommendations are based on detailed studies of eight development banks in the region.

The reasons for the disappointing performance of the SPDBs vary, but certain common threads need to be addressed, namely:

- In addition to the standard risks associated with lending for commodities sold on volatile world markets, low levels of management prevail among lenders, social obligations can seriously affect loan repayments, labor in some areas is in short supply, and support from government extension services is erratic. Most important, land usually cannot be offered as security in the normal sense.

- Lack of adequate staff training results in poor loan appraisal and monitoring with consequent arrears problems.

- In some cases senior management is inexperienced.

- Research and development activities are inadequate to identify new and appropriate lending opportunities.

- There are problems in ensuring a smooth flow of funds, either equity or loan, from government or donor agencies to ensure uninterrupted operations.

- Customers have a poor understanding of obligations implicit in borrowing money.

- There are unreasonable expectations by governments and the public of their potential to assist development.

None of the identified issues, which detract from the operational efficiency of the SPDBs, is insurmountable. The Private Sector Project makes a number of specific recommendations for improving the situation, which fall in the following broad areas:

Training, at both the staff and borrower levels, offers the longer-term solution to reducing and getting arrears to a manageable level while at the same time increasing the level of lending to the agricultural sector. For staff members, training in project identification, appraisal, and monitoring is a priority need, particularly because the banks are required by necessity, and sometimes by legislation, to have regard to the prospects of a loan becoming successful rather than the security available. While various staff training programs are already in place, a more intensified and systematic effort is required. With respect to borrowers, no effort should be spared to inculcate into smallholders the importance of credit as an adjunct to development. Many loan failures could be avoided if clients were fully conversant with the purposes for which the loans were granted.

Support for commercial agricultural management and extension companies. It must be recognized that the cost of the necessary training is high and that the lags in the effects being realized are long. Thus some bridging measures are required. As previously discussed, the infusion of commercial management and extension services can have a more immediate impact on arrears and on the efficiency of agricultural lending to complement the training process. However, if private management and service companies are to have a significant impact on the development of Pacific island agriculture the SPDBs must play an active catalyst role. Thus the fortunes of management companies and the performance of the development banks in the agricultural sector are interdependent.

Research and development. Research and development must be an important function of the SPDBs in identifying new lending opportunities that support national economic objectives. Accordingly, adequate resources should be allocated.

A strengthened and expanded South Pacific Regional Office (SPRO). The ADB's SPRO can provide the level of support required by SPDBs. Since these proposals were made, there has been a substantial strengthening of the SPRO. A need was identified for the bank to modify its reporting and information requirements to be more in keeping with the scale of the SPDBs and their loans.

Fostering regional cooperation between DFIs. At an operational level there is a need to strengthen the links between the individual SPDBs and with multilateral institutions, particularly SPRO.

Considerable advantages can be gained in addressing the needs of the SPDBs at a regional level as well as at the individual institutional level. These advantages include substantial economies of scale, which could be achieved in the design development and delivery of specially tailor-made training programs for the different target groups, namely, (1) senior managers, (2) technical bank officers, and (3) client borrowers. The development of high quality training, based on a comprehensive needs analysis, will require a substantial resource commitment, which may be feasible for the individual SPDBs to undertake. In addition, educational advantages may be gained if some training is undertaken at a regional level to permit interaction among participants from different banks. This training may be particularly valuable for senior managers, as well as serve as a cost-effective means of delivering high quality training to a small group of participants.

There is a large degree of commonality in the subject areas that the SPDBs have identified as high priority for research. The integration of the research programs of the individual banks into a regionally coordinated program could avoid duplication and enrich each SPDB's own program through cross-fertilization of methodology and research findings, as well as provide a regular forum for the interchange of information and expertise. The planning, coordination, and monitoring of projects to strengthen the SPDBs could be a main responsibility of a regional corporate body of SPDBs—the establishment of which is recommended to link all the development banks in the region and to liaise with the SPRO of the ADB in Vanuatu.

A lead role for the ADB in a regional project focused on institutional strengthening and staff development and training. Although the idea of a regional financial institution acting either as a bank or a source of equity finance for private sector projects is no longer tenable, there is a pressing need for a regional facility, perhaps along the lines of the Caribbean Project Development Facility (CPDF), that could:

- Provide a bridge between the SPDBs and the international development finance agencies,

- Assist in the formulation of major projects and the identification of funding for their implementation,

- Develop training programs and materials for courses designed for SPDB staff and clients,

- Identify professional staff for technically complex appraisal and implementation projects,

- Support research and development units in the identification and evaluation of new lending and development opportunities.

Such a facility might evolve through the strengthening of the existing Association of Development Finance Institutions of the Pacific (ADFIP). The 1990 Port Vila annual meeting of ADFIP considered these proposals and made the following recommendations to their governments and to the ADB:

- That there is a need to establish a South Pacific Development Banks facility, similar to the CPDF, such a regional institution to be located in one of the existing development banks.

The facility would be particularly useful to small banks in conducting negotiations with multilateral agencies or corporations in areas where they would have limited expertise, particularly in acquiring access to equity funds.

To a limited extent the project identification aspects of this proposal are now accommodated by the International Finance Corporation's (IFC) South Pacific Project Facility (SPPF) recently established in Sydney. However, the scale of most Pacific island projects have serious limits to the effectiveness of this facility at least as it was initially conceived.

The establishment of a venture capital industry

The Private Sector Project investigated the feasibility of establishing a regional venture capital industry (Crocombe 1990). The author concluded that high national returns could accrue from such a program to stimulate small business development and new venture creation if the approach is systematic and has a long-term perspective, and it was recommended that Pacific island governments implement measures to stimulate the development of venture capital industries. The following specific recommendations were made:

A venture capital industry should be developed as a partnership between government and development agencies. In the Pacific island countries the government is the only institution able to take the very long-term macroeconomic view necessary to develop a venture capital industry. Thus the government should be responsible for raising the bulk of the initial capital and providing incentives to invest in preapproved venture capital companies. Long-term government loans could be provided to venture capital firms on the basis of four dollars of loans for every dollar of private capital invested. This would mean that private enterprise money would be at risk, thereby bringing maximum commercial judgment to bear on investments.

Each Pacific island country should make a plan for a long-term commitment to adequate levels of funding. Any effort to stimulate small business and new venture investment should take from eight to twelve years. Both the government's and the venture capitalist's own funding sources should match the long-term nature of the venture investment.

A structure should be created that facilitates partnership between foreign and local capital and expertise. Foreign venture capitalists should be encouraged to establish venture capital firms as joint ventures with the local private sector. These firms will not only attract foreign capital but also provide access to contracts in overseas markets, management expertise, and technology.

Each Pacific island country should prepare a plan with strategies to stimulate all aspects of the entrepreneurial development process. This should include training programs to upgrade the skills and technical ability of both local entrepreneurs and venture capitalists, as well as the establishment of business incubators.

The ADB should provide both technical and financial assistance. Advantages could be gained from adopting a regional approach to venture capital development with the ADB initiating the establishment of a regional venture capital scheme. Such a scheme could provide the individual Pacific island countries with long-term loans for on-lending to private venture capital firms. In addition, the ADB could provide expert technical assistance to support the development of venture capital markets in activities such as staff development and specialized training.

chapter 7

Selected trade and investment opportunities

Trade and Investment Research

Chapter 1 showed that over the past decade the growth in the region has generally been low, with declining growth in exports and declining productivity of investment. It was further established that the long-run terms of trade have moved significantly against Pacific island bulk export commodities and are expected to continue to do so in the future, despite an anticipated improvement in commodity prices in the medium term.

Thus there is a need to increase the efficiency and reduce the production costs of traditional export commodities if the standard of living of rural populations is to be maintained. However, it is also vital for the Pacific island economies, as part of a long-term structural adjustment strategy, to diversify their output and exports toward commodities with more favorable production and demand characteristics, such as various types of manufactures, high-value horticulture and marine products, and service activities such as tourism. The opportunities and requirements for developing these types of export commodities was the focus of the Private Sector Project. Investment opportunities for non-traditional agricultural exports, export manufacturing, marine exports, tourism, and gold were specifically appraised.

The results of these sub-studies are reported in McGregor et al. (1990) and summarized briefly in this chapter.

Horticultural and Agricultural Niche Market Exports

In varying degrees the countries of the region were found to have certain inherent advantages in the production of horticultural and other niche export commodities. These stem from the region's climate, southern hemisphere location, relatively pest-free and unpolluted environment, quarantine status, trade agreements, and the linkages with tourism. Selected opportunities that were identified for the various Pacific island countries are summarized in Table 7.1. A modest trade has developed in commodities, mainly to New Zealand, North America, and more recently Japan. The performance details are also summarized in Table 7.1.

Yet the overall horticultural export performance has been well below the expectations of planners. The reasons for the gap between performance and perceived potential lie mainly with supply, not with demand. Marketing, which includes the quality and continuity of supply and not markets per se, has proved to be a paramount constraint to horticultural export development in the Pacific islands. Contributing factors have been the adverse impact of direct government involvement, inadequate institutional and infrastructure support, and in some cases problems associated with land availability and tenure. In this environment private investment has been slow to materialize, and thus management has been a major constraint. These issues were touched on in Chapter 6 and dealt with in detail in McGregor and Coulter (1991). Some of the constraints to horticultural development, together with recommendations for their alleviation, are summarized in Table 7.1, together with some suggestions for appropriate aid and technical assistance.

The Private Sector Project's major findings and recommendations relating to increasing the level and productivity of investments in non-traditional agriculture are:

- Priority in resource allocation needs to be given to safeguarding the quarantine status of island countries.

- Horticultural export industries, even extending into post-harvest treatment, need to be privatized.

- Exporters and processors need to provide their own extension services to contracted farmers.

- Government has a crucial role in creating an environment for sustained private investment.

- Aid should be redesigned and directed toward the private sector rather than traditional government avenues. A major contribution can be made by Hawaii, in post-harvest treatment, and New Zealand, in perishable export commodities.

Table 7.1 Status and prospects for horticultural and other high-value niche commodity exports from the Pacific islands

Commodity	Current status	Growth prospects	Growth constraints and requirements	Opportunities for aid and technical assistance
FIJI				
Ginger – Fresh	Mature industry based on North American market (fob value approximately F$2 million).	Modest in medium term with improvements in quality and marketing arrangements. Real value could double over the next decade.	• Need for quality improvement. • Institutional reform in industry required.	• Assistance to Fiji Fresh Ginger Exporters Association's extension service. • Facilitation of technical cooperation between Hawaii and industries.
– Processed Immature	Long-standing industry that has experienced recent expansion in exports to Japan (fob value around F$1.5 million).	Substantial if Japanese market can be stabilized. A sizable market is available in the EEC. Market opportunities are likely to exist in the U.S.	• Consistent high quality required. • Capital investment in processing. • Privatizing of processing and marketing. • Management upgrading.	• Identification of possible joint venture partners. • Market identification and market assistance for U.S. market.
– Puree	Some off-grade mature ginger sold to Hawaii-based buyer for processing in California.	Fresh convenience products a rapidly expanding market in U.S. With the large percentage of off-grade mature ginger, prospects are good for producing ginger puree.	• Technology and capital investment. • Foreign investor or joint venture partner probably required. A large spice company such as McCormick should be approached.	• Assistance in project preparation. • Evaluation of market prospects and requirements. • Identification of potential investors.
Papaya	Industry in place for several years and given high priority in government development plans. However, achievements to date have been disappointing (fob value around F$150,000).	Market prospects outstanding, initially in Australia and eventually in Japan.	• Antiquated post-harvest facilities operated by government a major weakness. • Need for export quality standards to be established and enforced. • Improved industry organization to ensure orderly marketing.	Assistance in: • Introduction of modern treatment technology to the private sector, which would involve strengthening government enforcement capability, • Establishment and operation of a commercial fruit exporter.

(continued)

Table 7.1 (con.) Status and prospects for horticultural and other high-value niche commodity exports from the Pacific islands

Commodity	Current status	Growth prospects	Growth constraints and requirements	Opportunities for aid and technical assistance
FIJI (con.)				
Off-season export & hotel vegetables	Small but encouraging private sector involvement in the Nadi area.	Excellent if quality standards can be maintained and projected growth in tourism materializes.	As with papaya.	As with papaya.
Organic cocoa	Promising prospect for Fiji's low productivity cocoa industry, particularly cocoa processing (powder and butter) in Vanuatu for organic (no fertilizer or chemicals) chocolate. Fiji 's own developed confectionary industry provides some interesting possibilities for chocolate products, which also could involve ginger and macadamia nuts.	Has promise. If Vanuatu's venture is successful, Fiji could follow suit-- either selling organic beans to Vanuatu or establishing downstream processing venture.	• Viability of the organic cocoa market still to be proven. • Development in Fiji cocoa industry constrained by inefficient government marketing monopoly and poor standards of dry bean processing. • Industry privatization with appropriate regulation required.	• Regional project to provide a market assessment of extent and requirements of organic beverage (cocoa and coffee) market. • If Vanuatu venture is successful, facilitation of intraregional technology transfer.
Macadamia nuts	No macadamia nut industry. Indications are, however, that Fiji has conditions that are suitable for successfully growing macadamia nuts.	Has promise. Fiji could establish significant macadamia nut industry based on expanded tourism sector. FAO currently is funding a major macadamia nut potential study.	If agronomic suitability is proven, qualified investors needed to establish and develop industry.	• Project preparation and identification of suitable private investors to establish and operate the industry.

Commodity	Current status	Growth prospects	Growth constraints and requirements	Opportunities for aid and technical assistance
PAPUA NEW GUINEA				
Floriculture	No floriculture industry.	Unique combination of altitude and latitude for floriculture and horticulture development in the Highlands. This would not be a niche development and would require major investment in support infrastructure.	• Development to be sufficiently large and profitable to justify dedicated air freighting. • Substantial agribusiness investment and expertise needed for development.	• Project preparation for presentation to potential agribusiness investors. • Identification of agribusiness investors.
VANUATU Root crops	Well-developed traditional industry. Export backloading opportunities now exist with Air Vanuatu flights to Brisbane and Melbourne, Australia.	Particularly good for yams due to superior quality and storability. Taro would face stiff competition from W. Samoa and Tonga. Substantial exports might be expected over the next decade, particularly if the expected growth in tourism is realized to provide backloading capability.	• Significant air freighting depends on anticipated introduction of 767 by Air Vanuatu. • Improved southbound shipping necessary but not anticipated in the near future.	• Assistance to commercial groups and management companies in export marketing. • Assistance in establishing export quality standards and packaging requirements.
Kava	Well-established traditional crop. In recent years the substantial domestic commercial industry has been based on urban "nakamal" (kava salons). Vanuatu is looking to establish a major export industry based on herbal and pharmaceutical markets.	Widest range of commercial cultivators in the Pacific located in Vanuatu. Technology now exists to produce soluble kava for a "ginseng" type product. If the herbal and pharmaceutical markets can be realized, potential exists for establishing a multi-million dollar industry.	• Considerable and skilled effort required to develop significant herbal beverage market (promotion and packaging will be critical). • Supply expansion to be carefully managed due to cultural sensitivities to traditional crop.	• Guidance in development marketing of new herbal and organic products. • Facilitation of marketing contracts and possible identification of joint venture partners.

(continued)

Table 7.1 (con.)   Status and prospects for horticultural and other high-value niche commodity exports from the Pacific islands

Commodity	Current status	Growth prospects	Growth constraints and requirements	Opportunities for aid and technical assistance
VANUATU (con.) Black pepper	Government sponsored series of pepper development projects. Farm production has been disappointing; however, superior quality pepper has been grown in several more remote areas. The crop is suitable for smallholder villages.	Has promise. Pohnpei pepper industry experience provides a model for niche market pepper development. Vanuatu has the additional advantage of being able to build industry development around supplying a growing tourist market. Vanuatu's labor supply situation is far better than that of Pohnpei.	• Industry organization lacking. • Intensive extension effort required. • Private sector involvement in processing and marketing required.	• Assistance (packaging, promotion, etc.) in developing tourist-based marketing. • Provision of in-depth assessment for the U.S. gourmet pepper market. • Assistance in preparation of materials to enhance quality standards (grower extension processing, storage, grading). • Assistance to commercial industry groups and management companies, particularly in extension. • Facilitation of links between industry and U.S. spice companies, which would involve marketing and possible joint venture investment.

Commodity	Current status	Growth prospects	Growth constraints and requirements	Opportunities for aid and technical assistance
VANUATU (con.)				
Vanilla	Vanuatu expected by government to develop Tongan scale vanilla industry. The French horticulturalist from the Tongan industry was brought to Vanuatu. Performance to date has been disappointing. Disease has affected plantings on the major islands of Efate and Santo.	Thrives in certain microclimates--particularly Malakula. Thus if well-managed a significant industry could be developed, although probably not on the Tongan scale. A$1 million export industry over the next decade seems a reasonable target.	• Careful sight selection necessary. • Industry organization focused on extension and marketing.	• Assistance in establishing commercial industry groups, with particular emphasis on extension and marketing. USAID could draw on the experience of FIMCO in Tonga. • Support for preparation of quality standards manual for vanilla.
Organic bulk commodities – Cocoa	Cocoa processing machinery directed at organic chocolate installed by Vanuatu-based entrepreneur with proven export marketing record.	Cocoa suited to Vanuatu farming systems. The smallholder-based industry produces around 2,500 tonnes and continues to grow despite low world prices. The quality is good. A production base for this venture thus exists. If successful, the value of cocoa exports, which currently stands at around US$2 million, could double.	• Need for processed organic product to be produced and market tested. • Need to determine extent and requirements of organic market.	• A regional project to provide market assessment of extent and requirements of organic beverage (cocoa and coffee) market. • Assistance in meeting requirements for organic products to meet U.S. and other importer standards. • Assistance to Vanuatu, as pilot scheme, in acquiring additional equipment for adequate test marketing.

(continued)

Table 7.1 (con.) Status and prospects for horticultural and other high-value niche commodity exports from the Pacific islands

Commodity	Current status	Growth prospects	Growth constraints and requirements	Opportunities for aid and technical assistance
VANUATU (con.)				
− Coffee	Coffee processing project being proposed by Tanna Coffee Development Company. It will be directed at organic exports and high-value packaged cocoa for the tourist market.	High-value processing expected to offer longer-term viability to Vanuatu's small but troubled coffee industry. With expanding tourism, Hawaii's Kona coffee has become the model for Vanuatu. Coffee generates farm value sales of around US$7 million in Hawaii.	• As with cocoa. • Need for vertically integrated private investment to be attracted to the venture.	• As with cocoa. • Assistance in applying Kona experience to the Pacific (tourist-based industries not in direct competition with Hawaii). • Particular attention given to marketing and promotion. • Assistance in identifying suitable joint venture partners.
TONGA Vanilla	Tonga's most important agricultural export industry, having surpassed both coconuts and bananas. The value of vanilla exports currently is around T$3.5 million annually.	Production base of industry firmly established, marketing largely in private sector hands. The value of exports could be expected to double over the next decade (if vanilla prices remain reasonably firm).	• Establishment and enforcement of standards. • Consolidation of exporting in hands of one or two industry-based exporters.	• Vanilla industry--a major beneficiary of assistance from USAID to FIMCO. FIMCO experience provides a basis for marketing technical assistance to other countries.
Squash	Substantial export industry supplying the seasonal niche in Japanese market. The value of exports for the 1990-91 season was T$4.8 million.	Mature T$6 million export industry a reasonable expectation if industry is consolidated.	Consolidation needed in place of current rapid expansion. Consolidation requires: • increasing the yields and profitability of existing farmers, improving quality, with particular emphasis on post-harvest handling, • improving coordination of marketing arrangements.	• Assistance to commercial Tongan Pumpkin Association in marketing and extension efforts. • Assistance in preparation of material promoting quality improvement and grading.

Commodity	Current status	Growth prospects	Growth constraints and requirements	Opportunities for aid and technical assistance
TONGA (con.) Root crops	Recently a steady growth in root crop (taro and yam) exports, principally to NZ. The official value of these exports stands at T$8 million (likely to be significantly underestimated).	Sound production and market base for sustained growth. Thus the real value of exports could be expected to double over the next decade.	• solving transportation constraint to expanding North American market.	• No direct assistance expected but preparation of regional quality standards material needed.
WESTERN SAMOA				
Taro	Major export earner and region's largest exporter. Prior to hurricane Ofa the value of exports officially stood at WS$6 million (likely to be underestimated).	Exports growing rapidly since 1987. The market is undersupplied, and Western Samoa is a low-cost producer that is well-located relative to major markets. A reasonable expectation over next decade is WS$15 million.	• Transportation a constraint to expanding North American market.	• No direct assistance expected but preparation of regional quality standards material needed.
COOK ISLANDS				
Papaya	Major agricultural export industry, fob value around NZ$0.5.	Auckland papaya market saturated, cannot profitably be expanded. Australia offers a large market if tourist-driven air links are created.	• Auckland papaya market saturated. • Air cargo links to other markets. • Introduction and operation of new generation post-harvest treatment facilities.	
Organic coffee	Small coffee industry being developed.	Market basis for development in tourism sector and high-value gourmet coffee markets in U.S. and elsewhere.	• Substantial investment in marketing (particularly packaging and promotion) required.	Same as Vanuatu.

Marine Exports

Frequent reference is made to "regional fisheries." However, this term masks the very great diversity between the various countries in the region, their fisheries, and the products of these fisheries. The marine environments vary from the rich estuaries of Papua New Guinea, to the mangrove swamps of Fiji, to the oceanic "deserts" of the atoll countries. Products range from single specimen shells worth US$2,000, to 60 kg tunas valued at US$30 per kg, to dried seaweed worth US$0.20 per kg. In terms of internal capability to successfully develop their resources, the regional countries are also comparatively very differently placed. Thus it is not possible to draw any regionwide conclusions on the state of marine products development or to prescribe any one set of solutions to "regional" problems. The existing opportunities, however, can be evaluated in terms of resource and market availability. How regional countries can best exploit these resources and tap the markets is necessarily a country-specific problem.

The Private Sector Project made projections to the year 2000 of marine product exports for all the Pacific island countries. These were based on resource base, current production, and marketing considerations. These are briefly presented in Table 7.2 and Table 7.3.

Several Pacific island countries are forecast to enjoy significant growth in marine exports before the year 2000, particularly in the tuna area. Tuna stocks in the region are currently judged to be underexploited, with the exception of the larger yellowfin and bigeye, which are thought to be approaching the limit of sustainable yield. Even in the case of these species, however, increased catches by regional countries could be made, if necessary, by reducing the catches of the distant water fishing nations through existing licensing mechanisms.

In terms of availability of markets for processed products, a worldwide shortfall of seafood is forecast for 2000 by the United Nations Food and

Table 7.2   Marine product export projections, Year 2000 ($'000)

Product	Cook Islands	Fiji	Kiribati	PNG	Sol. Is.	Tonga	Vanuatu
Tuna canning material	600	-	3,900	14,000	28,000	2,000	-
Processed tuna	-	30,000	-	18,750	30,000	-	-
Sashimi tuna	-	400	5,000	-	-	-	-
MMPs	1,400	2,000	-	1,500	2,000	-	250
Fresh fish	100	1,000	-	-	100	500	125
Other	-	-	-	9,000	-	-	-
Total	2,100	33,400	8,900	43,250	60,100	2,500	375

Table 7.3   Marine product export projections, Year 2000

Product	Cook Islands	Fiji	Kiribati	PNG	Sol. Is.	Tonga	Vanuatu
Tuna canning material (mt)	300	-	6,000	20,000	40,000	1,000	-
Processed tuna (cases)	-	1,000,000	-	750,000	1,000,000	-	-
Sashimi tuna (mt)	-	50	1,000	-	-	-	-
Fresh fish (mt)	20	150	-	-	20	100	25

Agriculture Organization (FAO), while increases in processing within the region represents only a re-location of processing effort, not an increase in overall production levels. Accordingly, individual country development figures will not be constrained by resource or market problems. However, as with horticultural exports, marketing will be a major constraint.

Future private sector investment opportunities

Industrial scale vs. entrepreneurial venture

Marine product investment opportunities can be broadly grouped into two categories: industrial scale and entrepreneurial. Apart from the tuna fishery, few marine resources are currently available to regional countries that would support industrial scale enterprises. Bêche-de-mer, for example, which probably has the greatest volume harvested in the region after tuna (excluding subsistence catches), is highly labor intensive in both harvesting and processing; the product is viable when harvested as a cash-generating adjunct to a subsistence economy, but it would not support an industry where the participants were paid wages. Other examples of marine products that, while viable in this mode of exploitation, would not survive the transition to an industrial-scale commercial activity are mother-of-pearl shell, specimen shell, cultured seaweed, and possibly marine aquarium fish, depending on the species mix achieved.

Many other marine products will remain small-scale entrepreneurial operations due to the limited resource base. Deep bottom snapper, for example, are never likely to have the volume to support a commercial enterprise, but they are likely to remain activities carried out by a few dedicated individuals at the owner/entrepreneur level. Snapper, like bêche-de-mer is a fragile resource, and to avoid over-exploitation there is a need for appropriate government regulation.

Aquaculture is an area that has potential for significant investment and production volumes sufficient to support industrial-scale private sector investment; however, there has been a continued absence of commercial viability in regional aquaculture projects.

In summary, there are few viable industrial-scale private sector investment opportunities in marine product export development other than those associated with tuna. This is not to say that other marine products will not continue to remain viable to the entrepreneur or that they would not benefit from development assistance. Rather, they do not represent opportunities for industrial-scale private sector investment. The role of government and external agencies in promoting exports in these areas, where commercial forces are "muted," is likely to be greater than in those areas where private sector development should be of sufficient scale to be self-sustaining.

Tuna catching

To date, private sector investment in the regional tuna fishery has been concentrated in the catching sector, where the export product is whole frozen fish. This basic raw material is able to access several commodity markets where, if basic quality standards are met, it is guaranteed a sale, even though the seller has virtually no control over the price. The "portability" of fishing vessels is also an attractant. For the external investors, who might encounter problems ranging from a change in the political climate to the failure of a fishery, the knowledge that they can walk away from these problems, if need be, is very effective in reducing perceived risk. The domestic investors likewise know that their risk is diminished by the frequent ability of vessels to move between fisheries or, if ultimately necessary, to be sold offshore. None of this is true of, for example, shore-based tuna processing plants, particularly in a regional setting where a large proportion of the establishment costs are in irrecoverable infrastructure development.

For these and other reasons, particularly the free entry to most tuna fisheries, there has historically never been a shortage of catching effort, and consequently the returns to fishermen and boat-owners are low and, due to the "hunting" nature of tuna harvesting, uncertain.

For the short term at least, investment in tuna fishing vessels designed to harvest pelagic tunas as canning material is unlikely to be viable. However, if such vessels are owned by the Pacific island countries and they can benefit from domestic concessions such as the waiving of license fees, they might possibly succeed. In particular, if they are integrated into a processing/marketing framework, as is the case in Solomon Islands, then the chances of success are considerably enhanced. There is a significant funding threshold in the tuna industry. A new purse seiner, in the medium-size (500 mt) class, for example, would cost at least US$10 million. A medium-size cannery, of 15,000 mt input capacity, would cost at least US$15 million. Furthermore, for many reasons, including the need for vertically integrated operations, economies of scale, and adequate infrastructure, successful investment must include the creation of the full support facilities from the outset. Many regional fishing activities have failed because they confused the acquisition of a fishing vessel with the establishment of a fishing industry.

Tuna processing

An analysis of the viability of processing sashimi tuna into loins prior to shipment to Japan concluded that because of technical difficulties and the demanding nature of the market it could not immediately be recommended for the Pacific island countries. For those countries that have access to a sashimi tuna resource, successfully exporting whole fish will depend on the availability of air transport to Japan. Recent developments in regional fresh sashimi fisheries, particularly those based in Guam, indicate that sufficient volumes are becoming available to justify the initiation of dedicated air-freight services to transport the fish to Japan. In 1988 it has been estimated that 7,000 mt of sashimi tuna was flown from Guam to Japan. On a much smaller scale, the recent development of yellowfin exports from Fiji to Japan and Hawaii is encouraging.

The processing of the sashimi tuna catch should be restricted to handling practices that ensure the whole fish arrives at market in the best possible condition. Investment would be required in ice-making equipment, cool-storage facilities, and infrastructure for servicing the vessels. Investment in freight-only aircraft dedicated to sashimi tuna shipment to Japan is viable for regional countries close to Japan but does not appear practical for any of the South Pacific countries. Thus development of this industry will depend on growth of tourism to create essential air cargo capacity at competitive cost.

Several Pacific island countries have investigated the possibility of establishing tuna canneries. There is already a 15,000 mt tuna cannery in Fiji and a 5,000 mt cannery in Solomon Islands with a second 10,000 mt plant currently being commissioned. Several studies have assessed the potential viability of tuna canning operations at various other locations in the region. Without exception, these studies have shown that the profits from processing operations were inadequate when the input fish was costed at market value. Accordingly, it can be concluded that investment in tuna canning will be viable only when the vertical integration of the catching and processing sectors allows tuna to be passed to the cannery at catching cost.

Tuna marketing

Fiji canned tuna, which holds 11 percent of the U.K. market, is an example of a superior product that has been successfully marketed to capture at least part of the price premium for the processor. Generally, however, canned tuna has not been differentiated at the producer level. In general, producers have operated as offshore suppliers of a commodity product.

The second major tuna market is for sashimi. It could not be recommended that the Pacific island countries attempt to establish their own distribution in Japan or that they attempt to improve returns by bypassing the traditional Japanese system of tuna importation and trading by seeking to deal with agents further along the distribution chain. Marketing activities for sashimi tuna in Japan should concentrate on ensuring consistently high quality on delivery to the agent, continuity of supply, and a relationship of trust with the Japanese partner cultivated over time. Any private sector investment in the sashimi fishery should accordingly be restricted to catching/processing.

Aquaculture

It can be concluded that while aquaculture is a prime candidate for high levels of development expenditure and technology transfer, this transfer of technology, and its funding, has proved insufficient in the region to generate marketable products that can pay their way in the international marketplace. Until this situation is reversed, it would be imprudent to consider private sector development expenditure in this sector.

Other products

The constraints to successful artisanal/commercial marine products enterprises, catching and processing, both at the entrepreneurial level in the region are becoming more widely appreciated. Many of these constraints are structural in nature, and little, if anything, can be done to ameliorate them. Among these constraints are the generally low productivity of tropical waters, the large variety of species presenting both harvesting and marketing problems, the toxic nature of some species offered for sale, the restricted domestic demand from small, often remote, cash economy centers with associated transport costs, and the difficulties with fishing access for other than traditional owners.

All these factors conspire to hinder the orderly development of regional marine resources. Nonetheless, particularly in domestic markets, significant volumes of artisanal catches will continue to be traded. However, these volumes are never likely to be sufficient to require significant private sector investment, and export volumes will remain low.

Major conclusion

Within the range of the marine resources available to the Pacific island countries, tuna is the only one capable of absorbing significant private sector investment. The creation of a full industry, from the outset, will take considerable confidence on the part of investors and lenders, as well as considerable funds. However, the alternatives are (1) no development at all, with continued reliance on foreign fishing and license revenue collection; or (2) continuation of the attempts at entry to the tuna fishery on a piecemeal basis, which has already proved frustrating and unprofitable in nearly every one of the Pacific island countries.

Export Manufacturing

Most island countries in recent years have viewed export manufacturing as a means of diversifying their economic base. The region offers the investor the following advantages: market access (particularly SPARTECA), generous incentives, generally low wage structures, and a readily trainable labor force. Yet despite these apparent attractions the progress in export manufacturing has been generally disappointing. The last five years, however, have seen two significant developments that confirm the region's comparative advantage in certain lines of manufacturing: (1) the successful establishment of Tonga's Small Industries Centre and (2) the dramatic growth in Fiji's garment exports. These developments, due to their importance for manufacturing investment in the region, were analyzed in McGregor et al. (1990). The findings are summarized below:

Tonga's Small Industries Centre (SIC)

Export manufacturing in Tonga has been actively promoted in Tonga through the creation of a Small Industries Centre (SIC) that was financed by an ADB loan. Standard factory sheds are provided, together with infrastructure such as roads, sewerage disposal, water, and telecommunications at reasonable cost. Leases are for 50 years, at subsidized rents. A major value of the SIC has been in the provision of long-term access to land in a situation where foreigners cannot own land. An important benefit of the SIC is that it has provided foreign investors with tangible evidence of the government's sustained commitment to manufacturing investment.

The SIC is supported by a standard set of fiscal incentives and customs duty exemptions. An important feature of the Tongan system is that a sole government agency deals with all bureaucratic requirements needed to establish a manufacturing enterprise, which has avoided the long delay experienced in many other island economies.

The foreign investor response to these initiatives has been excellent and has far exceeded the expectations of the planners, and there is now a waiting list for sites. A range of export manufacturing enterprises have been established, including luxury fiber glass yachts, light excavating machinery, leather jackets, and knitwear.

The individual manufacturing enterprises have enjoyed varied success. Garments have been the lead manufacturing sector, with knitwear being most successful. The light excavator enterprise, while contributing substantially to Tonga's capability to support light engineering and industrial enterprises, has since ceased operations. Overall the manufacturing sector now accounts for over 30 percent of Tonga's exports, which were valued at T$3.4 million in 1989-90.

The Tongan knitwear industry is based on a single firm that imports New Zealand wool and exports high-quality handcrafted sweaters to New Zealand, North America, and Australia. This is a high quality product of enduring market appeal; hence a small range of garments in traditional/classical styles are produced. All products have a special label that indicates the prestigious combination of New Zealand wool and Tongan craftsmanship. A successful place in the high-risk, high-profit, fluid "boutique" market would not be feasible for a producer in Tonga, considering distance from the market in terms of both shipping and fashion information.

Tonga's market share, particularly in North America, is minute, and there are excellent prospects for sales in European markets. Thus Tonga faces a virtually unlimited market for expansion. However, the labor supply is a serious constraint to growth. Outmigration and an exceptionally high rate of remittances mean that Tonga does not have a large pool of low cost labor available. Labor shortages have led to increasing mechanization, which has allowed for an increased output from a decreased labor force.

The viability of the Tongan knitwear industry has been based on a combination of factors, including:

- A highly skilled foreign entrepreneur/owner/manager based in Tonga.

- The South Pacific Regional Trade and Economic Cooperation Agreement (SPARTECA) trade agreement.

- Productive female labor, with a high level of weaving skills. However, as the enterprise has expanded, this labor has become in increasingly short supply.

- A government policy and administrative environment conducive to entrepreneurial investment. The government's administrative machinery generated quick decisions on the investor's proposals, which was a crucial factor for an entrepreneur having limited working capital and facing alternative investment opportunities.

Most of the islands in the South Pacific, in principle, offer equally suitable locations for this type of manufacturing enterprise. They all are a party to SPARTECA, offer a similar package of incentives, most have low-wage structures, and have an adaptable female labor force. Countries like Tuvalu and Kiribati are obvious examples. Furthermore, these microstates, unlike Tonga, have an abundant supply of labor, with limited outmigration options. They also have a well entrenched weaving and craft tradition. On the negative side the transportation constraints are even greater than they are in Tonga. The two fundamental limiting factors, however, are the identification of suitable entrepreneurs who are willing to invest their capital and skills in the Pacific islands and the administrative systems that can expeditiously accommodate such investors.

Fiji's Tax Free Factory system

In 1987 the government actively promoted a Tax Free Factory (TFF) system to restore investor confidence following two military coups. The scheme provided approved investors with a generous package of incentives, including a 13-year tax holiday. The introduction of Fiji's TFF system coincided with changes being made to SPARTECA, which significantly improved the access of manufactured goods from the Forum countries to the Australian and New Zealand market. Garment manufacturers in Australia and New Zealand responded quickly to the combination of incentives and improved market access. Fiji now supplies major brand names to these markets. The Fiji garment industry operates on a "cut make and trim" (CMT) basis whereby raw materials and patterns are supplied by the buyer who is often a joint venture partner.

Since the inception of the TFF scheme, until the end of the third quarter of 1990, 253 projects have been approved. Of the 104 projects implemented

70 (67 percent) were in the garment sector. Fifty percent are locally owned, 19 percent were local/foreign joint ventures, and 31 percent totally foreign owned. The fact that most of the tax free enterprises are locally owned or joint ventures is an unusual feature of the Fiji TFF sector. Most local enterprises are owned by Fiji-Gujarati entrepreneurs often in joint ventures with New Zealand and Australian investors. Investors from these two countries account for almost 70 percent of the foreign investors. Some developing countries such as South Korea, Malaysia, and Hong Kong also have some investment in the tax free sector.

The gross value of garment exports in 1989, according to government trade statistics, stood at F$100.7 million and is estimated to reach F$123 million in 1990. This will make garments Fiji's second largest export earner after sugar (however, the import requirements of garments are approximately 40 percent of sales). This compares with F$35 million in 1988 and $8.5 million in 1988. In 1982 exports were less than F$100,000.

Most exports are directed at the New Zealand market and, to a lesser extent, Australia. Fiji now has a sizable market share in these markets for certain garment lines such as men's trousers (14.5 percent of imports) and men's shorts (34 percent). Garment (mainly night-wear) exports to the United States are also important, currently accounting for 10 percent of all garment exports. This is likely to expand sharply with the recent increase in the "voluntary" quota to that market.

The development of Fiji's tax free exports has differed from the international norm in two important respects: (1) it has occurred without the supporting physical infrastructure of an export processing zone, and (2) it has not been dominated by foreign capital.

A crucial feature of the Fiji system has been the support provided by the Fiji Trade and Investment Board (FTIB). The package of incentives offered to foreign investors was vigorously promoted by the FTIB, and through it the administrative and approval procedures were streamlined.

The Fiji garment industry will face a watershed in 1995 when Australia will remove all garment quotas, leaving only tariff barriers on imports from non-Forum countries. Fiji will thus be in direct competition with low cost Asian exporters. This change could affect the development of the Fiji industry well before this date, depending on how investors perceive its impact. However, Fiji is expected to remain a competitive location for companies that have already invested there. While it has a higher wage structure than some competing Asian countries, this may be of only marginal significance because wages make up only an estimated 17 percent of Fiji's production costs. An ability to make quick adjustments in product lines, due to smaller production runs and proximity to the market, is seen as a major advantage. Fiji has proved itself to be a quality producer even in the face of the rapid expansion that has occurred. High quality Fiji garments are now penetrating the U.S. market where no special concessions are enjoyed.

There is need, however, to diversify from the CMT garments where there is limited value added and competition is acute. It is important to ensure that the incentives given to the garment sector do not lead to an industrial "monoculture" that is not sustainable in the long term. Excellent opportunities have been identified for higher value added lines of activity such as high fashion and island-type exotic clothing that uses local design capability. A long standing Fiji company is making encouraging progress in this area.

The wood/furniture and footwear exports have also grown under the tax free system. In 1989 there were nine wood and furniture projects and seven footwear projects. They accounted for 400 and 270 jobs, respectively. Yet these sectors have not achieved the substantial expansions expected of them. The prospects for wood and furniture products, based on Fiji's unique indigenous species, remain particularly good. The value added contribution of this industry is significantly higher than for garments. Electronic assembly industries were predicted as a major growth area under the tax free system. This has not yet materialized despite the trainability of Fiji's labor force.

Lessons from the Tonga and Fiji experience

The important lessons for potential investors and Pacific island policymakers that emanate from an analysis of export manufacturing in Fiji and Tonga are:

- Smallness and isolation are not insurmountable constraints.
- Expeditious administrative procedures are of crucial importance.
- Active investment promotion yields substantial benefits.
- A strong domestic manufacturing sector provides a strong basis for export manufacturing development.
- Significant export manufacturing development can be initiated without investment in industrial estates.

- Small industry centers can, however, make an important contribution (developing such infrastructure is an appropriate use for aid and technical assistance funds).

- SPARTECA has been the key ingredient in the establishment of export manufacturing in the region. However, the inflexibility of the Agreement's rules of origin continues to act as a brake on development. Any bona fide manufacturing operation in the islands should fall within the duty free provisions.

Tourism

The Pacific islands have an outstanding potential for tourism growth considering their tropical ambience and exotic image, natural beauty and cultural attractions, and an outstanding unpolluted marine environment. Yet with the exception of Fiji, and to a lesser extent the Cook Islands and Vanuatu, tourism in the Pacific island countries is not a major economic sector in terms of contribution to GDP and total employment.

Tourist arrival projections

According to the World Tourism Organization, global tourism accounts for over 1.5 billion travelers and US$2 trillion in expenditures. Over the past 12 years, East Asia and Pacific arrivals have grown at an average annual rate of 13.5 percent, exceeding the growth rates of established areas such as North America and Europe and making it the fastest growing region in the world. Tourist arrivals to the Pacific islands in 1989 are estimated at 608,000, or approximately 0.15 percent of the world total.

Central and South Pacific countries have not fully benefited from the rapid growth of the Asia/Pacific regional travel. Arrivals in the Central/South Pacific have grown at an average annual rate of 5.7 percent over the past 12 years, much of which can be attributed to the success of Guam and the Commonwealth of the Northern Mariana Islands (CNMI) in attracting Japanese tourists. The Central/South Pacific region is a two-tiered travel market, with Guam, the CNMI, Fiji, and French Polynesia accounting for 82 percent of travel to the region; the remaining countries have much less developed visitor industries and receive relatively few arrivals.

In all the Pacific island countries the trend in visitor arrivals since 1980 has been upward. Average annual growth rates since 1980 in total international visitor arrivals have ranged from a low of 0.5 percent for Solomon Islands to a high of 7.4 percent for Kiribati (Table 7.4), the latter being from a very low base. Despite the difficulties that tourism development in the Pacific islands has encountered over the past several years, the long-term forecast for arrivals is one of growth, with a conservative estimated figure of 1.6 million arrivals by 1993. Most of the Pacific island countries are forecasting growth rates of 5 percent or better over the next five years (Table 7.4).

The current global and regional tourism trends are favorable for the Pacific islands. The European market is set to continue its steady growth trends, while the Japanese market is now showing signs of strong revival. The considerable North American market potential will begin to be tapped as soon as adequate airline services to the region are reinstated and expanded. In a wider sense, the region's relatively late entry into the international tourism industry can be turned into a major long-term advantage. By adopting a planned and regulated development approach, the Pacific island countries are still in a position to expand their tourism sectors in a way that emphasizes environmental conservation and enhances the quality of the overall tourist experience in a way the rapidly expanded CNMI industry has not.

However, a number of factors will affect the region's tourism growth: (1) limitations in the number and kind of tourist attractions in the Pacific island destinations, which currently depend primarily on the tropical environment and ocean-related activities; (2) continuing difficulties in maintaining stable air transportation routes and fares; (3) the level of accommodation facilities and services in the islands, with relatively few international standard hotels and restaurants; (4) the ability of the islands to develop infrastructure adequate for further tourism development, especially in the areas of water, power, and sewage; (5) marketing and promotion effectiveness, especially given the increasing competition from destinations

Table 7.4   Visitor arrivals in Pacific island countries, 1980-95

Country	Visitor arrivals				Growth	Projected
	1980	1987	1989	1995	1980-89	1989-95
Cook Islands	21,050	32,100	35,000	47,430	5.8	5.1
Fiji	190,000	189,870	264,400	372,000	3.7	5.8
Kiribati	2,090	3,740	4,000	5,230	7.4	4.5
PNG	38,770	34,970	42,000	54,940	0.9	4.5
Solomon Islands	10,520	12,560	11,000	18,550	0.5	9.1
Tonga	13,320	19,220	20,000	30,000	4.6	6.9
Vanuatu	21,970	14,640	23,865	50,560	0.9	13.3
Western Samoa	41,480	48,660	47,000	73,800	2.1	7.8

Note: Growth rates are compounded average annual rates.
Sources: TIM (1990).

around the globe, as well as the limited budgets and expertise of agencies responsible for tourism promotion in the Pacific islands; (6) shortages of trained manpower at all levels of skills in the tourism sector; and (7) other considerations including government support for the industry, the extent and quality of tourism planning, and the cost of visiting the islands.

Investment opportunities in tourism sector

Private sector tourism investment opportunities may be viewed as falling into two categories: (1) those that relate to the development of hotels/resorts and other types of accommodation, and (2) all other tourism related investment, including the formation and expansion of enterprises directly serving visitors (e.g., restaurants, retail establishments, and cultural centers) and in industries that support the tourism sector (e.g., agriculture, handicrafts, and business services). Other industries such as a horticultural exports industry can be developed as a byproduct of tourism development.

For most of the Pacific island countries the anticipated growth in visitor arrivals is contingent upon increased levels of investment, particularly in the accommodations and tourism-related services subsectors. Given the low level of domestic savings, increased foreign direct investment and official (multi- and bilateral grants and loans), capital assistance will be needed. A high level of foreign ownership of international standard facilities will thus be necessary despite the preference for local ownership and management by most hotel chains.

Even though informal estimates of average room occupancy rates tend to be on the low side in most Pacific island countries, the outlook for investment opportunities in the accommodations industry is considered fairly strong. This assessment is based on the lack of international standard hotel/resort facilities, the prevalence of substandard commercial lodging, and the demand for a mix of accommodation types in areas newly accessible to tourists.

Outside the Cook Islands, Fiji, and Vanuatu, much of the visitor inventory is substandard in terms of catering to international visitors, even those on small budgets. Inns, guest houses, and other facilities in this category frequently have served domestic travel demand and special transient groups such as merchant seaman and yacht crews. Continued growth in visitor arrivals can be expected to stimulate the upgrading and replacement of part of this segment of commercial accommodation. However, small resorts and guest house facilities located on islands or in rural areas away from district or urban centers are attracting increasing interest, both from the standpoint of local investors and tourists having special interests, e.g., diving, bushwalking, naturalists, folk art, and handicrafts. The smaller scale of such facilities enables indigenous participation in ownership and management of visitor accommodations. However, if such tourism is to make a significant contribution, effective links with marketing and management have to be made. The Private Sector Project makes specific proposals to this end (TIM 1990).

Although investment opportunities are the greatest in the accommodations industry, in a majority of the Pacific island countries, substantial complementary direct investment also will be required in restaurants, shopping facilities, cultural and other entertainment services, recreation and sports activities, personal services, support business services, transport services, handicrafts, agricultural and fishery products, and selected light manufactures. Most of these activities have been identified as ones that are likely to include many small-scale ventures, and as such they are expected to generate opportunities for indigenous entrepreneurs and small businesses. Larger-scale activities requiring substantial capital outlays, such as cultural centers, interisland cruise ships, golf courses, and sport fishing facilities, represent opportunities for foreign investment.

The investment climate

Government promotion of foreign investment in tourism generally has been somewhat deficient in its articulation, coordination, and responsiveness to industry, as well as in terms of the effectiveness of support programs and policies. Reluctance to rely too heavily on foreign investment stems from concerns about adverse economic, social, and cultural impacts. While governments acknowledge the substantial benefits of foreign direct investment in tourism, they have concerns about the ability to control the pace and nature of development, the market domination by outsiders with a corresponding inability of citizens to participate in ownership and management, the dilution of economic benefits through large leakages of profits and other factor payments abroad, the adverse environmental impacts, and the disruption of traditional values and lifestyles. In Kiribati, Solomon Islands, and Tonga (and perhaps to a lesser extent Western Samoa), there appears to be a significant sentiment favoring a policy that emphasizes a greater degree of domestic ownership and the smaller-scale and (implied) slower growth that would be entailed by the greater reliance upon domestic investment.

To mitigate the potential adverse effects of foreign direct investment, countries have unanimously endorsed the policy of encouraging joint ventures entailing substantive ownership participation on the part of local investors. In addition to attaining a wider distribution and enhanced level of benefits for residents, this approach can be expected to increase domestic investment, to facilitate technology transfer and the strengthening of intersectoral linkages, and to avoid or lessen adverse social and cultural impacts.

Policies, incentives, and programmatic support for tourism development

Given the relatively recent emergence of tourism in the Pacific island countries and the lack of a private sector base upon which to build the industry, governments will continue to play a vital role in shaping tourism and its place in their overall economic development. Government policies will have a great impact on the industry and in many cases provide the leadership for tourism development. Although this situation poses many challenges for governments, it also provides an opportunity to shape the industry in a way no longer available to most advanced countries.

Investment initiatives are needed that:

- Define tourism objectives with respect to foreign investment,

- Establish programs to channel donor funding into financial assistance to tourism,

- Bolster domestic production of tourism goods and services,

- Revise land use laws, foreign investment regulations, and fiscal incentives,

- Implement zoning laws applicable to tourism,

- Encourage tourism joint ventures,

- Explore government investment in equity shares in private enterprises.

It is important that governments explicitly recognize that maintaining a large degree of domestic tourism industry control is likely to involve a fundamental tradeoff. That is, to obtain the benefits associated with maintenance of domestic industry control (e.g., smaller-scale accommodation facilities that enable greater participation of citizens in ownership and management, stronger linkages between tourism and other industries, and less expected adverse environmental and sociocultural impacts), it must forgo the income, employment, and technology benefits of more rapid tourism growth. A clear understanding of this tradeoff is more likely to result in the formulation of a tourism sector investment policy that is consistent with overall national development goals and at the same time is unambiguous to prospective investors.

It is recommended that the Pacific island countries substantially increase their effort in tourism investment promotion. One approach to investment promotion is to establish joint private sector/public sector Tourism Development Corporations responsible for planning and promoting joint venture tourism investments in new resorts and support businesses. Aid donor Joint Venture Schemes could participate with the National Tourism Development Corporations to provide funding for development corporation/government equity in new investment projects.

Even though governments in principle favor joint ventures, few provide specific incentives to encourage such ventures. In addition to financial support, other industry or government sponsored programs designed to facilitate joint ventures could be expected to improve the investment climate, particularly in regard to mobilizing domestic resources. Forms of assistance likely to increase the rate of joint venture formation are represented by identifying potential domestic joint venture partners; enabling local investors to provide land as equity contribution in joint ventures; providing management, marketing, and technical assistance to local investors involved in structuring a joint venture; and providing entrepreneurial and management skills training to residents interested in entering joint ventures.

In a number of countries, particularly the Cook Islands, Tonga, and Western Samoa, large numbers of citizens have chosen to live abroad and have acquired management and entrepreneurial skills. Many of these residents ultimately return to their home countries or desire to do so. Some of these citizens would be interested in joint venture opportunities but need to be put in contact with appropriate foreign investors. Providing management, marketing, and technical assistance to local investors specifically to help structure and negotiate a joint venture also is a service that is needed but generally not available in the countries. In the future with staff development and institutional strengthening, the development banks would be an appropriate vehicle for providing such assistance.

Land tenure systems in the Pacific island countries constitute constraints to tourism development in varying degrees. In most countries a large proportion of privately held land is customary owned. Often foreigners are prohibited from obtaining freehold interest in land and can acquire only long-term use rights through leasing. When leases are obtainable, length of lease, identifying available land, difficulty in negotiating lease terms with customary owners, and getting land and negotiated leases registered are very difficult and time consuming in nearly all the countries. Given these problems, government intervention is needed in providing land for hotel/resort development. In addition, to facilitate joint ventures, government could establish a mechanism to enable individual landowners to obtain a mortgage loan (e.g., from a development bank), the proceeds of which would be used for an equity interest in a venture, the land being used by the venture and debt service on the loan being paid out of venture operating revenues. However, for Papua New Guinea, Solomon Islands, and Vanuatu land registration and leasing procedures need to be developed to make long-term access to hotel sites generally available.

The scarcity of indigenous entrepreneurial and management skills is a major factor influencing investment climate, especially in those countries that have placed relatively more policy emphasis (typically not clearly articulated) on joint ventures. Prospective foreign investors experience great difficulty in finding joint venture partners with the requisite management skills to fully participate in operating an enterprise. The feeling of being obliged to include local ownership participation, and at the same time knowing the difficulty of obtaining productive participation, is a negative factor to prospective foreign investors. The scarcity of indigenous business skills is also a major constraint in the formation of wholly resident owned tourism and support sector enterprises.

The small business component of the Private Sector Project addressed the problem of providing skills training and management/technical assistance to entrepreneurs and small businesses. It is proposed that a regional approach utilizing the extension network of the University of the South Pacific be adopted. The details are presented in Briscoe et al. (1990). It is also recommended that integrated packages of services for small-scale tourism development be provided. Here the Tourism Council of the South Pacific (TCSP) and the development banks would play a lead role. One such integrated package of services proposed for tourism would be modeled after Vanuatu's Plantation Support Association (PSA). In this case, a Tourism Support Association (TSA), structured as a cooperative association with membership fees being based on volume of sales sold through the association, could consist of a network of village-based bed and breakfast accommodations. Both technical and management training specific to operating the accommodation facilities would be provided by the TSA.

The TSA would include a development arm to promote expansion of the chain, which could also provide such services as access to financing and consultant services, act as a marketing and booking agency, provide tour guides, and coordinate transportation services. The TSA concept could, of course, be applied to a number of different tourism-related products and services such as handicrafts and entertainment. Further details are presented in Briscoe et al. (1990) and in Chapter 9.

Minerals
Current situation and outlook

Gold has long been known to occur in the Southwest Pacific chain from Papua New Guinea to Fiji, which lies on the so-called Pacific "Rim of Fire," the boundary of the earth's tectonic plates (Pacific Plate and Australia-India Plate). International attention for large-scale mining and exploration in the region started with the development of the Bougainville Mine in Papua New Guinea in 1972. Other world class gold and silver deposits have since been discovered in the region. Currently, Papua New Guinea now produces some 40 tonnes of gold, Fiji about 5 tonnes, and Solomon Islands less than a tonne. The development of Ok Tedi mine in 1984, at a cost of approximately US$1.5 billion, made Papua New Guinea the world's fourth leading gold producer and ninth among copper producers. To date, Ok Tedi remains the largest gold mine operating in the world outside of South Africa and the Soviet Union.

Over the past five years, gold production from the Southwest Pacific has increased by about 50 percent, from 890,000 oz to 1,330,000 oz, and by mid-1990 this figure is expected to more than double. By the mid-1990s the entire Pacific region including Australia, the Philippines, and Indonesia is expected to surpass the United States, Canada, and Brazil in annual gold production and become the second largest producer after South Africa. Papua New Guinea alone has the potential to produce some 2.7 million oz (84 t) of gold valued at some US$1 billion, at today's gold price, during the early 1990s. The major mineral deposits of the Southwest Pacific are summarized in Table 7.5.

The long-term outlook (five years plus) for gold in the Southwest Pacific will be positive because of the expected gold prices and the nature of the gold deposits in the region, i.e., epithermal gold (gold occurring near the surface where it can be mined by open pitting, which is usually much more economical than underground mining). The anticipated development of new gold mines will attract more mining and exploration companies in the region, which would initiate further vigorous exploration and, in turn, increase the possibility of more new discoveries.

Table 7.5   Major mineral deposits of the southwest Pacific

Deposit Name	Tonnage (Million tonnes)	Cu %	Au g/t	Ag g/t	Status	Comments
Papua New Guinea						
Panguna	530	0.4	0.46	-	mine	Bougainville
Ok Tedi	300	0.75	0.6	-	mine	production
Misima	56	-	1.38	21	mine	production
Mt. Kare	unknown	-	-	-	mine	alluvial mining
Lihir	167	-	3.43	-	prospect	feasibility stage
Porgera	85.8	-	5.7	11.9	mine	production
Hidden Valley	47.5	-	1.63	24	development	await govt. approv.
Lakekamu	27.7 m³	-	154 mg/m³	-	prospect	advanced expl.
Laloki	0.37	3.93	3.75	10.76	prospect	advanced expl.
Wild Dog	0.65	-	7	-	prospect	advanced expl.
Tabar	5.4	-	1.95	-	prospect	advanced expl.
"	1.25	-	7.78	-	"	
Woodlark	1.4	-	3.7	-	prospect	advanced expl.
"	0.8	-	5.4	-	"	"
Frieda River	592	0.5	0.34	-	prospect	advanced expl.
Solomon Islands						
Gold Ridge	1.34	-	3.86	-	development	await govt. approv.
Chovohio River	20 m³	-	0.3-2 g/m³	-	prospect	out to bid
Vanuatu						
Taoran	not evaluated	-	-	-	prospect	grassroots expl.
Amethyst	not evaluated	-	-	-	prospect	grassroots expl.
Tafuse	not evaluated	-	-	-	prospect	grassroots expl.
Fiji						
Emperor	1.2	-	6.4	-	mine	production
Nasomo	0.3	-	14	-	mine	production
Mt. Kasi	0.5	-	6	-	prospect	advanced expl.
"	0.7	-	2	-	"	"
Faddy's	2	-	2	-	prospect	advanced expl.

Papua New Guinea

Landwise, Papua New Guinea is the largest and is geologically the most favorable for gold occurrences. Gold will continue to play a leading role in economic development to be the largest export earner for the country, despite the Bougainville crisis. At least three medium to large gold mines (Lihir, Hidden Valley, and Mt. Kare) are coming into production within the next three years, and also with the country's first commercially viable oil field development at Iagifu-Hedinia in the Southern Highlands, the immediate mineral outlook for Papua New Guinea is very promising. Oil reserves at Iagifu-Hedinia are put at well over 100 million barrels, and production is expected to start in 1992.

The announced gold projects and exploration are expected to result in the following expenditures during the next five years:

- US$2.25 billion (1990 dollars) for capital expenditures associated with buildings for at least six gold projects.

- Annual expenditures of at least US$100 million for exploration.

- At a production level of 3 million oz per year, some US$500 million per year is anticipated to be spent on operating costs.

These developments will bring with them business opportunities in the following areas:

- *Financing.* Investment banks and financial institutions will need to raise the US$2 billion to finance the capital expenditures for gold mining and milling facilities over the next five years.

- *Equipment and technology sales.* These include carbon-in-pulp, which will be used at Misima, and pressure oxidation for the refractory ores at Porgera and Lihir.

- *Modular equipment.* Many of the smaller deposits in Papua New Guinea will be in remote areas. The building of infrastructure will be impractical. The use of modular infrastructure and modular processing plants will be a likely solution.

- *Warehousing/distribution.* Each large project takes care of supply procurement, warehousing, and distribution. A central warehousing/distribution network is feasible.

- *Grassroots exploration.* Much of the country can be considered as "virgin" for gold exploration due to the rough terrain and logistics. Although currently some 250 licenses are in force, many geologically favorable areas are still open to exploration.

- *Local business.* There will be opportunities for a range of local business, e.g., supermarkets, local farm produce distribution, and local technical contracts.

Solomon Islands

Currently, gold production is limited to alluvial mining by landowners using hand panning and crude sluicing. In 1989 a total of some 2,000 oz of gold was produced. A mining lease is now negotiated for the Gold Ridge deposit. Although Gold Ridge Mine will be a small mine by world standards, it will play a significant role in the economic development of

Solomon Islands. Currently, the mining sector contributes less than 1 percent of the country's export earnings. With the development of Gold Ridge in 1992, export earnings for gold for the year are expected to be about US$12 million. The mine, however, is expected to be short-lived with a mine life of about five years. Solomon Islands gold reserves are estimated to be some 1.3 million t of about 3.86 g/t Au, valued at some US$40 million at today's gold price. The announcement of the new mine will generate further exploration interest in the country, boosting exploration expenditure and increasing the chances of new gold discoveries. The country is currently considering new mines and a mineral bill, which retains the basic concept of state ownership of minerals but will change the regulations governing the acquisition of surface access rights for prospecting and mining.

Fiji

The Emperor Mine has been in production for 55 years, and geological reserves have been defined for another eight years. The mine continues to produce around 135,000 oz of gold per year (valued at around $50 million at current prices), which is not expected to decrease over the next five years. However, the mine is currently in the midst of a major industrial dispute. At Mt. Kasi, in Vanua Levu, results to date indicate a possibility of a small gold mine being developed. If the Mt. Kasi mine was developed, it is expected to be short-lived (five years) and to contribute about 16,000 oz of gold per year. In addition, should the price of copper remain high, there is a possibility of the Namosi copper prospect being developed. This will be a major mine development because the Namosi copper deposit ranks as a world class size deposit. Development costs would be in the US$1 billion range. Fiji maintains mining legislation that will continue to attract international mineral exploration activity.

Investment environment

Political fragility has been tested in the last three years in both Fiji and Papua New Guinea. Yet investment in the region's mineral sector has continued to grow because of the extremely high rate of potential returns and government support and active encouragement of foreign investment.

Togolo (1989) provides a valuable analysis of the lessons to be learned from the "Bougainville Crisis," which he described "as the most threatening event to national unity since independence, as well as being expensive in terms of lost government revenue and export earnings." Lessons appear to have been learned by investors, central governments, and landowners. Investors are now more cautious and are less likely to go ahead with projects that are marginal in terms of the economic rate of return on investment. In addition, more resources are devoted to risk avoidance strategies such as a more thorough analysis of traditional land ownership issues, options for landowner equity participation and employment, relationships with provincial and central government, environmental impact analysis issues, and sociocultural impact issues. There is now more of a recognition from both mining companies and governments that feasibility studies, negotiations, and mine development plans must focus on the local, rather than the national level, and must address issues of land, economic expectations, environmental impacts, revenue sharing, and mineral ownership. A major finding of the Private Sector Project was that the Pacific island countries need to formulate a national gold policy that is specifically tailored to its medium- and small-scale gold mines.

chapter 8

Creating business opportunities through privatization

This chapter provides an overview of the scope for privatization in the Pacific island countries. The emphasis of the Private Sector Project's research was on accelerating private sector growth in the Pacific islands through the implementation of privatization policies. This approach is a departure from the usual focus of privatization policy, which has been on reducing government expenditure rather than on creating private sector growth and business opportunities. This overview is based on the detailed research findings in McMaster (1990c).

The involvement of Pacific island governments and statutory authorities in economic activity has been all pervasive, particularly in the smaller countries such as Kiribati. State owned enterprises (SOEs) have commonly ranged from the usual public utilities to shipping and ship building, commodity marketing, agroprocessing, forestry, and fishing companies. Some governments have even owned and operated hotels (Tonga, Kiribati, Solomon Islands, and Western Samoa), breweries (Western Samoa), and trading companies and retail stores (Kiribati and Western Samoa). The high incidence of government involvement in economic activity in the Pacific island countries tends not to be based on ideology, although its origins can be traced to the colonial era. Governments often initially established enterprises because local entrepreneurs with the financial or managerial capacity were not available. However, this has usually ended up stifling entrepreneurial development, and there are numerous examples of SOEs that have continued to operate even when they could reasonably have been passed on to the private sector. Excellent examples of this that emerge from the Private Sector Project are Fiji's National Marketing Authority (NMA) and the former Tonga Commodities Board (TCB). Furthermore, government involvement in joint ventures with foreign investors has often arisen from a desire to play a "watch dog" role. Solomon Islands provides an example and reflects a general ambivalence among the Pacific island countries toward foreign investment.

Over the last decade there has been an increasing interest in privatization among Pacific island policymakers. This has been a period in which the SOEs experienced increasing financial losses, governments faced more difficult budgetary circumstances, and the island economies failed to grow at rates necessary to maintain living standards. In recent years privatization has also become high on the agenda of international agencies (ADB, World Bank, and IMF) and bilateral donors (USAID) in their policy dialogue with Pacific island governments. In some cases the introduction of privatization policies have even became a condition in loan negotiations (e.g., the ADB's agricultural program loan with Western Samoa and the World Bank's structural adjustment loan with Papua New Guinea).

Considerable research, consultancy, and technical assistance effort has already gone into privatization in the Pacific island countries. The last few years have seen, in varying degrees, this move toward an implementation phase. Thus there is now valuable practical experience available in implementing privatization programs in the somewhat unusual and sometimes difficult circumstances of the island countries. The current privatization activities and implementation experience in the individual countries are reviewed in McMaster (1990c).

Objectives of Privatization

The most commonly stated objectives of privatization policies are to:

Reduce the size of government. This objective is to relieve the financial and administrative burden of government. Generally, this has been the main justification for privatization and has been a leading factor in generating interest in privatization in the Pacific island countries.

Dispose of government businesses that produce private goods at a loss. This objective arises from the first objective above. Most Pacific island countries have established government-owned businesses to produce goods and services that normally would be the domain of the private sector, including a wide range of agricultural, fishing, agroprocessing, and commodity marketing enterprises, as well as transportation companies. Many of these enterprises have operated with substantial losses, and their continued operation requires substantial subsidies or other forms of protection. In some cases they are in direct competition with private sector firms that are operating profitably and have the capacity to increase their market share.

Form new business and accelerate economic growth to stimulate private sector growth. The transfer of selected public services to the private sector can create new business opportunities for local entrepreneurs and can be directed toward stimulating a faster rate of economic growth. The resulting entrepreneurial activity usually has some multiplier effects as new entrepreneurs use profits to finance further growth and diversity into new areas of business. This should be regarded as the prime objective for privatization in the Pacific island countries.

Reduce the cost of public services to the consumers. Research studies on the economic impact of privatizing government activities have found that in many cases substantial cost savings have resulted after privatization. These savings, if realized, could be passed on to consumers in the form of lower prices or user charges or by reducing taxes. Many government functions are performed in a noncompetitive environment, which can result in slackness and general inefficiency, misuse of government resources, or lack of responsiveness to consumer needs. However, efficiency benefits do not necessarily arise when privatization means converting a government monopoly to a private monopoly. This is an important consideration in the Pacific islands where the privatization of public utilities is being contemplated.

Develop a wider business ownership. In some island countries where only a small group of entrepreneurs exists, government may aim to expand business ownership areas by selling shares in government businesses. Employee buyout schemes can provide a useful mechanism for achieving this objective.

Generate revenue from the sale of unused or underutilized public assets. Government may wish to mobilize revenues through the sale of assets such as underutilized buildings, plant, and land. There are many examples in the Pacific islands of foreign aid providing equipment, such as fishing gear in Tonga, a cool storage building in Western Samoa, and ice making facilities in Fiji that could be more efficiently used by the private sector.

Overcome constraints to private sector activity by the withdrawal of inefficient government services. Situations exist where government has a monopoly in the provision of an essential business support service but performs the service poorly—the provision of inefficient postal services, the failure to provide adequate communication (telex and fax) services, and irregular and unreliable shipping and electricity services. The private sector should be able to compete with the government in the provision of these services or the government should withdraw entirely. An example identified in the Private Sector Project is in the operation of post-harvest treatment and quarantine facilities. Here government involvement has proved a major constraint to the development of significant horticultural export industries in the Pacific island countries.

Satisfy unmet needs for public service. The mobilization of community groups, non-government organization (NGO), and private firms provides services that traditionally have been the responsibility of government. Many examples show voluntary community groups having provided recreation facilities, libraries, community halls, street cleaning, fire protection, security patrols, refuse collection, tree planting, maintenance of playing areas and parklands, tree pruning, lawn mowing, cleaning of roadside gutters and drains, bus shelters, parking lot operations, and school bus transport. In addition, many NGOs provide social services, such as child day care, foster home care, group home care, adoption, institutional care for the sick, elderly, and incapacitated, rehabilitative services, family crisis centers, women's shelters, youth centers, sheltered workshops, retraining centers, family counseling, family planning, child protection, homemaker services, and legal aid for the poor. In the Pacific island countries, a decade or so ago, it was common for village communities to provide food and other support services to boarding schools. Now such responsibilities tend to be assigned to governments. A reversal of such trends would be a fruitful target of any privatization program.

Restructure the economy. One of the fundamental objectives of privatization is to achieve a restructuring of the economy. Privatization can be used as a measure to reduce the size of ailing sectors of the economy that have been supported by government ownership of enterprises but that have lost any comparative advantage they had in world trade.

Scope for Privatization in the Pacific Island Countries

Limited interest has been expressed regarding the privatization of public utilities; however, this interest mainly takes the form of rationalization and commercialization of these enterprises or partial privatization through management contracts and joint ventures with foreign companies that have access to substantial technical expertise and experience. Less interest has been expressed in the greater use of contracting out government services as a method of stimulating the formation of new business enterprises for local entrepreneurs searching for feasible business opportunities. A worldwide trend exists for the greater use of contracting out of government services, and substantial cost savings have been reported in both developed and developing countries. Contracting out is by far the most widely used form of privatization and the one that has the greatest scope in the Pacific island countries.

Basic Methods of Privatization and Their Scope in the Islands

1. The outright sale of SOEs to the private sector

To date, privatization in the Pacific island countries has focused mainly on the divestment of unprofitable business enterprises that produce private goods, such as government shipping companies, timber mills, agroprocessing ventures, plantations, and hotels. Western Samoa has probably taken the lead in this respect.

However, privatization in the sense of straight out selling off larger SOEs to the private sector is often not practical in the island countries because the local entrepreneurs with cash resources and experience are simply not available. Capital markets are underdeveloped. Only Fiji and Papua New Guinea have stock exchanges, and even here these can be regarded as only share "trading posts." Furthermore, there can be a policy conflict between the sale of an SOE to the private sector and the objective of greater indigenous economic control and indigenous entrepreneurial development. The latter represents an underlying constraint to the implementation of privatization policy in Fiji. Consequently, commercialization as a strategy in the Pacific island countries can often be more appropriate than privatization.

2. Commercialization to improve the performance of public utilities

Commercialization is particularly well suited for the larger statutory type of public utility service. This usually takes the form of commercially rationalizing these enterprises or partial privatization through management contracts and joint ventures with foreign companies that have access to substantial technical expertise and experience. An excellent example of commercialization of a public utility in the region is the Fiji government program wherein the post and telecommunications sector has been converted into a corporation. Basically, what was previously the government Post and Telecommunications Department is attempting to operate in the same way as the private sector with a focus on profit and cost recovery, loss minimization, cost analysis, demand analysis, etc., and with more flexible use of human resources. This is being undertaken with technical assistance from the World Bank. In this case complete privatization would not have been feasible due to the lack of politically acceptable local capital.

3. Commercialization of state-owned enterprises

Many state-owned enterprises in the Pacific islands are in urgent need of management improvement programs and staff development, as well as the full commercialization of their policies systems and procedures. Commercialization is a process of introducing the commercial management practices that are common in well-managed, large private companies to private sector organizations. It emphasizes management by objectives and is result oriented. Performance is regularly monitored, and a cost analysis is undertaken of all aspects of the production and operation of the enterprises. The first step usually is a comprehensive audit of the organization—objectives, organizational structures, lines of authority, staff utilization, operating systems, unit costs of production, levels of client needs, etc. It involves identifying the strengths and weakness of the organization and the opportunities and threats posed by its operating environment. The main findings of the management and organization audit provide a platform for the development of a comprehensive corporate planning system.

The Papua New Guinea Government has had some success in implementing commercialization policies, and this experience provide some useful lessons for other Pacific island countries. In 1983 the government introduced a new Public Enterprise Policy for four main institutions known as the commercial statutory authorities (CSA). The CSAs were the Electricity Commission, Air Nuigini, the Post and Telecommunications Corporation, and the Harbours Board. The key elements of the package, which would be applicable to the island countries, are:

Objectives. The government announced that the primary objective of the authorities is to become commercial profit-making organizations and that the pursuit of non-commercial objectives was no longer to be used as an excuse for poor financial performance.

Investment criteria and subsidies. The authorities should only undertake new investment projects for which they expect to earn a specified real internal rate of return. Should any project fail this rate of return test but is desirable for other political or social reasons, the authority should make a submission to the cabinet that indicates the level of subsidy necessary to make the project viable. If the cabinet approves the project, an explicit subsidy is paid by government to the authority.

Price control. The need to generate profit requires effective price tariff systems that eliminate hidden subsidies and cross-subsidies. Prices have to be set to earn an accounting rate of return on existing assets specified in the range of 16 to 22 percent.

Taxes and duties. The CSAs are fully liable for the payment of corporate income tax, customs, duties, and import levies. This measure was introduced to place CSAs in the same situation as other commercial enterprises, thus reducing distortions in the allocation of resources between the public and private sectors.

Dividends. CSAs are expected to pay regular dividends of up to 50 percent of after-tax profits.

On-lending aid loan and grant funds. Any foreign aid grants or concessional loans that are directed to CSAs to finance their projects are on-lent by the government on standard, near commercial terms. In this way government receives the grant element in foreign aid rather than the CSAs.

Corporate plans. The CSAs are required to submit rolling five-year corporate plans to the cabinet that comply with key financial parameters set by government.

Contract approval. The limit on CSA contracts requiring the approval of the Minister of Finance was raised from K$100,000 to K$300,000.

Hiring and firing of employees. Prior to the 1983 package the personnel functions of CSAs were controlled by the Public Service Commission. The reforms gave CSAs the authority to hire and fire their own staff, thus giving them greater flexibility to effectively manage their use of human resources.

Government board representation. The Department of Finance and the National Planning Office were given ex-officio membership on all CSA Boards.

Management reviews. The government has instituted a system of regular five-year management reviews to be conducted by independent management consultants to assess the overall performance of CSAs. This review process is also designed to check the pricing policies of CSAs to ensure that they are not exploiting their monopoly power.

4. Contracting out of government activities

Contracting out is by far the most widely used form of privatization and probably the most appropriate for the Pacific island countries, particularly the smaller countries. Contracting out government services has an important role to play in situations where there are limited opportunities for the formation of small businesses with low levels of capital requirement and relatively simple technology. Such a situation is demonstrated in the island countries by the lack of viable small business projects reported by commercial banks and the development finance institutions. Evidence points to an excessive entry of new entrepreneurs into business sectors that already suffer from overcrowding, such as small retail stores in Tarawa, Kiribati, and taxis in Suva, Fiji.

The popularity of contracting out government activity stems in part from the existence of legislative guidelines for the procurement of goods and services and the greater control that the government retains over a service under this form of privatization. Moreover, substantial cost savings have been reported in both developed and developing countries through the contracting out of government services. The most obvious areas in the island countries amenable to this type of privatization would include a range of activities undertaken by the Public Works Departments and municipal councils. These include building and road maintenance, garbage collection, and the maintenance of parks, gardens, and the compounds of government buildings.

5. Management contracts

This is a particularly suitable form of privatization for the Pacific island countries that wish to improve the performance of given debt-owned enterprises yet still leave the assets under government ownership. This technique is valuable in a situation where the government entity has a natural monopoly and supplies essential services such as electricity, postal and telephone service, water supply, sewage treatment works, landfill garbage disposal sites, parks, and airports. Under this technique the management functions of the enterprise are contracted to a firm that usually has a track record of quality management as well as technical expertise. The contractor assumes responsibility to manage the enterprise and is given authority and operational control powers. The government continues to bear full responsibility for the commercial risk and the provision of working capital, as well as debt financing. Unlike a lease, the government receives any generated profits and absorbs any losses. This technique is often a very effective means of acquiring highly skilled management resources that may not be available from the public sector. The management contract usually has built-in performance and incentive payment schemes as part of the overall compensation package, which provides a strong incentive for the management company to control costs and fully commercialize the operations of the enterprise.

A comprehensive list of public services that could be considered for contracting out would include:

Public works and physical environment

- Solid waste collection (residential and commercial),
- Wastewater and sewerage treatment.

Transportation

- Road/street maintenance and repair,
- Maintenance of government vehicles and plants,
- Construction of new urban subdivision and farm access roads.

Parks and recreation/cultural and sporting facilities

- Maintenance of recreation facilities,
- Operation of sporting complexes,
- Park maintenance.

General municipal services

- Buildings and ground maintenance,
- Street cleaning and grass cutting,
- Legal services,
- Urban planning services,
- Ambulance services,
- Fire prevention services.

Not all these areas would be suitable for contracting out in all Pacific island countries. However, the list gives an indication of what might be feasible with creative thinking and good planning.

To date the management contracts have found their widest application in the tourist and hotel industries in the region. Management contracts often can be used as an intermediate solution for improving the performance of ailing state-owned enterprise that in the long term is listed for privatization of ownership. Using this approach, government is likely to be able to sell the entity at a much higher price than it would have received prior to a successful management contract period. This approach also can be used as a tool for commercializing the management practices of a moribund SOE.

6. Other commonly used techniques for privatization

These include the public sale of shares in SOEs; the private sale of shares in SOEs; the sale of complete parts of the whole enterprise (partial privatization); the sale of a portion of the whole operation (partial privatization); the sale of a government enterprise to the work force (management/ employee buyout); the reorganization of a SOE into several component parts (fragmentation); the leasing of government enterprise facilities; the use of management contractors; the sale of government assets, buildings, plants, and equipment; the deregulation of government monopoly; the complete withdrawal of the provision of a government service; franchises; grants; vouchers; the mobilization of an NGO to take over government service; and self-service.

A summary of privatization options

The following table summarizes the main areas of government activity that offer scope to privatization and the methods that are likely to be the most suitable.

Type of Authority	Method of Privatization
Privatization of public utilities:	
Electricity Authority	Management contracts
Water Authority	Restructuring and commercialization
Post and Telecommunications	Joint ventures with foreign
Department	companies with technical expertise
Civil Aviation Authority	Contracting out
Government enterprises that produce "private goods" and services:	
Hotels, plantations	Sale of the entity to local private firms, management contracts
Factories and fishing companies	Management contracts, employee buyouts, leases
General support services:	
Government printing	Contracting out
Maintenance of government buildings, quarters, schools, and hospitals	Contracting out
Maintenance of government vehicles, plants, and equipment	Contracting out
Office cleaning services	Contracting out
Public works and infrastructure construction:	
Construction of new roads, bridges, airports, ports, and buildings	Contracting out
Industrial estate construction	Contracting out
Rural and urban infrastructure development	Contracting out

Services provided directly to the public and industry:

Agriculture extension services	Transfer responsibility to private sector, industry association
Agricultural marketing services	Transfer responsibility to private sector, industry association
Agricultural fumigation services	Transfer responsibility to private sector, industry association
Fisheries extension services	Provide grant to industry association if warranted; greater use of charges and fees for service

Health and human services:

Hospital management, nursing homes,	Management contracts
welfare services	Contracting out

Planning for Privatization

The preparation and planning for privatization is a complex process requiring a range of specialized, professional skills, some of which are not readily available in the Pacific island countries. An important lesson that emerges from the worldwide experience with the implementation of a privatization program is the value of comprehensive detailed analysis and planning. Because privatization is not a simple solution, detailed planning needs to occur from the outset. An indication of the complexity of the privatization planning process can be seen in the stages of the implementation process shown below:

1. Preparing for privatization.

    - Develop and define privatization policies;

    - Assess opportunities, threats, and scope for privatization;

    - Create private sector interest;

    - Develop program guidelines and strategies.

2. Detailed planning on selected government state-owned enterprises and activities targeted for privatization.

    - Enterprise diagnostic analysis,

    - Audit of legal obligations and requirements,

    - Financial restructuring,

    - Review of situation of the enterprise workforce,

    - Determine future ownership options.

3. Implementation

- Undertake legal requirements for the sale of the enterprise, or the establishment of shares, franchise agreements, management contracts;

- Estimate the market value of the entity or services to be performed;

- Issue conditions for a transfer to the private sector;

- Evaluate proposals against criteria and select a successful bidder;

- Negotiate with the bidder and execute a legal transfer;

- Announce the transfer arrangements and educate the public on the implications for consumers.

4. Monitoring and evaluation

- Develop performance appraisal systems;

- Establish a database to enable the comparison of quality, service, and efficiency performance;

- Compare the performance data against targets, standards, and milestones, and identify shortfalls and possible corrective measures;

- Modify and adjust the program and regulations in light of the findings on the monitoring and evaluation program.

Comprehensive country privatization strategy studies should be undertaken in each island country prior to governments embarking on privatization programs. A start has already been made with privatization studies completed for Western Samoa, Solomon Islands, and Kiribati.

Role of International Agencies and Aid Donors in the Privatization Process

Technical assistance from the international agencies and aid donors is required for the planning and implementation of privatization programs in the Pacific island countries.

The main areas in need of professional technical assistance services are:

- Preparation of national privatization strategies and sectorial studies,

- Preparation of guidelines and procedures manuals,

- Preparation of manuals on contract administration,

- Preparation of detailed privatization plans for selected SOEs,

- Preparation of training manuals on privatization,

- Professional assistance with the implementation phase,

- Assistance with the establishment of monitoring and evaluation systems,

- Assistance with the establishment of public enterprise management units,

- Support for training and the development of management education programs to support privatization.

The ADB, the World Bank, and USAID have shown enthusiasm for playing a lead role in promoting privatization in the Pacific island countries. The ADB has financed privatization identification studies in Western Samoa and Solomon Islands and industry specific studies in Fiji and is to provide technical assistance to Tonga for the privatization of the TCB. The World Bank currently is financing technical assistance to assist with the commercialization of Fiji's Post and Telecommunications Department and the Housing Authority. The World Bank is also actively involved in Papua New Guinea's privatization and commercialization program. USAID has financed a major regional conference on privatization and has undertaken a study on privatization in Kiribati. However, much more is required from the international agencies and donors.

Apart from providing technical and financial assistance the international agencies have a policy dialogue role to play in promoting the case for privatization and the need to simultaneously introduce appropriate deregulation measures to promote competition and productivity improvement in the private sector. Both the ADB and the World Bank have been prepared to use progress in privatization as a condition in negotiating loan programs in the region. The ADB's Agricultural Sector Loan to Western Samoa is an example. Such conditionality can prove important in maintaining the necessary long-term political commitment to privatization programs.

Apart from specific privatization programs, aid donors could also play an expanded role in projects to strengthen the private sector and by so doing make privatization efforts more effective. The Private Sector Project has identified five possible types of such projects that could be financed by aid donors:

1. *Training programs.* These are needed to strengthen private sector capacity in the areas of entrepreneurial development, small business management, commercialization strategies, corporate planning, export market development, international marketing, marketing for small businesses, new product development systems, product quality control systems, cost analysis and financial planning, production plant layout, human resource management, and productivity improvement systems.

2. *Assistance with appropriate technology transfer and application.* This could include:

   • The secondment of business experts (retired executives) to local firms;

   • Support for the establishment of technology centers to provide technical assistance to firms on production technology, productivity improvement, new product development systems, licensing of technology, plant layout, storage and materials handling systems, and stock control systems;

   • Support for the establishment of technology parks, innovation centers, and research and development activities.

3. *Support for business development.* This would usually involve providing consulting services to small businesses. These services are known by a variety of names, such as small business centers and business development units. They provide small firms with assistance and training in financial management and accounting; business management practices; and marketing, sales, promotion, and advertising advice.

4. *Financing for privatization.* This is usually via the provision of grant funds to the development banks for this purpose.

5. *Support for infrastructure development.* Aid donors have been heavily involved in financing public sector infrastructure development such as roads, ports, and airports, all of which are essential for efficient private sector operation. Donors also could play a more direct role in funding the development of industrial estates and factory buildings for rent to the private sector by government. These industrial estates could be developed as nursery factory schemes or incubator centers where new entrepreneurs receive a high level of support services from a central office at the industrial estate. Under these systems the small firms in the industrial

estate receive assistance with product quality testing, marketing, procurement of supplies, access to finance, and production planning.

Financing Privatization

This section discusses some of the financing techniques that can be applied to compensate for the weaknesses of the local financial markets in the Pacific island countries. However, it is of note that the experience, to date, with privatization in the island countries indicates that access to finance has not been the major constraint. A greater obstacle to privatization typically has been the lack of local entrepreneurs with the necessary background and business experience.

The public offering of shares in government-owned enterprises is difficult due to the absence of organized share markets and the lack of local investors with cash savings for the purchase of shares. The major sources of finance for privatization are therefore most likely to come from:

- Development finance institutions,
- Commercial banks,
- Institutional investors,
- Provident funds,
- Established local entrepreneurs with funds to invest, or
- Foreign investor funds.

Development banks

Privatization programs that provide new opportunities for entrepreneurs for establishing businesses to undertake contract work for government could lead to an increased demand for funds from the South Pacific Development Bank (SPDB). In addition, established companies with sound track records will likely need development bank financing to buy government business enterprises that are producing private goods or services.

Because many government-owned companies have had a history of poor performance, it is important for development banks to carefully assess financing proposals for the acquisition of government privatization projects. The management and technical skills of the entrepreneur is an important factor in assessing the capacity of the entrepreneur to convert the business into a profitable operation.

A representative from a development bank should be included on the planning team when the financing of privatization proposals is being developed; this would ensure that development banks have a thorough understanding of the privatization program and their role in financing projects.

Institutional investors

Measures could be taken by the governments of some Pacific island countries to modify the laws governing national provident funds, pension funds, and insurance companies to allow them to invest their financial resources in the shares of selected government enterprises targeted for partial or complete privatization. Institutional investors are likely to be particularly attracted to the purchase of equity shares in secure public utilities that operate in a natural monopoly environment.

Tax incentives

Tax incentives are another policy measure that could be applied to encourage investors to buy equity in public enterprises that are participating in a national privatization program. For example, tax concessions might include a reduction in the taxable income of investors by a specified percent of the value of shares purchased in government enterprises as well as tax free dividends on selected shares held in companies included in the privatization program. However, the costs and benefits of such a measure must be carefully assessed in terms of its budgeting cost in tax revenue forgone.

chapter 9

An integrated program for private sector development

Drawing on the major recommendations of the various studies of the Private Sector Project, McMaster (1990a) presents an integrated set of programs and projects designed to accelerate private sector development. This chapter summarizes this program and makes specific recommendations for its implementation.

An integrated approach to private sector development is recommended because it allows for consistency of government policies and support programs and projects. In particular, it will facilitate achieving maximum benefits from available aid funds and allow for implementation and follow-through.

It is recommended that each Pacific island country should implement an integrated private sector development program based on a comprehensive private sector development plan. The main components of such a program are summarized in this chapter. Indicative costings and program implementation are also discussed.

The international agencies and aid donors are seen to play a crucial role in implementing this program. The main components identified will require expert technical assistance and efficient organization and financing, which realistically could be obtained only through assistance from the international agencies and donors. The international agencies have recently expressed the intention to provide greater assistance to private sector development and have indicated their willingness to allocate a much higher proportion of their assistance to projects that directly promote private sector growth. However, to date, implementation has been slow to materialize. The proposals presented here are seen as a practical way of converting these good intentions into concrete programs of action. The main ways are examined in which the international agencies could assist private sector development in a coherent integrated fashion.

Provision of Finance Facilities to the Private Sector

Strengthening the development banks

Training was identified as the need most crucial to the effective operation of the South Pacific Development Bank (SPDB). Training should be conducted at three equally important levels: (1) senior management, (2) technical bank officers, and (3) borrowers—perhaps the most crucial level so as to instill in clients an understanding of the responsibilities and obligations resulting from the granting of credit. In many respects these requirements represent a consolidation and a focusing of the ongoing efforts of the ADB.

Extension services are necessary to educate customers to introduce new husbandry practices, but they can be minimized if effective management is clearly demonstrated through training programs.

Research and development must be an important function of the SPDBs in identifying new lending opportunities that support national economic objectives. Accordingly, adequate resources should be allocated to this function.

Smallholders are perhaps the most important SPDB clients. Their needs, ambitions, and problems should be identified and addressed.

Commitment on the part of borrowers is an essential prerequisite to success. Thus equity and realistic security should be an important component of all loans.

Regional cooperation should be fostered between the SPDBs and multilateral institutions, particularly the ADB's South Pacific Regional Office (SPRO). A corporate body should be established to link all SPDBs and to liaise with the SPRO in training, research and development, loan management, and other issues affecting the efficient operation of the SPDBs.

These recommendations could be formulated into a major regional project for the advancement of the SPDBs. The international agencies and particularly the ADB could play a leading role in such a project focused on institutional strengthening and staff development and training.

Although the idea of a regional financial institution acting either as a bank or a source of equity finance for private sector projects is no longer tenable, there is a pressing need for a regional facility, perhaps along the lines of the Caribbean Project Development Facility (CPDF), that could:

- Provide a bridge between the SPDBs and the international development finance agencies,
- Assist in the formulation of major prospects and the identification of funding for their implementation,
- Develop training programs and materials for courses designed for SPDB staff and clients,
- Identify professional staff for technically complex appraisal and implementation projects,
- Support research and development units in the identification and evaluation of new lending and development opportunities.

It is recommended that such a facility be developed through the strengthening of the existing Association of Development Finance Institutions of the Pacific (ADFIP). The 1990 Port Vila annual meeting of ADFIP considered these proposals and made the following recommendations to their governments and to the ADB:

- That there is a need to establish a South Pacific Development Banks facility, similar to the CPDF, such a regional institution to be located in one of the existing Development Banks.

That the proposed SPDB facility should have the following broad objectives:

- To work closely with individual SPDBs in both project preparation and finance identification. The facility would be particularly useful to small banks in conducting negotiations with multilateral agencies or corporations in areas where they would have limited expertise, particularly in acquiring access to equity funds.
- To provide a coordinating role both in the identification of financing and in the organization of training programs. Courses appropriate to needs could be developed or identified and materials prepared to provide a continuing basis for training. A valuable role for a regional facility could be in the design and production of training materials for borrowers and the development of programs to be used in media-oriented publicity of SPDB activities.
- To provide a clearing house for new ideas, problem solving, and cooperation in both regional and national development.
- A professional staff of, say, three (manager, training officer, and research officer) is envisaged. They would be located at one of the existing development banks.

Establishment of credit guaranteed schemes

The Private Sector Project recommends that those Pacific island countries that do not have a credit guarantee scheme—designed to encourage the commercial banks to lend a higher proportion of their funds to the small business sector—should establish such a scheme as a matter of priority. In this respect the proposal, under consideration by the ADB for Vanuatu, to create a development fund from which both the development bank and commercial banks can borrow should be monitored with the view to replicate elsewhere.

Development of venture capital schemes

It is recommended that the Pacific island governments should consider measures to stimulate the development of venture capital industries. The international agencies could provide both technical and financial assistance to support this development. In addition, advantages could be gained from adopting a regional approach to venture capital development. Such a scheme could provide the individual SPDBs with long-term loans for on-lending to private venture capital firms. In addition, the ADB could provide expert technical assistance to support the development of venture capital markets in activities such as staff development and specialized training.

Expansion and improved promotion of the joint venture schemes

The Australian Joint Venture Scheme and the New Zealand Pacific Islands Industrial Development Scheme provide a sound approach to stimulating private sector development; however, they have been relatively underused and have not achieved their full potential as instruments for stimulating new joint venture businesses. Both schemes have been recently reviewed and modified so that they are more attractive and useful to entrepreneurs. It does appear that these schemes have not been widely advertised to the business community and that an effective promotional campaign is now needed to raise the level of awareness of the considerable benefits offered by these schemes. In addition, the annual budget allocations to these schemes should be progressively increased over the next few years so that they can play a larger role in channeling resources directly to financing private sector growth.

Introduction of a banking and finance degree program

The Private Sector Project recommends that an undergraduate degree program in Banking and Finance should be established at the University of the South Pacific (USP) under the direction of the Economics Department.

This degree program should be specifically designed to meet the staffing needs of the banking, finance, and insurance sectors of the Pacific island countries. The financial sector's demand for such graduates over the next decade is of sufficient size to justify the development of a new professional degree program in development finance.

Export Market Development and National Marketing Support Services

The building of a South Pacific Regional Trade Commission network

A central recommendation of the Private Sector Project is for the building of a South Pacific Regional Trade Commission (SPRETCO) network. The study of the export marketing activities and current support agencies found that most Pacific island countries will never be able to afford their own overseas trade commissions. Considerable economic benefits could be gained through the development of a network of regional trade commission offices, building on the success of the South Pacific Trade Commission (SPTC) in Sydney and the recently established South Pacific Trade Office (SPTO) in Auckland. The concept is to build on parts of the network that are already in place.

Rather than create another regional institution, SPRETCO would be a rationalization and development of existing services. It is recommended that SPRETCO be based in the Trade Division of the Forum Secretariat, which is best qualified to act as a central reference point for trade promotion activities and to coordinate an expanded network of trade commission offices. The establishment of regional trade commission offices in the markets of importance to exporters that are currently not adequately covered by the existing range of agencies is recommended. The Private Sector Project recommends the establishment of trade commissions in Tokyo, Los Angeles, Vancouver, Hong Kong, and Brussels as part of the SPRETCO network. It is hoped that the Los Angeles link will develop under the USAID's Market Access and Regional Competitiveness (MARC) project.

These new SPRETCO trade offices could be developed by using principles and funding mechanisms similar to those in the successful models of SPTC and SPTO. These principles and mechanisms are as follows:

- Funding for the establishment and operating costs of the SPRETCO trade commission would be the responsibility of the host government as a South Pacific regionally aid funded project.

- The trade commission should be staffed by a mixture of expertise from the host country and the Pacific island countries.

- A minimum of bureaucratic red tape and a maximum accessibility for Pacific island exporters should be the distinguishing characteristics of these offices.

The establishment of the new proposed regional trade offices is in keeping with the trend toward the support of regional programs rather than bilateral ones and would assist aid donors that wish to raise the percentage of aid to Pacific island countries in their global aid program.

The formation of SPRETCO could achieve the following advantages:

- Opportunity for regional coordination in trade and investment development.

- Economies of scale and cost efficiency in the provision of overseas trade services.

- Opportunity to consolidate produce at a central point to achieve bulk consolidation and transportation economies.

- Capability of providing a regional approach to marketing of the region's fresh produce in Japan and other new markets.

- Capability to provide a strong continuous promotional program for island exports in important overseas markets.

- Provision of regional trade data bank and information services.

- Participation in trade fairs and expositions of relevance to island exporters.

- Cost-effective provision of regional investment promotion activities.

- Cost-efficient provision of market research including the evaluation of foreign market potential for the selected island products.

- Provision of a focus for the establishment and operation of a computerized regional trade data bank and information service.

- Provision of office services and marketing assistance to visiting island exporters.

Institutional strengthening of export marketing agencies

Several Private Sector Project studies recommended that the Pacific island countries need to substantially strengthen their national trade and investment promotion institutions. The Fiji Trade and Investment Board (FTIB) provides a sound model for other Pacific island countries to emulate.

International agencies could play a valuable role in organizing the design and funding of institutional strengthening projects to develop national trade and investment promotion agencies. In most cases, international agencies could provide national trade and investment agencies with the following forms of technical assistance:

- Preparation of an institutional development plan including organizational design, staff development plans, training needs analysis, and systems design.

- Expert assistance with the production of investment promotional materials such as films, videos, booklets, and promotional kits.

- Expert assistance with the development of international marketing strategies, marketing research, and analysis of the export potential of specific markets.

- Design and preparation of training programs for private sector managers on export development processes and requirements.

- Professional assistance with the implementation of staff training and development programs in the more complex areas of trade promotion and investment analysis.

- Upgrading of the hardware and software of information systems and the provision of specialized training in marketing information systems, the maintenance and updating of databases, and management information systems.

Introduction of an export market development scheme in each Pacific island country

It is recommended that those Pacific island countries that wish to promote non-traditional exports to new markets should consider the introduction of an Export Market Development Scheme, which is similar to the scheme operating very successfully in Singapore. The aim of this type of scheme is to provide firms with a cash grant to assist them in paying for the costs associated with export market development. Grants could be given to firms to finance up to a given percentage of eligible costs incurred for activities such as:

- Investigating new export markets and the costs of market research studies.

- Redesigning products and packaging to suit the special needs of export markets.

- Setting up overseas offices, funding the cost of identifying agents, and developing distribution systems and networks.

- Visiting overseas markets and participating in overseas trade fairs, conventions, and trade missions.

- Providing promotional materials to support export marketing, production of samples, catalogs, displays, videos, promotional films, and other promotional material.

- Providing or purchasing professional services to assist with export development, training of staff in export procedures, and export marketing.

However, international experience has shown that such schemes need to be well designed and closely monitored if they are to be successful.

Regional training program on export marketing procedures and techniques

This regional training program involves the development of high quality training courses for private entrepreneurs on the procedures and techniques of export market development. The international agencies could provide financial support to the Trade Division of the Forum Secretariat to conduct such training programs and to train the trainers from the Pacific island countries.

Export credit financing scheme

The introduction of an export credit financing scheme in the island countries that do not have such a scheme and the revision of some existing schemes to make them more effective are recommended.

Investment promotion activities

The review of foreign investment promotion found that the FTIB is the most professional investment promotion agency of the Pacific island countries. It provides potential investors with a comprehensive range of services and serves as a "one stop shop," which provides information, undertakes feasibility studies, and identifies local and overseas joint venture partners. The FTIB has been active in organizing investment seminars and trade fairs, providing trade publicity for Fiji exports, and producing investment handbooks and promotional material. It serves as the focal point for applications for approval of new investment projects and industry concessions.

It is recommended that there be institutional strengthening of the agencies involved in the administration of foreign and local investment promotion and approval, business licensing, fiscal incentives, and new business feasibility studies. It is also recommended that the development of a "one stop shop" agency approach is essential if services to clients are to be improved. Priority should be given to targeting former Pacific island nationals living in Australia, New Zealand, and North America, as investors in small to medium sized businesses. For Polynesia in particular this group represents a rich source of potential investment funds and entrepreneurial capability.

Enterprise Support Organizations (ESOs) and Entrepreneurial Development

The establishment of a regional network of Small Business Centers (SBCs)

A regional network of SBCs should be established. The network should consist of a coordinating regional SBC (RSBC) and a network of autonomous (but cooperating) national SBCs.

The principal tasks of the RSBC will be to:

- Promote and facilitate SBC development at the national level.
- Facilitate regional cooperation in small business development.
- Coordinate those resources and services that can be effectively developed and used on a regional basis.
- Provide training programs for staff of national SBCs.
- Inform governments and international agencies of the appropriate legislative and macroeconomic measures required for the facilitation of small business development.

The principal purpose of national SBCs will be to provide entrepreneurs and small business operators with easy access to a comprehensive range of development resources and services. To fulfill this purpose the SBCs will have to perform the following kinds of tasks:

- Provide a first contact point for entrepreneurs and small businesspeople seeking assistance.
- Maintain a library of self-instructional materials.
- Identify and maintain a register of existing enterprise support services and other sources of assistance.
- Provide appropriate information, advisory, consulting, and training services.

- Provide mobile advisers who can take the services of the SBC into remote areas.

- Identify gaps in existing services and develop strategies to fill them.

- Multiply the impact of the SBC by identifying potential small business trainers and development workers and by training them in the skills required to offer assistance to entrepreneurs and small businesses—target audiences for such training would include the staff of non-government organizations (NGOs), fieldworkers of organizations like the YMCA, government fieldworkers, community groups, associations, service clubs, loan officers of banks, and professionals and technical experts who interact with small businesses.

- Solicit secondments from the private and public sectors as well as volunteers prepared to donate time for counseling and working with developing entrepreneurs.

- Provide integrated development packages geared to the needs of significant target groups and industrial sectors.

A role for USP and its extension network

To facilitate the cost-effective establishment of the network, the RSBC and the national SBCs should seek access to the extension infrastructure of the USP on a cost-sharing basis. This procedure would greatly facilitate communication between the SBCs of the region and enable them to take advantage of the substantial training and educational resources available in the institutes and schools of USP.

In many countries the national SBC could be located at or near the local Extension Center of USP, enabling the SBC to share the communications, library, classroom, and office facilities of the Extension Center.

Other educational institutions in the region, such as Solomon Islands College of Higher Education, are also making valuable contributions to business development and could offer valuable assistance to the SBCs.

Private/public/NGO partnership

To ensure that the SBCs make effective use of local resources, each center should be operated as a partnership between private, public, and voluntary sectors. Each SBC should be incorporated as a non-profit association or community development corporation, with individual and corporate (institutional) members who participate actively in setting its objectives, monitoring its performance, and evaluating its success.

Integrated development packages

A principal function of the SBCs will be to develop integrated packages geared to the development needs of specific target groups and industrial sectors. These packages typically comprise the following elements: (1) relevant information, (2) appropriate education and training, (3) advisory and consulting services, and (4) finance. Integrated programs can be designed for specific industrial sectors (e.g., machine repair workshops, agribusiness, and tourism), or they may be aimed at specific target groups (e.g., women, young people, technical school graduates, and communities with severe economic problems). Examples of such development packages already successfully operating in the region, and reviewed by the Private Sector Project, are the Plantation Support Association, the Small Mechanics Workshop Programme in Solomon Islands, and the highly successful Stret Pasin Stoa (trade store) Scheme of Papua New Guinea. There is considerable scope for replicating this experience elsewhere in the region.

A priority sector for the implementation of an integrated development program is the tourism industry. It is recommended that a Tourism Support Program be developed to foster the growth of locally owned tourism businesses. Such a program could be delivered through a Tourism Support Association (TSA) modeled on Vanuatu's Plantation Support Association (PSA) and acting as a voluntary chain to support the development of a network of village-based bed and breakfast accommodations.

A priority target group to assist in business development would be unemployed young people. An integrated development package should include assistance in the following areas:

- Idea generation.
- Training in market research and business plan development.
- Appropriate technical training.
- A "Starter Pack" on operating a business.
- Basic start-up resources.
- Continuing back-up and support.

Implementation

A suggested approach to getting started is as follows. Clearly, this approach will have to be adapted to match available resources, as well as the priorities identified by the SBCs in individual countries. The following steps are in approximate chronological order.

1. Regional Small Business Center (RSBC)

The RSBC will initially be located in Suva to have easy access to the resources of USP's main campus and the head office and communications facilities of the USP Extension Services. Initial catalyst roles could be played by appropriate personnel from USP (e.g., Continuing Education staff, Institute of Social and Administrative Studies, Coordinator of Business Studies, and/or head of Management). As the network develops, the USP staff will take a less central role in its operation. The initial basic staffing should consist of one director and support staff.

2. National Steering Committee (NSC)

An NSC will be set up in each country. It will consist of representatives from private, public, and voluntary sectors and will be chaired initially by the local USP center director. The NSCs will advise the regional director on appropriate groups to work with in each country—particularly those groups that are already performing some functions of an SBC.

3. Local SBCs

Funding will be solicited to set up and staff new organizations, consisting initially of the director, support staff, drop-in extension center service, and basic resources. Each SBC will be located, where possible, at or near the local USP Center. In some cases, an existing organization will be designated as the national SBC, on the condition that it is prepared to establish and work with a multi-sectorial advisory committee to oversee and contribute to its activities.

4. RSBC training for personnel of SBCs

The RSBC will also identify training and other resource materials that can be easily tailored to the needs of local SBCs.

5. SBCs' open drop-in advisory and referral service

In addition to providing a sounding board for entrepreneurs, the SBCs will offer consulting support and complementary skills to entrepreneurs and new ventures. The SBCs will maintain a register of enterprise support services and resources available elsewhere in the community and will make referrals as appropriate. Traveling consultants will visit new firms and periodic clinics in outlying districts. To assist the SBC staff in these tasks, the center will solicit secondments from established firms, as well as volunteers such as service club members, retired executives, and members from professional associations.

6. SBCs' in-country (or sub-regional) training programs

This program will include training of trainers for the volunteers and part-time resource people working for the SBC and other ESOs, a workshop to create entrepreneurial networks, and a workshop to identify promising entrepreneurs for more intensive programs. The SBC will also establish a library of learning resources.

7. Identification of priority industrial sectors and target groups

Initial research programs and database creation will focus on priority industrial sectors. The aim will be to produce usable market data and how-to packages geared to the needs of specific industries. These materials can provide the basis for establishing the integrated development programs mentioned in the next step.

8. SBCs' integrated development programs for specific sectors and groups

In effect, these programs provide entrepreneurs with an apprenticeship program, providing industry-specific information, training, consulting services, and access to finance and other resources. Each of these programs will probably be conducted by a separate spin-off organization like a TSA (a voluntary chain for tourism businesses) or Instant Muscle (a quasi-franchise organization to help young people start businesses).

9. Inclusion of business studies material in educational programs at all levels

Such business studies curricula should emphasize action learning or learning by doing. Primary school children can operate a school mini-shop. Groups of high school students can run their own short-term income generating projects in competition with one another. Technical students can be encouraged to consider the option of self-employment after graduation. A graduate enterprise scheme can stimulate the entrepreneurial talents of students in tertiary institutions.

10. Evaluation of the SBC network

An important task of the various steering committees will be to evaluate the performance of each SBC and the RSBC at least once a year. In addition to more subjective criteria, quantitative criteria (costs per business started or costs per job created in small businesses) should be devised to enable the steering committees to measure the relative performance of the different SBCs and compare their performance from year to year.

Costs of the proposal

It is estimated that the average annual cost of operating an SBC would be approximately US$50,000. This estimate is based on figures provided by USP Extension Services and are an estimate of meeting the operating costs of an SBC based at a USP Extension Center for the first year of its operation. Thus the operating cost of the complete network would be approximately US$550,000. This would allow for a modest but adequate level of operation. The ability of the SBCs to offer the range of services and programs recommended would then depend on the entrepreneurial talents of each SBC director. Particularly crucial would be his or her ability to elicit resources and assistance from the public, private, and voluntary sector organizations.

The benefits that might accrue from this modest investment are not easy to quantify but are likely to be considerable. The following kinds of results could be expected:

- Improved coordination, effectiveness, and use of existing enterprise support services.

- Improved access for potential entrepreneurs to appropriate, multi-dimensional support services.

- Development of new integrated programs that are tailored to the needs of promising industrial sectors and priority target groups that offer continuing support to new businesses.

- Stimulation of an approved entrepreneurial climate through new programs in the educational system and by the active involvement of more of each community's human resources in enterprise development.

- Generation of more useful and appropriate business development data and training materials.

- Improved regional coordination of research, development, and training activities.

These are just some of the benefits that are likely to lead to an increased rate of development of locally owned small businesses as well as the improved effectiveness of existing businesses. Governments, private sector organizations, and NGOs throughout the region are eagerly exploring ways of increasing small business development.

Establishment of private sector staff development assistance schemes

Very few indigenous businesses in the Pacific island countries invest sufficient resources in conducting their own in-house training programs, although almost all would benefit from increased work skills and labor productivity through training and other forms of staff development. An incentives system based on the scheme adopted in Singapore is proposed.

Manufacturing Development

Development of small industry centers

The development by the Pacific island governments of industrial estates has proved to be an effective measure to stimulate industrial development. Tongan's Small Industries Centre (SIC), which was developed with ADB assistance, is an example of the successful use of this strategy. The case for government involvement in industrial estate development mainly relates to the comparative advantage that governments have in the following:

1. Ability to acquire land through compulsory acquisition,

2. Authority to rezone land,

3. Power to plan and execute the provision of all the public sector infrastructure services.

The development of well planned and located industrial estates with the proper mix of infrastructure and technical support services is a complicated exercise requiring the professional services of experts in areas such as civil engineering, urban planning, environmental planning, and financial analysis.

Most Pacific island government ministries do not have the necessary professional expertise to undertake industrial estate development without the services of foreign technical assistance. In most cases, international agencies could play a valuable role in providing such technical assistance as well as loan or grant funds to support the development of industrial estates.

Well planned industrial estates can overcome a major problem for small enterprises by providing suitable factory buildings at reasonable rental rates. In addition, industrial estate development can enable the government to efficiently provide a range of ancillary support services to businesses located at the estate. By comparison, disbursed industrial development of factories in widely scattered locations in urban areas can increase the cost of providing support services. Centralizing small manufacturing enterprises on an estate generates economies of scale in the provision of a range of support services such as:

1. Technical support services in areas such as plant design and layout, materials handling systems, equipment repair services, appropriate technology advice, assistance with installation and setup of equipment, trouble shooting on plant breakdown, etc.;

2. Materials testing services and quality control services;

3. Industrial waste collection and disposal services;

4. Computing services, telecommunication services, fax, telex, etc.;

5. Public utility services.

Recently, some innovative approaches have been developed to assist the development of small manufacturing firms that should be considered for their applicability in the Pacific island countries. They are seen as particularly appropriate for facilitating local business involvement in manufacturing development. These approaches include incubator centers, nursery factory schemes, and village factory schemes.

The new business incubator model

The new business incubator concept is attracting widespread attention in the United States, Europe, Japan, and Southeast Asia. A new business incubator is a center for cultivating the growth of new companies during their start-up phase. The definition of the word "to incubate" is to maintain under prescribed and controlled conditions an environment favorable for hatching or developing. It has interesting connotations when applied to new business development. An incubator is a facility for the maintenance of controlled conditions for cultivation.

In the new business incubator center, the controlled conditions usually include four types of resources: secretarial support, administrative assistance, facilities support, and business expertise including accounting, financial management, marketing, and general management advisory services. The business incubator seeks to effectively link technology, capital, talent, and business know-how to accelerate the growth of new enterprises. The number of incubators in the United States has grown rapidly during the 1980s and now numbers about 150. Incubator centers have various names including "Innovation Center," "Enterprise Center," "Business and Technology Center," and "Technology Park."

The basic aim of incubator centers is to assist small businesses during their first few years of operation when their chance of failure is highest. Small businesses fail for many reasons, including under-capitalization, lack of a market for their products, high cost of raw materials, inappropriate technology, economic recession, low level of labor skill and productivity, and poor management.

The village factory model

An innovative model for export market development has recently been established in Malaysia by the Furniture Manufacturers Association (FMA). Under this Village Factory Scheme, the FMA has organized a group of furniture manufacturers to relocate their factories alongside each other at an industrial estate, which is called a "furniture village." The co-location of small factories producing the same type of products has generated considerable economic advantages in the supply of support services. The members of this furniture village share the costs of a furniture design service and special professional assistance to improve quality control, assistance with the acquisition and use of new technology for the production of high quality knock-down furniture, and assistance with international marketing. The design unit has helped village members to re-design their products to suit the particular needs of their overseas market segments for doors and furniture. The central unit provides service to village members for production, management assistance, marketing, packaging, transport, and quality control. The Malaysian Iron and Steel Industry Association is also adopting a similar village-type concept for foundries.

Public Utility Services

The international agencies have traditionally provided substantial technical assistance, loans, and grants to support the development of public utility services. There is a continuing need for a major involvement of the international agencies in this sector to ensure that private sector growth is not constrained by inadequate and costly public utility services. At present, technical assistance is especially needed to improve management and productivity programs in public utilities, which have been given high priority by some Pacific island countries and which are already receiving assistance from the ADB and the World Bank.

Most island countries are committed to implementing programs of public utility productivity improvement through the introduction of commercialization strategies, more effective corporate planning, rationalization, corporatization, and institutional strengthening. In addition, the public utilities are under considerable financial pressure to improve their financial performance by implementing efficiency measures to reduce operating costs and by improving resource mobilization efficiency. In most cases, technical assistance has been to provide expertise in financial management areas involving reviewing cost structures and improving pricing policies and charging systems, as well as other aspects of revenue administration such as billing and collection efficiency improvement.

The external agencies have traditionally provided the island countries with funds and technical assistance to support the development and upgrading of public infrastructure, which provides essential services to the private sector. All the main forms of public infrastructure have received substantial assistance including ports, ships, ship repair yards, sea transport, and marine facilities; cargo handling facilities; airports and terminal facilities; roads and highways; electricity generation and distribution systems; water storage and distribution systems; postal and telecommunication systems; land and industrial estate development, etc.

The national development plans of the Pacific island countries clearly outline the future public sector infrastructure development objectives, polices, priority programs, and individual projects. Several countries are almost entirely dependent on aid donors and international agencies for the financing of public sector infrastructure projects, and this situation is likely to continue for years.

Several Pacific island countries have engaged in a program to improve the productivity of their main public utilities by implementing programs of commercialization involving more efficient pricing and user charging policies designed to increase the level of cost recovery. For example, the government of Fiji has recently corporatized the Department of Post and Telecommunications to transform it into a separate corporation with the powers to operate on a commercial basis without the administrative restrictions associated with being a government department. The government has engaged the assistance of the World Bank to guide the implementation of the corporatization process.

The Private Sector Project found that substantial economic benefits are likely to accrue to all Pacific island countries if they implement commercialization programs to improve the performance of their public utilities.

Many of the necessary tasks in commercialization require a high level of management consulting skills, which are in short supply in some island countries and thus usually require the participation of the international agencies.

It is recommended that the international agencies engage in policy dialogue to encourage and support the island countries to implement policy reforms and institutional development programs to strengthen the management and improve the performance of their public utilities. High priority should be given to the human resource development aspects of the public utility sector.

The additional development of the private sector is heavily reliant on the firms' ability to purchase sufficient quantities of public utility services to meet their production requirement—at price levels and quality standards that are in line with those of their international competitors, either in the form of import competition or through competing on competitive export markets.

Projects that generate improvements in the cost efficiency and quality of public utility services and that lead to lower real prices, or to the containment of prices, are of direct financial benefit to the private sector and should be seen as an important element of private sector development strategy.

In addition, high priority should be given to continuing external assistance to fund the construction, upgrading, modernization, and maintenance of public infrastructure as an essential strategy for supporting and accelerating private sector development in the Pacific island countries.

Technology Acquisition

The adoption of an export-led growth strategy by some island countries requires local firms to develop high quality products specifically designed to meet the needs of overseas market segments. In many cases, firms need special assistance in the technical aspects of manufacturing, agroprocessing, post-harvest treatment, product improvement, and new product development, as well as in design, packaging, and physical distribution management. To overcome these difficulties two schemes are recommended.

1. Introduction of technology development assistance schemes

It is recommended that greater assistance be given to private firms to encourage them to acquire appropriate new technology, especially in the larger island countries that are promoting manufacturing and agroprocessing development.

One major problem experienced by manufacturing firms in the region is their lack of technical and design capacity to develop new innovative products to satisfy the unmet needs of consumer markets. Many of their current products are imitation products based on well established mature products that are often entering the declining stage of their life cycle. Canned coconut cream is an example. A successful new coconut cream venture would probably have to be based on an appropriate aspectic packaging rather than the traditional canned product.

A new product development assistance scheme could be considered by those island countries that wish to promote manufactured exports. This type of scheme aims to encourage firms to adopt new products and processes by providing them with financial assistance. Such a scheme could support the improvement of existing products and manufacturing processes as well as the development of new products. Emphasis should be given to improved design, product quality, packaging, and presentation for export.

2. Establishment of a mini-technology park

In Fiji and Papua New Guinea the practicality should be examined of establishing small technology parks directly linked to the universities or institutes of technology and located close to their campuses. These parks could provide an opportunity for the universities and institutes to develop applied research and development projects directly related to the specific technological development needs of the enterprises located in the parks. The technology parks could provide an ideal environment to assist firms in acquiring appropriate new technology and could cultivate the growth of new companies during their start-up phase by providing them with consulting services to assist them in applying manufacturing technology to their production processes.

Agricultural Development

Aid in the past has done little to accelerate private sector development in Pacific islands agriculture. At worst, project aid has actually weakened the position of the private sector by requiring the direct involvement of government agencies in production and marketing activities. However, redesigned foreign aid will be vital in facilitating horticultural development in the region. The project has identified a number of specific areas, including:

- Project and investor identification,
- Technical support for establishing and operating commercial industry associations, including assistance to industry-based extension and research,
- Assistance in establishing quality and grading standards,
- The provision of post-harvest treatment facilities and technical support,
- Private sector training,
- Market research and development and market intelligence.

These areas are summarized briefly below.

Facilitating agribusiness investment through project identification and formulation

Agribusiness investment could be accomplished in the following sequential stages:

1. Identify profitable export-oriented diversified agriculture projects that could be supported by small- to medium-sized joint venture businesses. Some possible projects would include the development of an integrated macadamia nut industry and the establishment of papaya and guava puree processing facilities.

2. Evaluate all such projects in terms of comprehensive feasibility studies and business plans, including emphasis on risk factors, market development, requirements for management expertise, extension and research support, and infrastructure development (i.e., essentially a turnkey approach). These evaluations should be performed to the most exacting requirements of international accounting firms and financiers.

3. Obtain an unequivocal commitment from the host government to afford guarantees that protect the interests of overseas investors within predetermined, agreed upon guidelines.

4. Identify potential joint venture partners, both local and overseas, who would be attracted to and capable of managing the project. This phase is not easy, and a high level of expertise is required in "tendering" the project to international local entrepreneurs.

5. Provide ongoing support for each project through training and the provision of specialized experts.

6. Provide loans to local shareholders to acquire the overseas equity once the project has been successfully stabilized.

A program such as the one outlined above would go a long way in maximizing the participation of foreign joint venture partners in the development of the region's horticulture industries. However, in the initial stages it must be recognized that attracting suitable new foreign companies for the development of smallholder-based diversification crops will be difficult, although not insurmountable, provided appropriate incentives and guarantees can be provided. The fact that these investors need not necessarily directly acquire land simplifies the process. Some of the more successful companies in Hawaii's diversified agriculture could be a potential source of investment in this area. However, by and large, it will be necessary to develop an in-country capability. In this respect, aid donors, technical assistance, and the development banks have an important role to play.

Technical support to commercial industry associations

Selected industry associations can provide a focus for developing an in-country capability. A strong commercially oriented industry association would be well placed to provide marketing, extension, and other services to its members and other suppliers. Strategically placed technical assistance can be crucial to the success of such organizations, as illustrated by the Friendly Islander Marketing Cooperative (FIMCO), which is now Tonga's largest exporter of vanilla beans.

Assistance in establishing quality and grading standards

Sustained horticultural industry development will depend on achieving continuity of supply to the specification required by the market. A necessary condition for achieving this continuity is to have in place quality and grading standards that are consistent with market requirements. Aid could be effectively used in the preparation and publication of a manual of quality standards, presentation and packaging, and quarantine requirements. As a part of this exercise, drafting instructions should be prepared to translate the standards into legislation to ensure their enforcement.

The provision of post-harvest treatment facilities and technical support

Throughout the region post-harvest treatment is undertaken in obsolete fumigation facilities operated by government departments. Investment is now required in facilities for the post-ethylene dibromide (EDB) era. EDB has been banned as a treatment for exports to the United States since 1984 and will soon be the case worldwide.

Post-harvest treatment technology presently is in a state of flux, with various forms of treatment under consideration, including various forms of heat treatments together with the controversial irradiation with gamma rays and the use of semipermeable shrinkwrap. Interest is primarily being focused on dry heat treatment (DHT) that involves forced air heating. The main technical difficulty has been to construct a large commercial unit that allows rapid and even heat distribution. This problem seems to have been resolved, and a number of Hawaii's papaya exporters have obtained United States Department of Agriculture (USDA) certification for commercial DHT-treated units.

The challenge facing the donors will be to get these facilities and the ancillary technical assistance into the hands of the private sector, with the government's role being confined to supervision and certification. The provision of technical support for export industries to operate these facilities will be essential. Support to government quarantine departments in undertaking their crucial certification role also will be necessary.

Commercial agriculture training

The premise underlying these proposals is that the transfer of technology is best achieved via agribusiness investors or commercial industry associations by using expert staff and on-the-job training of local personnel. Furthermore, technology transfers via government ministries, a course often followed due to the strictures of aid, have proved to be highly ineffectual and should be avoided. Scope exists for facilitating intraregional training utilizing private sector organizations. For example, the Plantation Support Association (PSA) in Vanuatu could send members to New Guinea Islands Produce (NGIP) in Papua New Guinea for on-the-job training.

Market research and development and market intelligence

Beyond broad market identification and market intelligence, a need exists for more detailed market and marketing development assistance for a select few products, preferably confined to situations in which an existing product could be tested in the market. Detailed market and marketing assessments would be linked to the project identification and formulation proposals made above.

Fisheries Development

The review and evaluation of the effectiveness of external assistance to regional fisheries development call for a major redirection of assistance and recommend that a higher proportion be allocated to human resource development and less to equipment and facilities.

Government actions in support of fisheries-related activities in general, and export promotion in particular, naturally vary widely between the various Pacific island countries. A general theme has been the enhancement of the efficiency of the artisanal fisherman. This often takes the form of extension work by Fisheries Officers, provision of fishing gear, establishment of infrastructure such as ice-making plants, and so on. Generally, this form of direct involvement by government in the artisanal fishery has proved effective.

Governments have also been active participants in marketing artisanal fish but with less success. More than one government-sponsored fish marketing operation in an island country has collapsed, in one case owing a considerable amount to its artisanal suppliers. In other cases operations have been maintained only by ongoing government subsidies, and criticism has been leveled at them as having a detrimental effect on the growth of market-driven distribution and marketing systems.

Often Pacific island governments have sought to initiate domestic participation in industrial fisheries by forming wholly government-owned corporations to operate fishing ventures, often using vessels and facilities obtained under external aid. Examples are National Fisheries Development Ltd. (Solomon Islands), Ika Corporation (Fiji), and Te Mautari Ltd. (Kiribati). In other cases vessels are operated on commercial lines directly by government departments, for example, the m.v. Lofa in Tonga. While such activities have created a cadre of experienced local fishermen, all of these enterprises are believed to have needed ongoing government support, in some cases measured in millions of dollars.

Governments have experienced more success in their participation in joint ventures with foreign companies, for example, the Solomon-Taiyo joint venture. In such cases government incentives and concessions to the foreign partner have included exclusive marketing rights, exemption from export taxes, and preemptive rights to all tuna caught in the country's Exclusive Economic Zone (EEZ). Such terms have tended to be negotiated on a case-by-case basis during the establishment or renewal of the joint venture agreement. Governments have seldom drawn profits from these joint ventures, but they have proved an effective vehicle of change and are likely to be pursued by other Pacific island countries as the opportunity occurs; Solomon-Taiyo, for example, employs nearly 2,000 Solomon Islands nationals.

There also is a need for Pacific island planners to recognize the practical realities of fisheries projects; in particular, they should be designed so that regional strengths can be capitalized on and weaknesses avoided where possible. Only in this manner can competitive advantage be gained. The procedure of simply following the example of the Distant Water Fishing Nation (DWFN) and attempting to make their solutions fit the region's problems is certain to fail.

Future role for aid donors and international agencies

These external agencies have played a major role in fisheries development in the region. Funds can be made available on a scale never possible for individual countries or in some cases for the projects themselves to sustain. Technical and human resources can be obtained at short notice from any of the advanced fishing nations, or specialist agencies, for long- or short-term projects.

With ownership of the resource now secure under the Law of the Sea regime, and with these aid-supported inputs of labor, technology, and capital, it is surprising that so little progress has been made; for example, most Pacific island countries have no significant domestic tuna fishery.

For "fisheries development" to gain momentum in the period up to 2000, the emphasis of external agencies (and domestic governments) must move away from "fisheries" and concentrate on "development." Fewer resources should be expended on these "fisheries" inputs, which run a wide gamut and include stock assessments, ice machines, computerized information systems, boat harbors, and so on. Instead, efforts should concentrate on developing the human resources that are required to drive these inputs. The only way that present progress can be consolidated and built on is from the enhanced capabilities derived from the mix of raw material, capital, and labor already present in regional fisheries.

This re-orientation of funding effort will require a move away from the high profile capital projects and toward funds expended on longer-term human resource development, the beneficial effects of which will be less evident, particularly in the shorter term. Changes will also be required in the background of the expatriate adviser who should reflect the developmental rather than the fisheries function. Frequently, the individual is well grounded in marine biology, for example, but has no experience in business management, personnel management, finance, marketing, etc., the very areas that would benefit most from external inputs.

Together with altering the orientation of aid toward general development rather than fisheries-specific work, an alteration in emphasis in the production/marketing system might also be beneficial. At present, in many cases the impetus is coming from what might be called "push" rather than "pull." Projects and development aid are usually focused on enhancing production, and marketing efforts are often a reaction to the production surplus, or "push." Market development work should be carried out with a view to identifying opportunities to satisfy the market demand with regional production. Once identified, these market forces should "pull" the product out of the production system—as opposed to marketing efforts that are simply a reaction to a product that is "pushed" onto it.

Because the Pacific island countries, and all the individual producers, will be unable to afford the costs of this market-driven approach, it is an ideal opportunity for external aid. Many of the potential markets, such as the United States and Japan, are already aid donors and thus would be supportive of market activities in their home countries. Effective marketing calls for a continued presence in the marketplace, and current volumes, even regionwide, would not be sufficient to support the necessary office and staff. The establishment of the proposed South Pacific Regional Trade Commission (SPRETCO) network would have a very positive effect on marine product trade, provided the staff members were knowledgeable and effective.

Tourism Development

Tourism in the region has received valuable assistance from the external agencies in recent years, especially since the establishment of the Tourism Council of the South Pacific (TCSP). However, given the importance of the tourism sector to the overall development of the private sectors of most Pacific island countries, a substantial increase in assistance to tourism is now warranted. The main areas where external assistance is required are summarized below:

Training and staff development

Training activities need to be substantially expanded to meet the workforce needs of the growing tourism industries in the Pacific island countries. An increased training effort is needed across all levels from senior management to junior staff. In addition, there is a need to provide specialized entrepreneurial training specifically designed to assist local entrepreneurs in establishing small-scale tourist resorts and support service businesses, including tourism business opportunities suitable for small-scale operations such as cultural entertainment, day tour activities, diving, fishing, and sailing, and other recreational businesses. Proposals are made for achieving this goal.

Tourism investment promotion, joint ventures, and institutions for tourism development

It is recommended that the Pacific island countries consider the merits of substantially increasing their effort in tourism investment promotion. One approach to investment promotion is to establish joint private sector/public sector Tourism Development Corporations responsible for planning and promoting joint venture tourism investments in new resorts and support businesses. Aid donor joint venture schemes, such as the Australian Joint Venture Scheme, could participate with the Tourism Development Corporations to provide funding for development corporation/government equity in new investment projects. Expatriate Cook Islanders, Tongans, and Samoans were identified as a significant source of joint venture partners for small-scale tourist development in their home countries.

The development banks could also provide loan funds to support joint venture, foreign, and local partnership projects sponsored by the development corporations. The external agencies could play a valuable role in assisting the institutional development of the proposed development corporations by providing technical assistance during the establishment phase, staff development training assistance, assistance with the design and delivery of investment promotion material, and financing of local equity in tourism joint venture projects.

Preparation and evaluation of national and regional master plans

An ongoing need exists for the preparation of comprehensive national tourism master plans and implementation strategies. The ADB has commenced this in a number of Pacific island countries. Tourism development in some countries has been constrained by a complex range of factors including the lack of physical land use and public infrastructure plans that provide an integrated framework to guide and direct the location and siting of new resorts and other facilities to the optimal locations. The location of new resort facilities should be planned and coordinated at a national level in the context of a master plan to ensure that the agglomeration economies associated with collocation of hotels and recreation facilities and the economies of scale associated with the provision of public utility services, as well as private sector entertainment services, are fully taken into account.

Gaining the maximum advantage of the natural environmental attractiveness of alternative potential resort sites is another important factor that has sometimes been neglected in the location and land use zoning for resort development. These factors need to be thoroughly evaluated and regularly monitored through the implementation of tourism master plans.

Privatization Programs

Provision of foreign technical assistance

The preparation and planning for privatization constitute a complex process requiring a range of specialized professional skills, some of which are not readily available in the region. A most important lesson that emerges from experience with the implementation of privatization programs over the last five years is the value of comprehensive, detailed analysis and planning. The preparatory phase is crucial because if done properly it sets the stage for successful implementation.

It is recommended that comprehensive country privatization strategy studies be conducted in each Pacific island country before governments embark on a privatization program. Such studies have already been undertaken in Western Samoa and Kiribati. However, in advance of these studies, it is necessary to have a firm political commitment and an understanding by government of the implications of adopting privatization strategies.

There is a continuing need for the international institutions and aid donors to provide additional technical assistance and finance to support the development of privatization programs in the Pacific island countries. The main areas in need of professional technical assistance services are:

1. Preparation of national privatization strategies and sectorial studies,

2. Preparation of guidelines and procedures manuals,

3. Preparation of manuals on contract administration,

4. Preparation of detailed privatization plans for selected state-owned enterprises,

5. Preparation of training manuals on privatization,

6. Professional assistance with the implementation phase,

7. Assistance with the establishment of monitoring and evaluation systems,

8. Assistance with establishment of public enterprise management units,

9. Support for training and the development of management education programs to support privatization.

Training in small business management and entrepreneurship is an essential aspect of privatization strategies. Most island countries do not currently have adequate systems for the development, training, and support of local entrepreneurs. A regional approach has been proposed for developing first-class training programs and materials.

Role of aid donors in supporting privatization programs

The policies of the current aid donors are all generally supportive of the concept of privatization, although most channel their tied aid directly for public sector projects rather than to private sector projects.

Aid donors could play an expanded role in supporting both specific privatization programs and general projects to strengthen the private sector and enable it to play a greater role in the economy. The following is a list of the possible types of projects that could be financed by aid donors over the next five years in the Pacific island countries. The list has five categories: (1) training programs, (2) technology transfer, (3) small business support and development, (4) financing privatization, and (5) infrastructure development.

1. Training programs to strengthen the private sector's capacity in:
   - Entrepreneurial development
   - Small business management
   - Commercialization strategies
   - Corporate planning
   - Export market development
   - International marketing
   - Marketing for small businesses
   - New product development systems
   - Product quality control systems
   - Cost analysis and financial planning
   - Production plant layout
   - Human resource management
   - Productivity improvement systems.

2. Assistance with appropriate technology transfer and application:

    - Secondment of business experts (such as retired executives) to local firms.

    - Support for the establishment of technology centers to provide technical assistance to firms on:

        - Production technology and productivity improvement,

        - New product development systems,

        - Licensing of technology,

        - Plant lay-out,

        - Storage and materials handling systems,

        - Stock control systems.

    - Support for the establishment of technology parks, innovation centers, and research and development activities.

3. Support for Small Business Center (refer to previous section on SBC)

4. Financing privatization

    Donors have provided financial assistance to private sector entrepreneurs indirectly by providing governments with grant funds to increase their equity in national development banks. These funds are then on-lent to private sector borrowers and could be used to finance privatization projects. In addition, donors have developed special schemes such as the Australian Joint Venture scheme to fund the governments' equity in joint venture companies with foreign partners from the donor country.

5. Support for infrastructure development

    Aid donors have been heavily involved in financing public sector infrastructure development such as roads, ports, and airports, all of which are essential for efficient private sector operation. Donors could also play a more direct role in funding the development of industrial estates and factory buildings for rental by government to the private sector. These industrial estates could be developed as nursery factory schemes or incubator centers where new entrepreneurs receive a high level of support services from a central headquarters at the industrial estate. Under these systems the small firms in the industrial estate receive assistance with product quality testing, marketing, procurement of supplies, access to finance, and production planning.

Economic Policy Reforms

Role of international agencies in policy dialogue and private sector program implementation

The international agencies have played a valuable role in promoting policy dialogue and funding technical assistance for a wide range of economic policy analysis and economic planning studies.

The implementation of economic reform measures is often a difficult and complex process involving activities such as the drafting of new legislation or changes to existing legislation; institutional change, which may involve the abolition of existing institutions; the establishment of new institutions; privatization and commercialization; institutional strengthening and development; and the design of new incentives and systems for their administration, etc. Many of these activities require the services of experts, which are not available locally. In addition, a high degree of coordination is required to ensure the consistency of various policies, programs, and projects.

Thus it is recommended that the international agencies and aid donors provide the Pacific island countries with expert technical assistance for the detailed formulation of national private sector development programs and for the implementation of the set of projects and policy reforms.

Macroeconomic policy

Over the last decade the IMF, the World Bank, and the ADB have conducted ad hoc macroeconomic reviews of Pacific island economies, mainly by sending teams of experts to visit the countries to work with staff of Ministries of Finance, etc., and to engage in policy dialogue. These reviews have played a very valuable role by providing the Pacific island countries with independent professional advice and assessment of the performance of their economies. Regular monitoring of the performance of the economies, as well as evaluation of their macroeconomic policies, is desirable to ensure that an appropriate macroeconomic environment for private sector development is maintained. It is recommended that a more regular process of macroeconomic reviews is now warranted, given the volatility of the external environment. To meet this need PIDP has embarked on a program of country economic assessments that will cover each country on a biannual basis and will provide material on economic performance, policy, and prospects. These reports have the advantage of being in the public domain, unlike economic assessments prepared by the ADB, the World Bank, and the IMF. Reports have been completed for Fiji, Tonga, and Vanuatu.

Microeconomic policy

Several of the sectoral studies undertaken for PIDP's Private Sector Project have identified areas where private sector development could be enhanced by reforming areas of microeconomic policy. These include proposals to deregulate labor markets, reduce barriers of entry into certain economic activities that have been dominated by government-owned monopolies, simplify tariff structures and reduce the level of protection, undertake tax reforms, eliminate price controls, reduce subsidies to agriculture, abolish export taxes, review price support systems, privatize the functions of commodity boards, eliminate or phase out import quotas, modify investment incentives, etc. These proposals are generally aimed at deregulating the environment in which firms operate and at increasing the level of competition.

As already discussed, the implementation of these recommended reforms will not be an easy task because some of the highly protected sections of the business community are likely to resist changes that will require them to improve the efficiency of their operations. The international agencies could assist governments in this regard by engaging in further policy dialogue and by providing experts to assist with the implementation of policy reforms, the drafting of legislation, and the preparation of comprehensive sector studies and sector development plans. An agency such as the ADB, through loan conditionality, can have considerable leverage in the acceptance and implementation of policy reforms. This is shown by the recent experience of Western Samoa's Agricultural Sector Loan.

A Program for Private Sector Development

To gain the maximum value from this type of policy analysis research it is necessary to follow-up the major recommendations from the Private Sector Project with each Pacific island government. This process involves policy dialogue, the initiation of economic reform measures, and the development and funding of national private sector development programs. PIDP has commenced the process with its regional Policy Analysis and Training Program in Private Sector Development.

Similar workshops at the national levels are also proposed that involve participation of donors. Each workshop should initiate the preparation of an integrated private sector development program that has consistent policies and programs, facilitates follow-up and monitoring, creates investor confidence, and maximizes the use of aid funds and technical assistance. The private sector must be actively involved in this process.

Technical assistance will also have a facilitating role to play. This exercise will require each Pacific island country to specify in detail the following:

1. A realistic set of private sector development objectives.

2. Detailed implementation strategy designed to achieve the specified private sector development objectives. The strategy should outline the roles and responsibilities of the public and private sector agencies in the implementation process.

3. An integrated set of projects designed to directly stimulate private sector development. The project should be specifically targeted at alleviating the main constraints to private sector growth.

4. A complementary set of policy measures and reforms designed to stimulate private sector growth including proposals for deregulation and privatization.

5. A financial plan indicating expected sources of funds including loan funds, grants, and revenue to be raised through the application of user charges for the provision of services, as well as the projected annual budgets and implementation schedule for the private sector development program, phased over a ten-year period.

   In some country situations, it may be desirable for the Pacific island countries to take up a sector loan with the ADB to fund a range of projects under the umbrella of the private sector development program. This procedure would provide the island countries with several significant advantages including professional technical assistance in detailed formulation, design, and appraisal. The involvement of the ADB would also help ensure sustained implementation. In addition, the ADB could play a valuable role in recruiting aid donors to co-finance the program.

6. An implementation chart and detailed network analysis of the steps and activities involved in the implementation of the plan. This step should include a systems chart showing the relationships and lines of responsibility of the various private and public sector agencies involved in the program.

7. An institutional development plan for each major public agency involved, such as the development banks, the investment promotion agency, and national small business centers.

Indicative costing of a private sector development program

This section illustrates the components of a typical national private sector development program and indicates the likely annual level of financial resources needed to support such a program. The amount of money that is necessary to fund the individual national private sector development programs of the Pacific island countries obviously will vary greatly from country to country, and the actual size of a country program will usually be constrained by both the availability of staff resources and funds. In particular countries some of the elements are already being implemented in various forms.

Table 9.1 illustrates the recommended level of funding and composition of an annual budget for a typical country's private sector development program, based on the needs of larger Pacific island countries. These budgets represent estimates of the annual level of funding desirable to implement these types of projects, assuming they are phased over a three- to five-year period. It assumes a total program of the type described was adopted, whereas in reality only a proportion is likely to be implemented.

The table shows that the implementation of a comprehensive national private sector development program in a large Pacific island country is likely to require an annual budget of as much as US$20 million. In the smaller countries such a program is likely to warrant an annual budget of US$3 to $5 million. For most island countries the funding of a comprehensive national private sector development program will require a major redirection of foreign aid to support such a national program. This redirection can be achieved only with strong leadership and commitment to private sector development on the part of the major international agencies and donors.

Table 9.1   Illustrative national private sector development program for
country x—program components and indicative annual budget

	(US$ '000)
1. Development finance project	
Strengthening of development bank (DB)	2,000
Increased government equity in DB	1,000
Staff development	500
Systems development	500
Establishment of credit guarantee scheme	800
Venture capital scheme	1,000
Project total	5,800
2. Export marketing project	
Institutional development of authority	800
Database development	300
Training in export marketing procedures	900
Establishing export credit scheme	1,200
Assistance to industry associations	500
Project total	3,700
3. Small business development project	
Strengthening small business center	1,500
Developing training material	500
New training courses	1,000
Project total	3,000
4. Investment promotion upgrading project	
Institutional development	600
Production of promotional material	400
Staff training and development	500
Project total	1,500
5. Export manufacturing development project	
Phase 1 small industries center development	2,500
Support to manufacturers associations	600
Technical assistance for product development	400
Project total	3,500
6. Technology development assistance project	
Research and development grant scheme	600
New product development scheme	300
Foreign technical assistance	500
Project total	1,400
7. Private agriculture development project	
Technical assistance to industry associations	500
Upgrading of quarantine system	500
Project total	1,000
8. Tourism development project	
Tourism development commission	900
Promotion campaign	1,000
Staff training	500
Joint venture equity	2,000
Project total	4,400
9. Private development program management cost	200
Total program cost for year	24,500

chapter 10

Major findings and recommendations

Introduction

The economic performance of the Pacific island countries during the 1980s has been poor compared with that of the 1970s. There has been a substantial slowdown in Pacific island export growth in the 1980s as compared with that of the 1970s. This slowdown has been accompanied by poor investment productivity and growth performance both absolutely and relative to many other developing countries. The generally poor performance of the last decade has been masked somewhat by substantial aid and, in the case of the Polynesian countries, by remittances from family members living abroad. The comparative analysis undertaken suggests that structural weaknesses in the Pacific island economies need to be addressed.

Diversification

A need exists to increase efficiency and to diversify outputs and exports toward commodities with more favorable production and demand characteristics. While the Pacific islands may have a "natural" comparative advantage in the production of traditional bulk commodity exports, these cannot alone provide the basis for sustained development in the future. Over the last two decades the terms of trade have moved significantly against Pacific island bulk export commodities and are expected to continue to do so in the foreseeable future. Thus there is a need to increase the efficiency and reduce the production costs of traditional export commodities if the standard of living of rural populations is to be maintained.

The Private Sector Project makes recommendations for achieving this goal, with particular emphasis on management. However, it is vital for the Pacific island economies, as part of a long-term structural adjustment strategy, to diversify their outputs and exports toward commodities with more favorable production and demand characteristics, such as various types of manufactures, high-value horticulture and marine products, and service activities. The opportunities and requirements for developing high-value exports have been a focus of the Private Sector Project.

Macroeconomic Policy

Macroeconomic policy has by and large created a stable financial system that has been conducive to private investment, but it has been less successful in providing a competitive cost and price environment. In almost all Pacific island countries, macroeconomic policies have generated a stable financial system. Through sound management these countries, for the most part, have been spared the foreign exchange shortages and the hyperinflation common to many countries in Africa and Latin America. Although macroeconomic policies in the Pacific island countries have in general been successful, they have been less than satisfactory in providing a competitive cost and price environment for private sector investment and growth. Specifically, policies are needed to ensure that the cost of labor reflects the market conditions.

Entrepreneurs

Governments have a key role to play in providing a decision-making environment conducive to the needs of entrepreneurial investors. This role goes beyond offering investors an attractive package of fiscal incentives. Although variations exist, the effectiveness of the incentive measures, which have been adopted to attract new investment, has been substantially reduced by cumbersome administrative measures associated with investment application and approval systems.

Government

An outward looking, and activist, role for government is advocated. A number of specific programs and projects are proposed to encourage investment and export oriented private sector development. These include institutions for export promotion, the establishment of export oriented small industry centers, and various measures and programs directed at enterprise support organizations. This process does imply a policy of judiciously selected protection—albeit with an outward-looking orientation. Governments, however, need to minimize their involvement in direct production and marketing activities. The Private Sector Project also strongly advocates against the high rate of protection of import substitution industries that has arisen in some Pacific island countries over the last two decades.

In manufacturing sector development, the Private Sector Project reviewed the concept of establishing incubator centers, mini-technology parks, and village factory models. Proposals are made for adopting these models for involving the region's entrepreneurs in export manufacturing.

Improvement is also needed in the efficiency and productivity and cost-effectiveness of public utility services. The public sector plays a very vital role in supporting the private sector so that programs directed toward commercializing or corporatizing public sector utilities can improve efficiency and deliver better quality services at the right time and the right place.

Extension Service

In the agricultural sector, government agencies have performed poorly in production and marketing activities. There is need to privatize some or part of the extension and research functions. However, a crucial role for government has been identified in creating the environment for sustained commodity development. Some vital responsibilities include (1) certifying that quarantine and quality standards have been met and (2) providing the institutional and legal environment to facilitate industry self-regulation and self-help.

Savings

Improvement in the level of domestic resource mobilization poses a challenge for the Pacific island countries whose rate of domestic savings has traditionally been low. A major problem of financing in years to come is how to control consumption and increase savings. Domestic savings have been low and, in some cases, even negative. With the help of private remittances and official grants, some countries have been able to maintain a high level of consumption in excess of their income. While this situation continues unabated, it is not sustainable in the longer term. Policies and measures to meet this challenge are proposed. In these recommendations, attention is given to cultural factors.

Financial Intermediation

Greater efficiency in financial intermediation is required in financing the private sector. Through aid transfers, domestic resource mobilization has not been a constraint on investment or growth. Yet this sizable source of financial resources has failed to generate growth and thus has been highly inefficient. A major challenge for the Pacific islands is how to funnel the large available sources of official aid to productive private sector activities. To date the process of financial intermediation has failed to establish an adequate conduit.

Development Banks

The development banks are key institutions in private sector development, yet they have not achieved the level of success expected of them. The region's development banks have been assigned a leading role in bridging the gap between savings and investment requirements. Yet these institutions have generally not, for various reasons, been particularly successful. These problems are not insurmountable, and recommendations for improvement are proposed. The human resource development aspects are stressed in the proposals to strengthen the development banks. The emphasis is on the key role of training with a strengthened regional institution.

Venture Capital

A successful local venture capital industry can provide the vital link between entrepreneurs, long-term finance, and management expertise. Proposals have been presented on how such an industry might be established, involving a partnership between government, development agencies, and the private sector.

The development of credit guarantee schemes to assist the commercial banks to provide more effective finance to the private sector is recommended together with suggestions for developing venture capital. The expansion and promotion and more effective use of the joint venture schemes, both the Australian and New Zealand Schemes, have great potential but as yet have not been fully utilized.

Small Business

Priority needs to be given to small and indigenous business development and promotion. In the Private Sector Project the emphasis moved from identifying problems and constraints for small business development to recommending policy programs and projects. A study of enterprise support organizations made detailed recommendations for expanding the role and improving the performance of small business. These recommendations include the use of the University of the South Pacific's (USP) extension network to facilitate small business development and entrepreneur training and the development of a regional network of Small Business Centers (SBCs).

In the area of small business development and entrepreneurial problems, proposals are presented for using the existing infrastructure at the University of the South Pacific. This program is extremely practical in its approach, and one that could play a very valuable role in assisting private sector development to strengthen national support institutions.

Exports

A greater political commitment to develop export capabilities is required. In large measure the responsibility for encouraging increased trade and investment devolves on the Pacific island countries themselves. A start in this direction can be made through aid resource allocations, government policies, and the region's institutional energies. Specific recommendations are made that focus on the establishment of the South Pacific Regional Trade Commission (SPRETCO) network. Elements of this network are already in place in Australia and New Zealand.

Also presented by the Private Sector Project is the concept of establishing a trade data bank and the importance of having marketing information and international marketing research, directed to the private sector. The national export marketing agencies need to improve their capacity and performance in delivering services to the private sector. In particular, new exporters need assistance into the export market through training and export procedures and assistance in that learning process as they move to exporting.

Regional training programs on export market development also need to be developed. Support for industry associations was identified as an appropriate use for technical assistance.

The trading partners of the Pacific island countries can also do more. For instance, the inflexibility of the rules of origin of regional preferential trade agreements continue to act as a brake on regional export development.

Investment Opportunities

Export oriented private sector investment opportunities in the region are greater than often perceived. Certain countries have outstanding prospects for large-scale mineral exploitation, while others have opportunities for major tourist plant development. Although these larger developments are important, the focus of this study has been on the opportunities for smaller countries and smaller firms and the actions required to successfully exploit these. Most Pacific island countries were identified, in varying degrees, to have a comparative advantage in marine products, in high value niche-market agriculture, and in certain lines of manufacturing such as quality garments and furniture. This advantage stems from a combination of location, trade agreements, labor costs, and in some cases linkages with tourism. Limiting factors have included the lack of suitable entrepreneurs who are willing to invest their own capital and skills and the absence of administrative systems that can expeditiously accommodate such investors. However, the recent experiences of Fiji and Tonga in export manufacturing illustrate what can be achieved by encouraging entrepreneurial investors.

International Agencies

Many international agencies have recently expressed the intention to provide greater assistance to private sector development and have indicated their willingness to allocate a much higher proportion of their assistance to projects that directly promote private sector growth. However, to date, little action has been taken to convert these good intentions into concrete programs of action. The Private Sector Project outlines the main ways in which the international agencies could assist private sector development, and it proposes that they could play a leadership role in the formulation and implementation of national private sector development programs for each Pacific island country.

The preferred approach for funding and managing a country program for private sector development is for the ADB to play the leading role in planning and coordinating external assistance for the program. This role may involve the ADB providing a sector or program loan to fund a set of private sector projects accompanied by the implementation of a set of new policy measures and reforms. The involvement of the ADB as the leading institution offers opportunities for the bilateral donors to contribute grant funds to such a program in a co-financing operation. The advantages to the Pacific island countries of this approach are substantial and well recognized by them. These advantages include comprehensive project management, monitoring, and control systems used in bank funded projects, as well as the thoroughness of the bank's approach to project formulation, preparation, and appraisal.

In addition, the policy conditionality attached to program loans provides a mechanism for ensuring that the government implements desirable policy reforms, which may otherwise be shelved or delayed because of the likely adverse political reaction to such measures by sections of the community having vested interests in maintaining the status quo.

The Private Sector Project recommends that the international agencies should coordinate their assistance to private sector development to avoid the duplication and waste that can result from a piecemeal, fragmented approach. The magnitude of the private sector assistance needs are substantial. It is recommended that at least 50 percent of external assistance should be directed to supporting the national private sector development programs of the Pacific island countries.

However, the provision of aid to the Pacific islands is a complex and vexatious issue. The high percentage of aid receipts has distorted the allocation of resources and has generated an attitude of dependency. Furthermore, despite the increasingly numerous policy pronouncements from bilateral and international agencies, the research showed that aid accomplished little to accelerate private sector development in the region. An important outcome of this research project is the specific set of recommendations that will enable these agencies to contribute in a substantial and coherent fashion to private sector development. The emphasis here is on human resource development. Some of the recommended program areas suitable for external technical and financial assistance include:

- Credit delivery to the private sector with particular emphasis on institutional support for the development banks,

- Export market development and national marketing support services,

- Entrepreneurial development and staff training,

- Investment promotion,

- Small industry centers and supporting infrastructure development,

- Technology acquisition and development.

Integrated Private Sector Development Program

Each country should prepare an integrated private sector development program. Drawing on the major recommendations of the various project studies, an integrated set of programs and projects designed to accelerate private sector development is presented. The program covers the following areas:

- Provision of credit facilities to the private sector,

- Export market development and national marketing support services,

- National Small Business Centers, entrepreneurial development, and staff training,

- Sectoral private sector support programs (e.g., manufacturing, agriculture, and fisheries development),

- Technology acquisition and development,

- Privatization and corporatization programs,

- Economic policy reforms.

An integrated approach to private sector development is recommended because it allows for consistency of government policies and support programs and projects. The preparation of a specific private sector development program would provide a focus for coordinating the involvement of the aid donors and international agencies in private sector development. To initiate this process it is recommended that in-country workshops be held involving both government and private sector participation. The aid donors and the international agencies would be invited to attend. The research from PIDP's Private Sector Project would provide the core resource material for these workshops.

Statistical appendixes

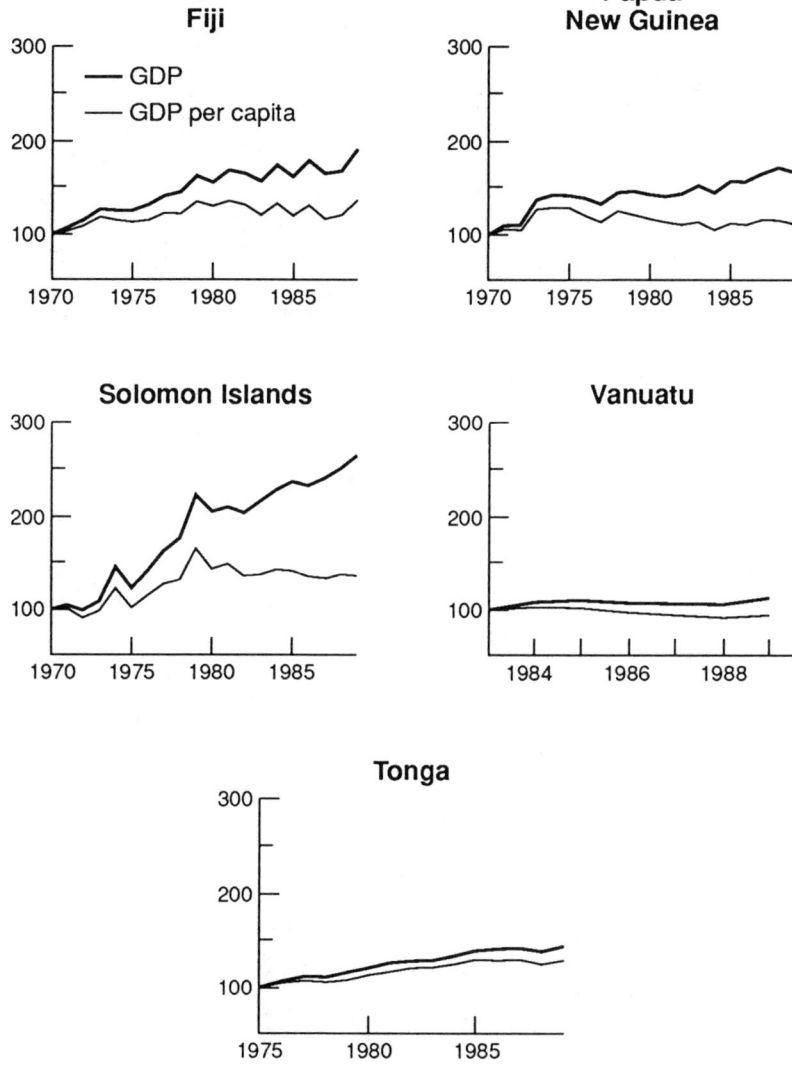

Appendix 1. GDP growth and GDP growth per capita for the major
Pacific island countries, 1970–89 (1970 = 100)

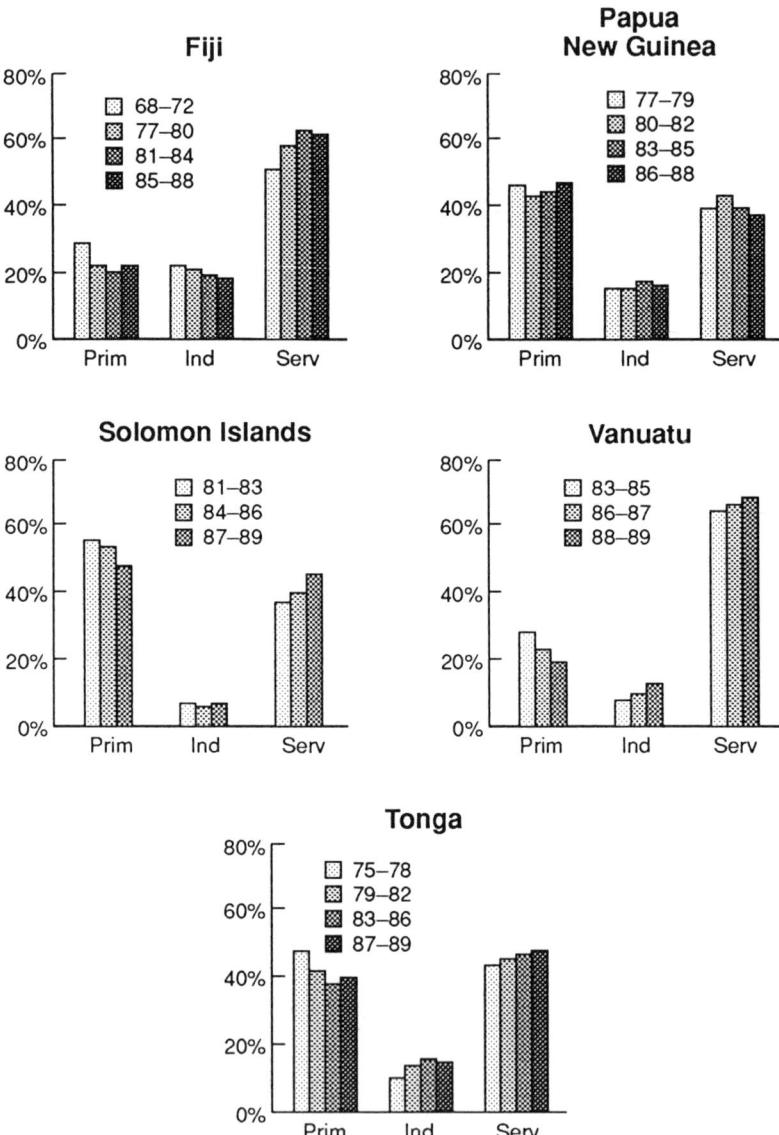

Appendix 2. Structural change by major sector for the Pacific islands for
selected years, percent of current price GDP

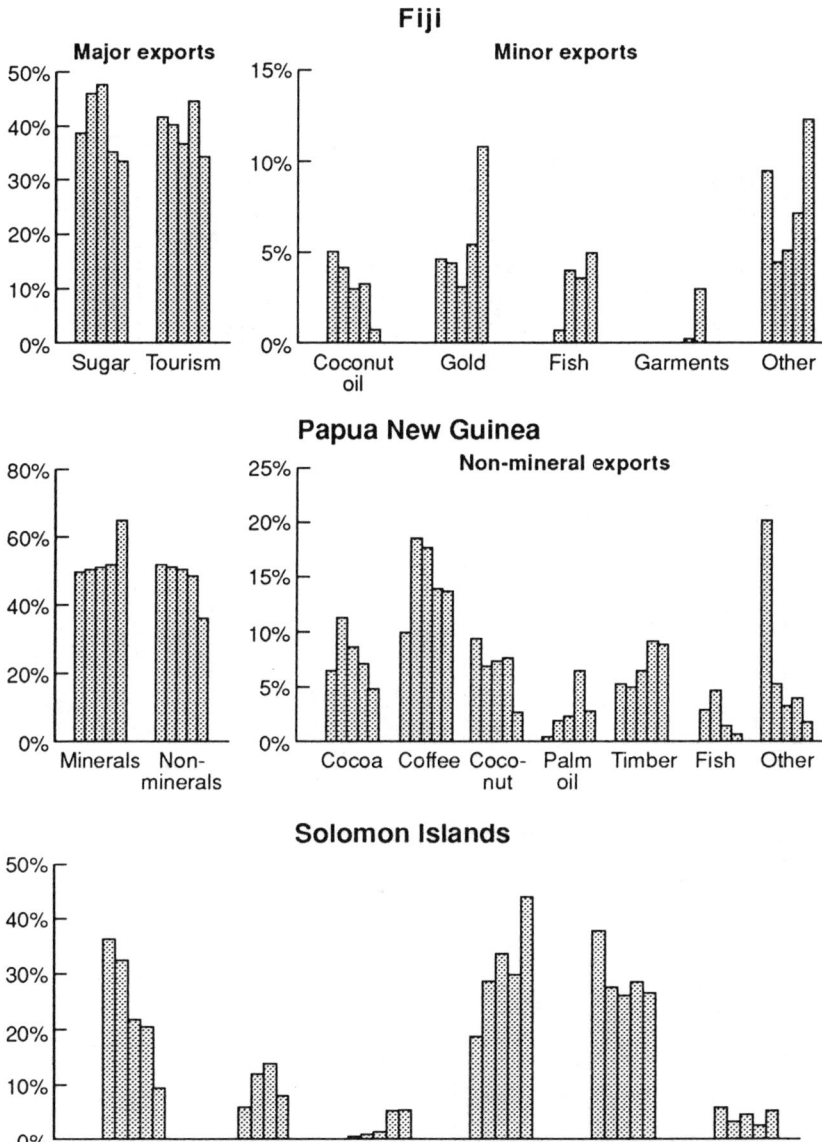

Appendix 3. Structural change in components of exports for the Pacific islands for selected years between 1970–89, percent of total exports. (Each bar refers to a four year group.) *Appendix 3 is continued on next page.*

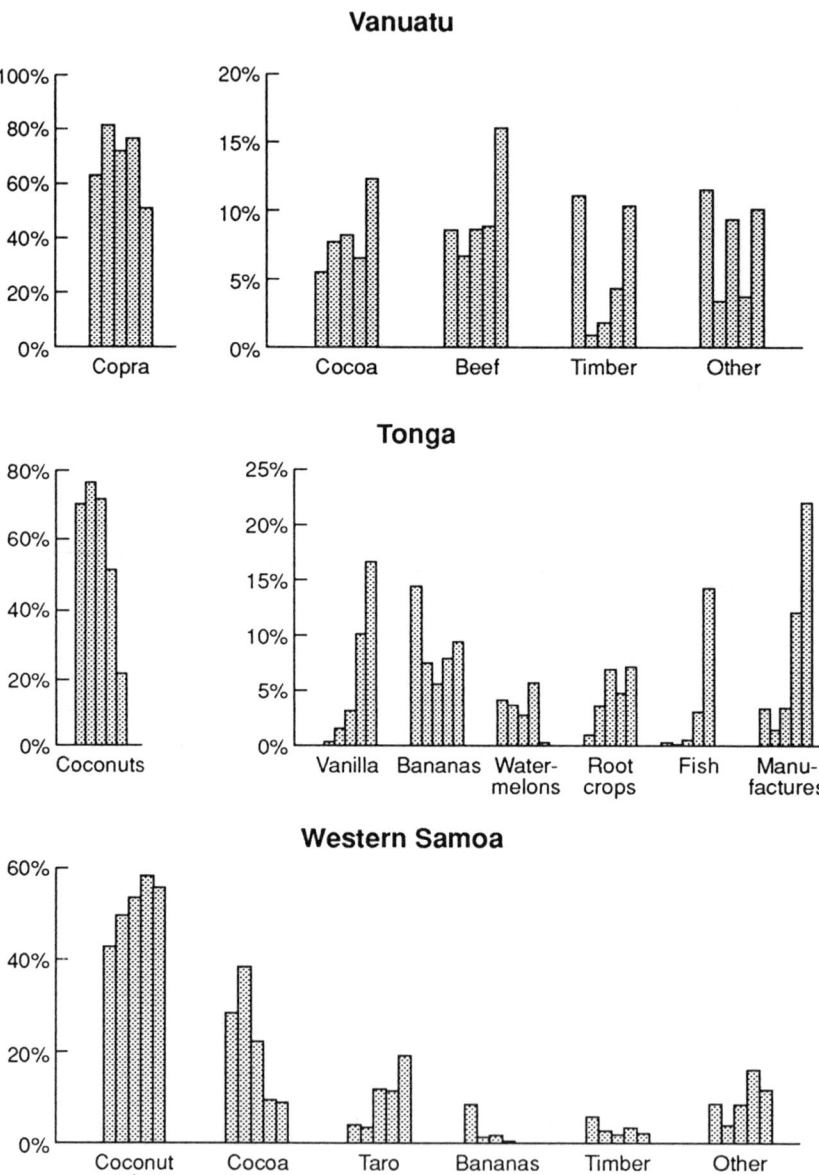

Appendix 3. *Continued from previous page.*

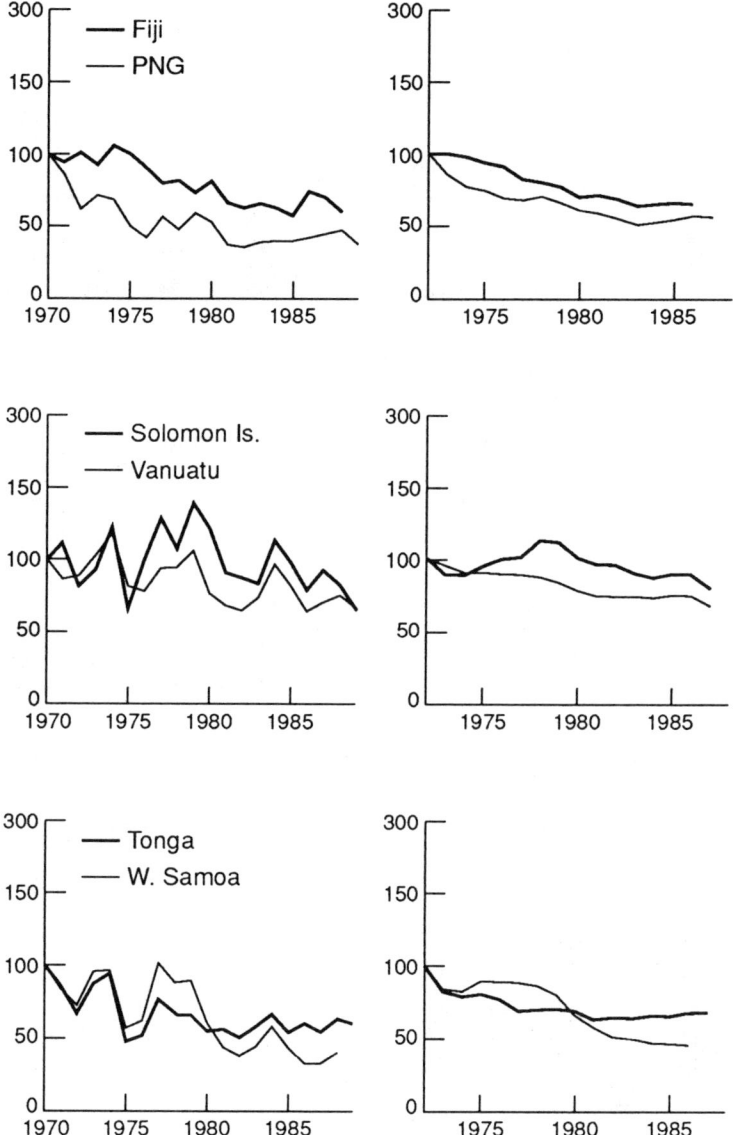

Appendix 4. Terms of trade for selected Pacific island economies, 1970–89
(1970 = 100); right-hand graphs five year moving averages
(1972 = 100)

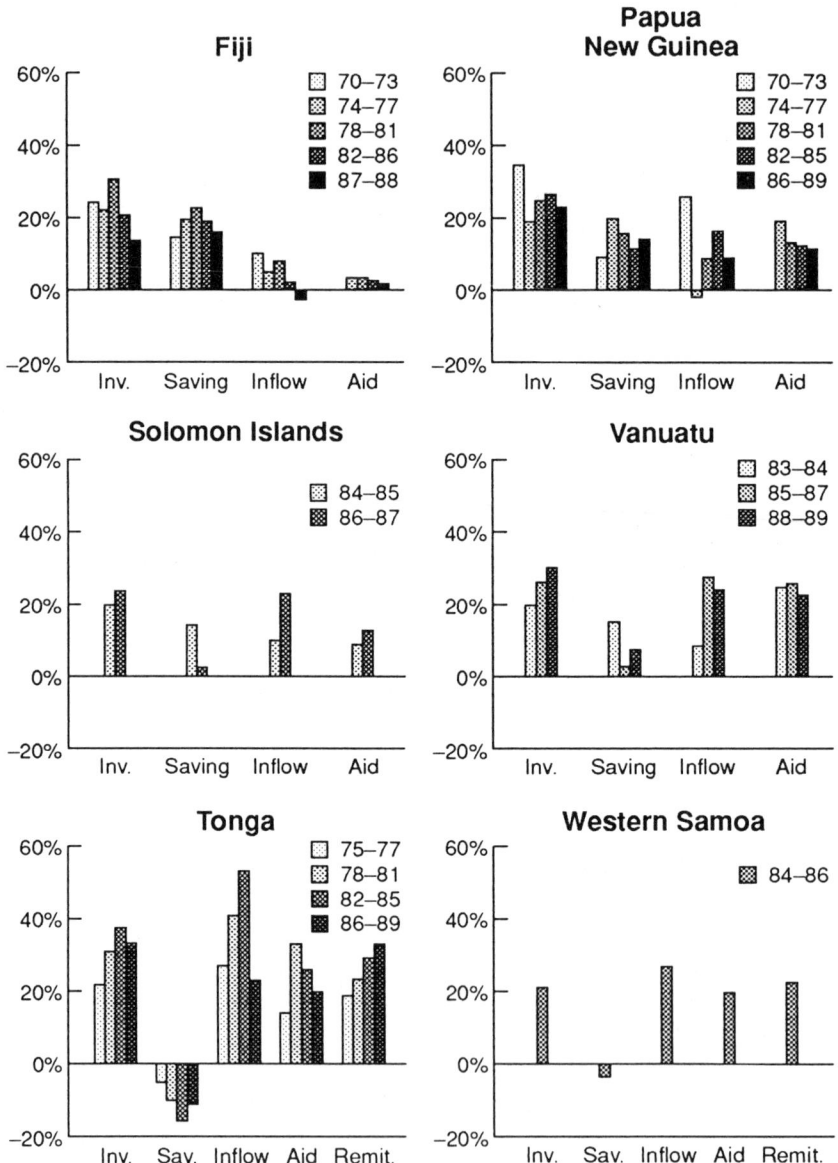

Appendix 5. Investment, savings, capital inflow, aid, and workers remittances as a percent of current GDP during the 1970–89 period

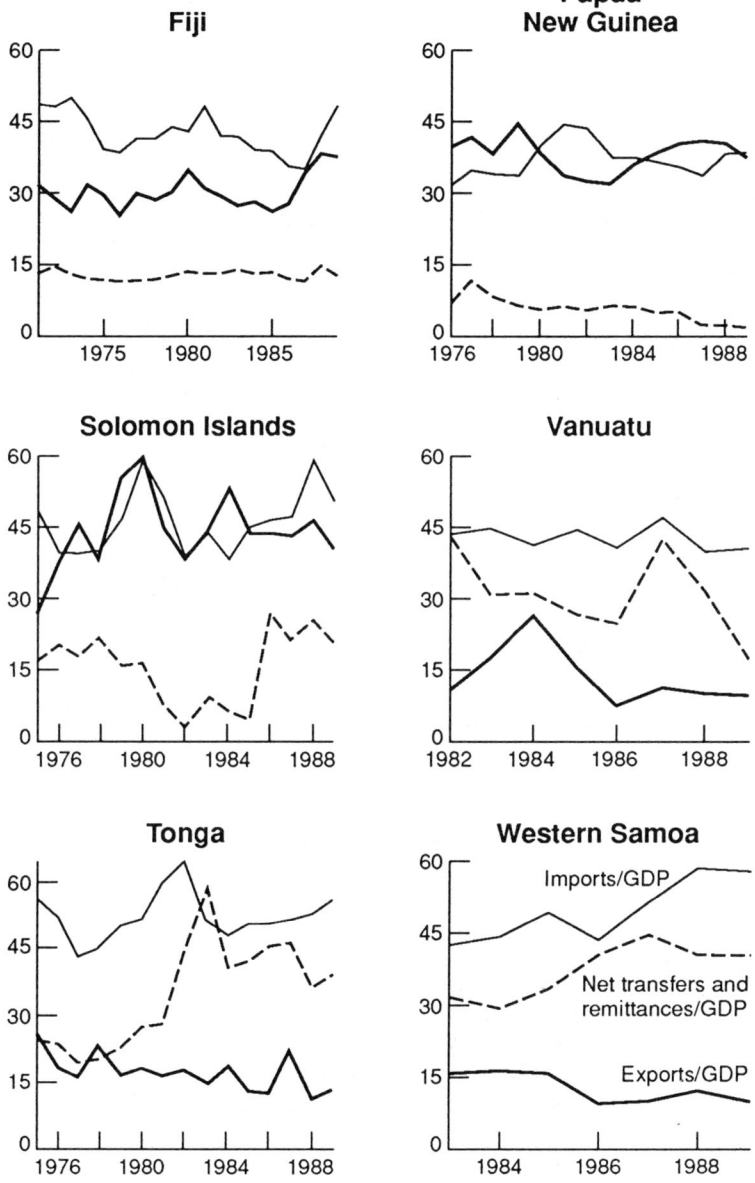

Appendix 6. The structure of the external account: ratios of exports, imports, and net transfers and remittances to GDP during the 1970–89 period

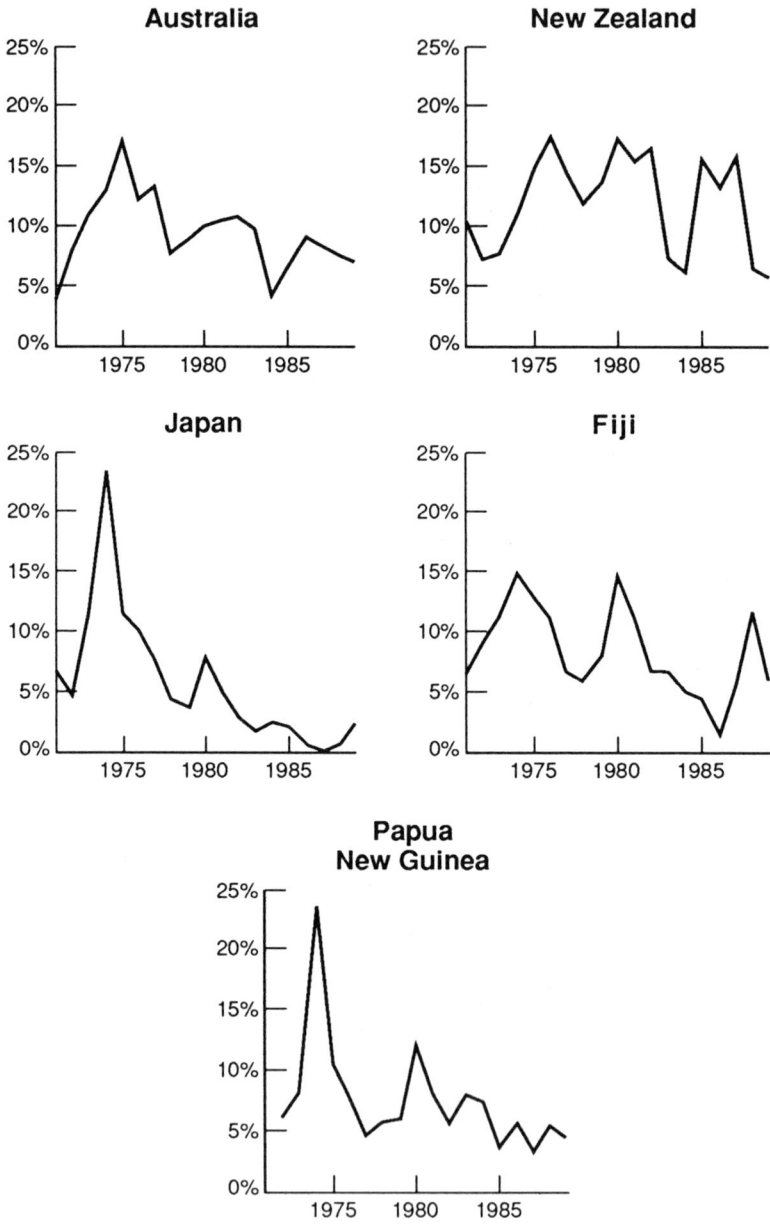

Appendix 7. Rates of inflation in the Pacific islands and their major trading partners, 1970–89

Solomon Islands

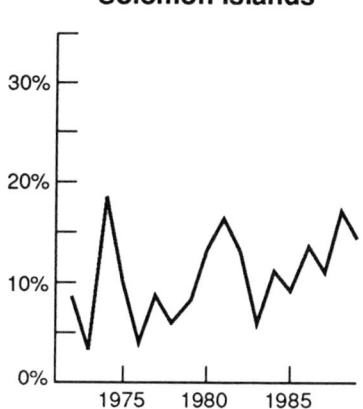

Vanuatu

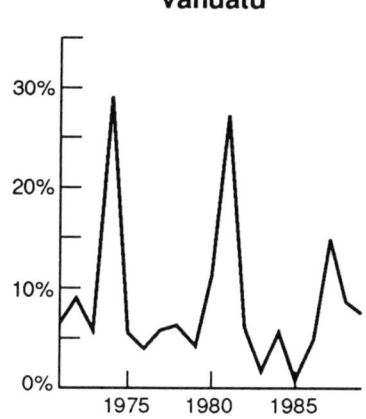

Tonga

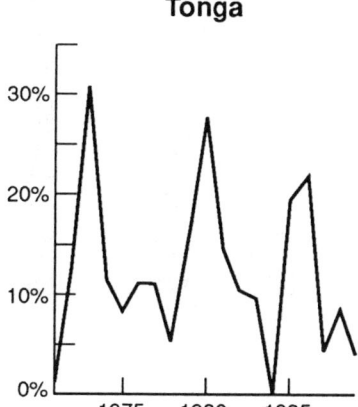

Western Samoa

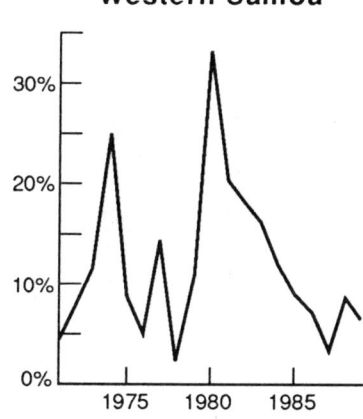

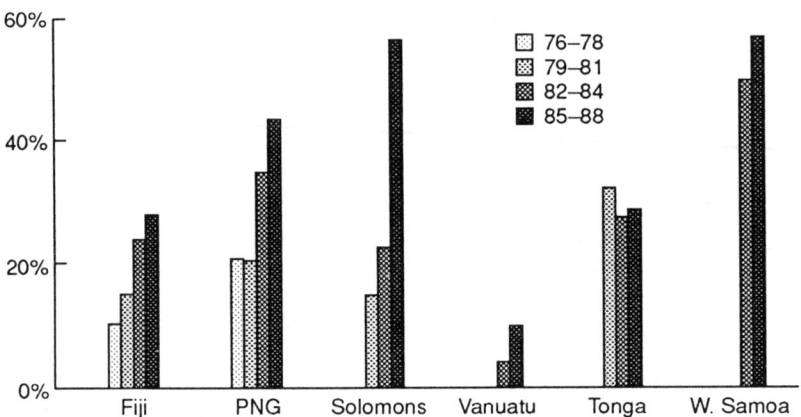

Appendix 8. External debt ratio to GDP, percent, 1976–88

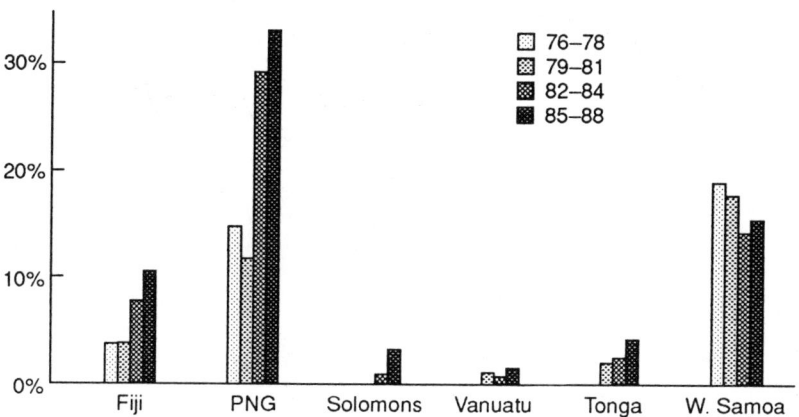

Appendix 9. Debt service ratio, percent of exports of goods and services, 1976–88 (includes both interest and principal repayments)

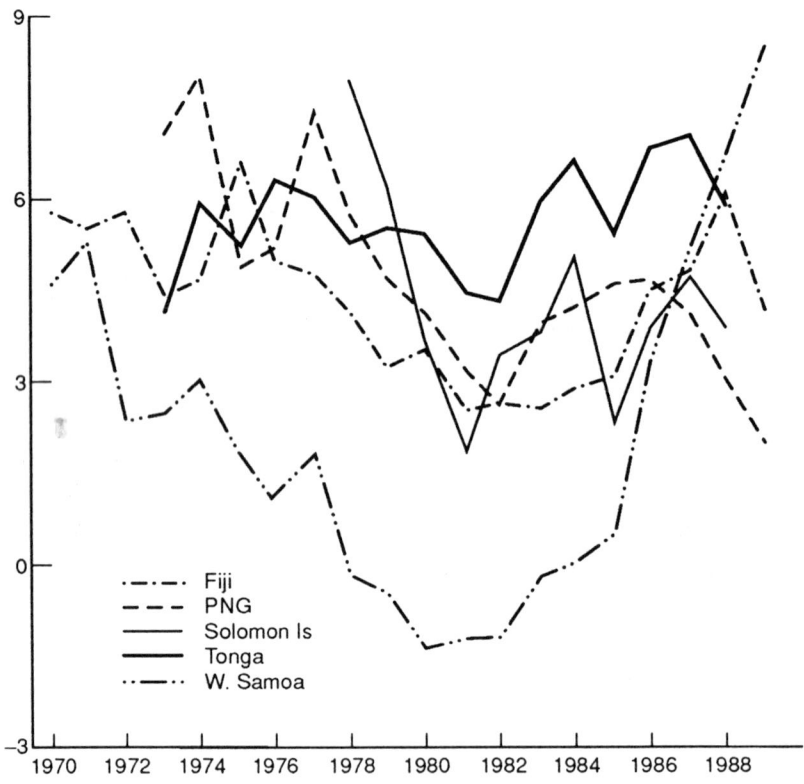

Appendix 10. Foreign reserve (net) import coverage, 1970–89 (net foreign
assets divided by monthly average imports)

Private sector project references

Briscoe, Robert, Godwin S. Nair, and Alex Sibbald
   1990   Enterprise Support Organizations for the South Pacific:
           Problems and Proposals. Research Report Series No. 13.
           Pacific Islands Development Program, East-West Center.
           Honolulu. 89 pp.

Carroll, John, et al.
   1990   Private Sector Development and Investment Prospects in
           Pohnpei State - Federated States of Micronesia. A Report by
           the College of Micronesia to the Pacific Islands Development
           Program, East-West Center. Honolulu. 179 pp.

Chandra, Rajesh
   1990   Fiji's Tax Free System. Pacific Islands Development
           Program, East-West Center. Honolulu. 71 pp.

Cole, Rodney V.
   1990   South Pacific Development Banks: Key Issues in their
           Future. Pacific Islands Development Program, East-West
           Center. Honolulu. 45 pp.

Coulter, Hugh K.
   1990a   Commodity Marketing Institutions in the Pacific Islands: A
           Case Study of Papua New Guinea. Published jointly with the
           Institute of National Affairs. 128 pp.

   1990b   Performance, Role, and Potential of Commodity Boards in
           the Pacific Islands: A Case Study of Papua New Guinea.
           Pacific Islands Development Program, East-West Center.
           126 pp.

Crocombe, T.
    1990   Blueprint for the Stimulation of Small Business Development
            and New Venture Creation. Pacific Islands Development
            Program, East-West Center. Honolulu. 27 pp.

Eaton, Charles
    1990   Prospects of the Private Sector's Participation in the
            Development of Smallholder Agriculture in Fiji and Vanuatu.
            Pacific Islands Development Program, East-West Center.
            Honolulu. 128 pp.

Garae, Augustine
    1990   A Study on the Private Sector Development In Vanuatu. A
            study submitted to the Pacific Islands Development Program,
            East-West Center. Honolulu. 71 pp.

Guest, James
    1989   The Macroeconomic Environment for Private Sector
            Development in Papua New Guinea. Pacific Islands
            Development Program, East-West Center. Honolulu. 162
            pp.

Kofe, Siliga A.
    1990   Role and Prospects of the Private Sector in the Economic
            Development of Kiribati. Pacific Islands Development
            Program, East-West Center. Honolulu. 93 pp.

Lum, Jackson A.
    1990   Gold Mining, Exploration, and Investment Opportunities in
            the Southwest Pacific: Papua New Guinea, Solomon Islands,
            Fiji. Pacific Islands Development Program and Minerals
            Policy Program, East-West Center. Honolulu. 27 pp.

Lum J. A., A. L. Clark, and P. J. Coleman
    1991   Gold Potential of the Southwest Pacific: Papua New Guinea,
            Solomon Islands, Vanuatu, and Fiji. Pacific Islands
            Development Program and Minerals Policy Program, East-
            West Center. Honolulu. 40 pp.

Manning, Michael
    1990   Development and Performance of Management Agencies in
            Papua New Guinea. Published jointly with the Institute of
            National Affairs. 106 pp.

McGregor, Andrew
    1988   The Fiji Fresh Ginger Industry: A Case Study in Non-Traditional Export Development. Research Report Series No. 10. Pacific Islands Development Program, East-West Center. Honolulu. 44 pp.

    1989   The Tongan Knitwear Industry: A Case Study in Export Manufacturing Development in the Pacific Islands. Pacific Islands Development Program, East-West Center. Honolulu. 29 pp.

    1990a   Agricultural Diversification in the Pacific Islands: Developing High Value Export Crops. Pacific Islands Development Program, East-West Center. Honolulu. 16 pp.

    1990b   Expanding Horticultural and Niche Commodity Export Trade between the Pacific Islands and the Pacific Rim. Pacific Islands Development Program, East-West Center. Honolulu. 49 pp.

    1990c   Marketing Horticultural and Niche Commodities from the Pacific Islands: Opportunities and Constraints. Pacific Islands Development Program, East-West Center. Honolulu. 15 pp.

    1990d   Requirements for the Development of New Export Crops: The Case of Papaya. Pacific Islands Development Program, East-West Center. Honolulu. 33 pp.

    1991   A Review of the World Production and Market Environment for Macadamia Nuts. Pacific Islands Development Program, East-West Center. Honolulu. 44 pp.

McGregor, Andrew and Hugh Coulter
    1991   The Institutional Environment for Agricultural Development in the Pacific Islands. Pacific Islands Development Program, East-West Center. Honolulu. 74 pp.

McGregor, Andrew M. with Charles Eaton
    1989   Developing a Viable Horticultural Export Sector in the Small Island Economies of the South Pacific. Pacific Islands Development Program, East-West Center. Honolulu. 86 pp.

McGregor, Andrew, Charles Eaton, and Michael Manning
1993   Commercial Management Companies in the Agricultural Development of the Pacific Islands. Research Report Series No. 15. Pacific Islands Development Program, East-West Center. Honolulu. 46 pp.

McGregor, Andrew, Peter Philipson, Jackson Lum, Robert Lucas, and Rajesh Chandra
1990   Selected Trade and Investment Opportunities in the Pacific Islands. Pacific Islands Development Program, East-West Center. Honolulu. 67 pp.

McMaster, Jim
1989   Foreign Aid and Private Sector Development in the Pacific Islands. Pacific Islands Development Program, East-West Center. Honolulu. 52 pp.

1990a   Future Role of International Agencies and Donors in Private Sector Development in Pacific Island Countries. Pacific Islands Development Program, East-West Center. Honolulu. 58 pp.

1990b   Incentives, Regulatory Mechanisms, and Risk Climate for Private Investment. Pacific Islands Development Program, East-West Center. Honolulu. 65 pp.

1990c   Scope for Accelerating Private Sector Growth in the Pacific Islands Through the Implementation of Privatization Policies. Pacific Islands Development Program, East-West Center. Honolulu. 72 pp.

Millett, John
1990a   Private Sector Development in Papua New Guinea. Published jointly with the Institute of National Affairs. 142 pp.

1990b   Special Initiatives of Development Banks in Entrepreneurial Development--The Case of Agriculture Bank of Papua New Guinea. Paper presented by Pacific Islands Development Program/ADFIP Development Finance Workshop, Port Vila, Vanuatu. 17 pp.

Nganga, Meto
Vanuatu Commodities Marketing Board and the Role of Private Investment in Pacific Island Agriculture. Report prepared for Pacific Islands Development Program/Asian Development Bank. 42 pp.

Philipson, P. W.
1989   The Future of Marine Product Exports from the South Pacific. Pacific Islands Development Program, East-West Center. Honolulu. 40 pp.

PIDP
1989   The Role of the Private Sector in Pacific Islands Development: A Summary of Preliminary Findings and Major Recommendations. Pacific Islands Development Program, East-West Center. Honolulu. 37 pp.

PIDP and Minerals Policy Program
1990a   Analysis and Review of Gold Mining Taxation in Papua New Guinea, Solomon Islands, and Fiji. Pacific Islands Development Program and Minerals Policy Program, East-West Center. Honolulu. 28 pp.

1990b   Gold Potential and Future Trends: Regulatory and Administrative Arrangements for Gold Development: Papua New Guinea, Solomon Islands, and Fiji. Pacific Islands Development Program and Minerals Policy Program, East-West Center. Honolulu. 64 pp.

Ramanlal, Soane
1990   Private Sector Development in the Kingdom of Tonga. Pacific Islands Development Program, East-West Center. Honolulu. 187 pp.

Rofeta, John
1989a   Incentives, Regulatory Mechanisms and Risk Climate for Investment in Solomon Islands. Pacific Islands Development Program, East-West Center. Honolulu. 49 pp.

1989b   The Investment Corporation of Solomon Islands. Pacific Islands Development Program, East-West Center. Honolulu. 43 pp.

1991   The Private Sector in Solomon Islands: Its Nature, Structure, and Performance. Pacific Islands Development Program, East-West Center. Honolulu. 200 pp.

Sevele, F. V. with H. Petelo
1989   Agricultural Export Marketing Institutions in Tonga: An Assessment of the Role and Consequences of Government Involvement. Pacific Islands Development Program, East-West Center. Honolulu. 41 pp.

Sturton, Mark
1990a   The Macroeconomic Environment for Private Sector Development. Pacific Islands Development Program, East-West Center. Honolulu. 60 pp.

1990b   Overview of Macroeconomic Environment for Private Sector Development. Pacific Islands Development Program, East-West Center. Honolulu. 12 pp.

1991   Economic Performance of the Pacific Islands. Pacific Islands Development Program, East-West Center. 23 pp.

1992   Tonga: Development through Agricultural Exports. Economic Report No. 4. Pacific Islands Development Program, East-West Center. Honolulu.

Sturton, Mark, and Andrew McGregor
1991a   Fiji: Economic Adjustment, 1987-91. Economic Report No. 1. Pacific Islands Development Program, East-West Center. Honolulu. 44 pp.

1991b   Vanuatu: Toward Economic Growth. Economic Report No. 2. Pacific Islands Development Program, East-West Center. Honolulu. 39 pp.

Thirlwall, A. P.
1991   Performance and Prospects of the Pacific Island Economies in the World Economy. Research Report Series No. 14. Pacific Islands Development Program, East-West Center. Honolulu. 76 pp.

Thomson, Peter W.
    1989   Trade and Investment in the South Pacific Islands: A
            Diagnostic Study.   Pacific Islands Development Program,
            East-West Center. Honolulu. 134 pp.

Togolo, Mel
    1989   Land, Mining and Redistribution: Panguna and Ok Tedi in
            Papua New Guinea. Pacific Islands Development Program,
            East-West Center. Honolulu. 35 pp.

Travel Industry Management (TIM), University of Hawaii
    1990   Pacific Islands Tourism Case Studies: Regional Summary.
            School of Travel Industry Management, University of Hawaii
            at Manoa. Honolulu. 160 pp.

World Bank
    1991   Toward Higher Growth in Pacific Island Economies:
            Lessons from the 1980s. Report No. 9059. Asia. January
            18, 1991.

Index

PACIFIC ISLANDS DEVELOPMENT PROGRAM

The purpose of the Pacific Islands Development Program (PIDP) of the East-West Center is to help meet the special development needs of the Pacific islands region through cooperative research and training. PIDP conducts specific research and training activities based on the issues and problems prioritized by the Pacific Islands Conference of Leaders, which meets every three years. The Standing Committee, composed of eleven island leaders, reviews PIDP's research projects annually to ensure that they respond to the issues and challenges raised at each Pacific Islands Conference. This unique process enhances the East-West Center's capability in serving the Pacific.

EAST-WEST CENTER

The East-West Center is a public, nonprofit education and research institution with an international board of governors. The U.S. Congress established the Center in Hawaii in 1960 with a mandate "to promote better relations and understanding between the United States and the nations of Asia and the Pacific through cooperative study, training, and research."

Some 2,000 scholars, government and business leaders, educators, journalists and other professionals annually work with the Center's staff on major Asia-Pacific issues. Current programs focus on environment, economic development, population, international relations, resources, and culture and communications. The Center provides scholarships for about 300 graduate students from the Asia-Pacific-U.S. region to study at the nearby University of Hawaii, and conducts faculty and curriculum development programs focusing on Asia and the Pacific for teachers from kindergarten through undergraduate levels. Since 1960 some 28,000 men and women from the region have participated in the Center's cooperative programs.

Officially known as the Center for Cultural and Technical Interchange Between East and West, Inc., the Center receives its principal funding from the U.S. Congress. Support also comes from more than 20 Asian and Pacific governments, private agencies and corporations and through the East-West Center Foundation.